# FISH ON FRIDAY

# FISH ON FRIDAY

## FEASTING, FASTING, AND THE DISCOVERY OF THE NEW WORLD

## BRIAN FAGAN

BASIC
**B**
BOOKS
A Member of the Perseus Books Group
New York

Set in Adobe Garamond by the Perseus Books Group

The Library of Congress has catalogued the hardcover edition as follows:

Fagan, Brian M.
    Fish on Friday : feasting, fasting, and the discovery of the New World / Brian
Fagan.
        p.   cm.
    Includes bibliographical references and index.
    ISBN-13: 978-0-465-02284-7 (isbn-13, hardcover : alk. paper)
    ISBN-10: 0-465-02284-7 (isbn-10, hardcover)  1. Fisheries—North America—
History. 2. North America—Discovery and exploration. 3. Fish as food—History.
I. Title.

SH219.F34 2005
639.2'2'097—dc22                                            2005021322

Paperback: ISBN-13: 978-0-465-022854; ISBN-10: 0-465-02285-5

10  9  8  7  6  5  4  3  2  1

*To*

Susan Rabiner

with thanks for inspiration and encouragement

Male and female created he them. . . .

Be fruitful and multiply, and replenish the earth, and subdue it: and have dominion over the fish of the sea, and over the fowl of the air, and over every living thing that moveth upon the earth.

Genesis 1:27–28

# Contents

## · PART THREE ·
## DISCOVERY

## · PART FOUR ·
## HARVEST AND SETTLEMENT

# PREFACE

## THE THOUSAND-YEAR JOURNEY

> The fascination of a fisherman's life is that he reaps his harvest
> from an unseen world through whose insecure and perilous
> crust he throws down his sacrificial gifts for a reward that may
> be small, or may be great, but is always uncertain. All that he
> knows of that obscure region beneath him is that it is inex-
> haustibly rich.
>
> Leo Walmsley[1]

"A brave wind is blowing and the caravels are rolling, plunging and throwing spray as they cut down the last invisible barrier between the Old World
and the New." Thus Samuel Eliot Morison conveys the drama of the mo-
mentous day—October 14, 1492—when Christopher Columbus, Admiral
of the Ocean Sea, made landfall in the Bahamas thinking he had reached
the outlying islands of Asia.[2] Five years later, a Venetian, John Cabot, sailed
confidently from Bristol across the North Atlantic and landed on Newfoundland on a warm June 24, 1497. James Williamson tells us that Cabot
walked no farther inland than a bowshot from the breakers, for fear of the
natives. "It must have been awesome, there in the heat and silence, surrounded by the great trees and undergrowth, and watched, as they might
guess, by hidden hostile men."[3]

The voyages of 1492 and 1497 made Christopher Columbus and John
Cabot icons of the Age of Discovery, explorers whose transatlantic journeys transformed global geography. Everyone knew that Europe, Africa,

and Asia were three contiguous continents, and most people believed the earth was spherical. Thus it was theoretically possible for them to sail directly from Europe to Asia by heading into the Atlantic, the empty and hazardous Western Ocean. Columbus and Cabot did just that, but instead of Asia they found a new continent teeming with unknown peoples and exotic animals. They had achieved geographic immortality.

Except for a small group of Vikings who created a short-lived settlement in Newfoundland during the late tenth century, Columbus and Cabot are generally assumed to be the first Europeans to reach the Americas. Both were expert mariners who came along at a time when academic knowledge of geography had been enriched by Marco Polo's explorations in Central Asia and China. Paolo Toscanelli of Florence had estimated the distance to China and speculated about possible rest stops along the way. The convergence of broadening academic knowledge, new designs of oceangoing ships, lust for the wealth offered by the spice trade, and sailors prepared to undertake the risky journey produced an impetus for discovery that was not present a century earlier.

But the familiar names of history, Cabot and Columbus, did not bring Europeans to the New World. The hard-won knowledge of the Western Ocean was acquired over many generations by people who did not talk freely about their experiences or share knowledge with others, least of all with scholars or government officials. I argue in this book that the finding of North America was not a brief moment of iconic discovery but a thousand-year journey fueled by Christian doctrine and a search for hardtack.

This is not a tale of kings, popes, and statesmen, but of merchants, monks, and fishermen who lived and worked far from the spotlight of history. In all but a few cases we shall never know their names, but their devotion and labor yielded greater wealth than the gold of the Indies. They led Europeans to North America to fish and then settle there, well before the Pilgrims landed on a continent said to be inhabited only by Indians. Much of this journey is cloaked in historical obscurity, owing to lacunae in official records as well as the silence of many of the players. We can follow their doings only by triangulation from diffuse and often indirect clues.

Abstinence, atonement, fasting, and penance lay at the core of Christian belief; from the earliest times fish had a special association with such practices. The traditional fasting days were Fridays and Lent, when Christians atoned for the suffering of Christ on the cross. As Christianity spread across Europe and religious communities proliferated, so did the number of holy days. By the thirteenth century, fast days took up more than half the year.

Once eaten on special occasions, by the eighth and ninth centuries, fish was a preferred food for abstinence days throughout Christendom. Fishing had always been an important subsistence activity for people living by lakes, rivers, and seashores. To supplement these resources, monks and nobles turned to fish farming to provide the catch for holy days. Eels were so commonplace that they became a form of currency. But as populations rose and the grip of Christian doctrine tightened, even thousands of hectares of fishponds proved insufficient to satisfy the demand on meatless days. By the tenth and eleventh centuries, fish had become not a catch but a commodity. The stage was set for the extraordinary journey to North America.

Sometime around the tenth century, Baltic herring fishers and Norse fisherfolk learned to preserve herring by salting it in brine-filled barrels. The Skänia fishery in southern Sweden spawned an industry that carried herring far inland to Vienna, Bern, and the Mediterranean. Customshouses high in the Alps stank of fish from distant oceans. Along the English coast great fairs arose that trafficked in millions of fish. Herring rapidly became a staple, not only on aristocratic and monastic tables but in poorhouses and cities. Herring nourished armies in an era of endemic warfare. Between the eleventh and fifteenth centuries, the European herring industry expanded rapidly, first in the hands of the Hanseatic League, then on an industrial scale with the Dutch, who took processing operations offshore in factory ships. But it was a local industry conducted mainly in shallow waters.

The Norse were the first to voyage deep into the Western Ocean. For thousands of years, the Lofoten Islanders of northern Norway had harvested white-fleshed cod, drying it in the sunshine and cold winds of late winter and spring. Dried "stockfish," light and easy to transport, was the perfect staple for Norse ships coasting deep into the Baltic, raiding England

and France, and sailing westward to Iceland and beyond. The Norse could not have sailed to Iceland, Greenland, and North America without stockfish, which enabled them to survive at sea for weeks on end.

Their voyages came during the Medieval Warm Period, a time when temperatures were at least as warm as today and ice conditions in the north were favorable for offshore voyaging. Until about 1250, ships could sail readily between Iceland and Greenland. With the onset of the Little Ice Age, however, skippers had to sail farther south and west to avoid the pack ice. At the same time (and here we are venturing onto untrodden scientific ground) changes in water temperature and the pressure gradients of the North Atlantic Oscillation must have affected the distribution of both cod and herring, though the precise relationship is little understood.

The great Norse voyagers sailed to Greenland and beyond in search of new places to settle and out of a wanderlust that was an integral part of a restless, violent society. They carried stockfish far and wide, and it proved a more palatable substitute for salted herring on holy days. A huge stockfish industry developed, centered on Bergen, where Hanse ships exchanged grain for dried fish. Archaeological excavations in the Lofoten Islands have pinpointed the moment around the eleventh century when cod became a lucrative trading commodity that supplanted herring on many dinner tables.

Bulk commodities meant bulk carriers, new ships with greater cargo capacity than Norse merchant ships had. Profound changes in ships and shipbuilding form another thread in our historical tapestry, beginning with lapstraked Viking ships and followed by the slow-moving Hanse cog, the first true bulk carrier, then the Dutch buss or herring factory ship, and new designs of offshore fishing vessels. The quest for new cod fisheries, notably off Iceland in the early fifteenth century, could never have happened without the development of the dogger, a craft that first carried North Sea fishermen far offshore as early as 1412. The dogger opened the doors of an entirely new fishery, whose practitioners were solely interested in supplying fish at a handsome profit to a rapidly growing marketplace.

By the mid-fifteenth century, the demand for fish of all kinds had brought massive growth to the fisheries of western England and southern

Ireland. The merchants of Bristol assumed a leading role in the Lenten fish trade, buying catches from Ireland and Iceland. By this time, the caravel, a full-rigged ship with a strong, rigid hull, had come into its own as the oceangoing ship for Atlantic sailors. I believe that Bristol skippers acquired an unrivaled knowledge of the North Atlantic from their experiences in the far north, where they learned about Greenland and perhaps the lands to the west. Many had also sailed to Madeira, the Canary Islands, and even the Azores. I argue that Bristol merchants sponsored expeditions in the 1480s and later that sailed westward in search of the fabled "Island of Brasil" and a route to the spices of Asia—almost twenty years before John Cabot.

Some of these voyages are recorded in customs records, but their results are not. Some vessels shipped out with cargoes of salt, presumably expecting to return with their holds full of salted cod. At least a few ships may have latitude-sailed westward, well south of Cape Farewell in Greenland, and eventually made landfall on Labrador or Newfoundland. There they found not spices but fish, returning home on the prevailing westerlies with profitable cargoes of salt cod. All this is speculation, flying in the face of prevailing historical opinion that credits John Cabot as the first person to make landfall on Newfoundland. But I find it hard to explain away the repeated voyages. Why would hard-nosed merchants keep sending their ships west if there was no profit in it? Cabot shipped out with at least two merchants on board, who may have known sailing directions to the Newfoundland fishing grounds.

It was fish, not spices, that led to the discovery of North America. The fishers may never have landed, or if they did, they built no permanent settlements until much later. Those who fished these distant waters before the Cabot voyage were there without royal sanction or official approval. Since their goal was not conquest or glory or empire but commercial advantage, they had no reason to trumpet their finds; they kept quiet, knowing that a lucrative fishery in hand was as valuable as any dream of spices.

Once the Newfoundland fishery became public, the huge international industry in dried and salted cod expanded effortlessly across the Atlantic. Rather than settle on an inhospitable shore, the fishers and whalers came and went each winter, spring, and summer, basing themselves in sheltered coves or remaining offshore on the Grand Banks. Individual fishers might travel one year to Iceland, the next to Ireland, the next to Newfoundland. The first attempts at settlement came in the seventeenth and eighteenth centuries, and even then they faltered because it was difficult to compete with the established economic interests of migrant fisherfolk.

While the Newfoundland fishery was a summer enterprise, the cod came toward shore in New England waters during winter. Inevitably people began to overwinter on islands in the Gulf of Maine, close to the cold-weather fishing grounds. New England was first settled not by Pilgrims escaping persecution in a land peopled only by native Americans, but by roistering cod fishermen schooled in the rough-and-ready world of the migrant fishery. In one of the ironies of history, it was these very cod fishermen who provided the starving Pilgrims with boatloads of fish in 1622. The journey that began with ancient traditions of fasting and penance ended with the permanent settlement of New England. The mythmakers of American origins, obsessed with virtuous Pilgrims, have written the morally flawed cod fishers out of the story—but that is often the fate of the men and women who labor in history's shadows.

# Author's Note

All measurements in the narrative are given in metric units, following international scientific convention. For recipes, both U.S. and metric measurements are given.

Place-names are spelled according to the most common usage. Archaeological sites and historical places are spelled as they appear most commonly in the sources I used to write this book. Some obscure locations are omitted from the maps for clarity; interested readers are referred to the specialist literature. *Fish on Friday* involved a search through numerous complex and rapidly proliferating literatures in a variety of disciplines from archaeology and anthropology to ecclesiastical history, fish ecology and fisheries history, maritime archaeology and ancient naval architecture, even novels about the Grand Banks. Only a small fraction of the articles, books, and monographs I consulted can be listed here; I have tended to reference those with comprehensive bibliographies, to allow the reader to enter the more specialized literature if desired.

The footnotes seek to identify animals, people, places, and occasionally artifacts and documents. They also define such arcane terms as *kipper, thole pin,* and *tun.*

Except where specifically stated, all recipes in this book have been tested. Since recipes are subjective and vary from one cook to another, those given here should be treated as guides, not scripture.

# RECIPES

## A NOTE ON THE RECIPES

Each chapter of the book has a recipe box (numbered consecutively throughout the book) that accompanies the narrative. The boxes include a short historical preamble or background information and, taken together, offer a (very) potted history of fish cookery. My colleague and friend Daphne Derven kindly tested all of the historical recipes and made sure that a relatively authentic version of each one could be prepared with modern ingredients. Supplementing the traditional with the modern, she has also included modern fish recipes contributed by well-known contemporary food authorities and chefs.

Then as now, cookery was an oral tradition, learned by apprenticeship as recipes were passed down from one generation to the next. Professional chefs rarely use the precise recipes found in cookbooks, relying instead on their instincts and experience. (Many of us amateur adventurers owe a debt as well to tolerant dinner companions.)

Here are some recommendations from Daphne, based on her efforts to approximate authenticity when cooking from the recipes:

- Heavy cooking dishes are recommended. They tend to change cooking times, but most closely approximate the cookware used originally.
- All ovens are slightly different, which can cause cooking times to vary. Please check the recipe and then use your own judgment as to cooking time.
- Today's chefs prefer shorter cooking times for fish than those used a few centuries ago. We have attempted to accommodate this change.

- Use stone-ground wheat flour when possible.
- Sourdough bread should be used when bread is called for.
- To be as authentic as possible, you should bake bread in a traditional brick oven, as are many artisanal breads.
- Use walnut oil with northern recipes, as was done in medieval times, and extra virgin Italian or Greek olive oil with southern ones. The correct oil is indicated for each recipe.
- Although recommendations for seasoning are given, your own judgment is all-important. Season to your own taste.
- Where butter is called for, use organic salted butter; for animal fat, use lard.
- Use smaller vegetables and heirloom varieties where possible.

Daphne's recommended readings, which she used to research the recipes, appear at the end of the book.


RECIPE CREDITS

The following chefs and food authorities kindly gave permission for their recipes to appear in this book:

8       Roman seafood stew. Adapted from Apicius, *De re coquinaria*.

21      Garum. No recommended recipe. Garum is not for modern tastes.

33      Smoked eel, bacon, and mash. Fergus Henderson, chef and owner, St. John Restaurant, London, and author of *The Whole Beast: Nose to Tail Eating: A Kind of British Cooking*.

50      Grilled mackerel with cameline sauce. Sauce from Chiquart's *Du fait de cuisine*.

67      Salt cod in parsnip gratin. Rowley Leigh, Kensington Place, London.

77      Baked salt-packed turbot with Sandefjord butter. Ingrid Espelid Hovig, Oslo.

# TIMELINE OF MAJOR EVENTS

| | |
|---|---|
| c. 1640 | First triangular voyage sponsored by New England merchants. |
| 1640s | New England settlers engage in cod fishery and exporting. |
| 1630 | Massachusetts Bay Company lands its first settlers in New England. Boston founded. |
| 1621 | Sir George Calvert founds the Ferryland settlement, Newfoundland. |
| 1620 | The Pilgrims establish Plymouth Plantation. |
| 1619 | Year-round fishing station on Monhegan Island, Maine. |
| 1614 | Captain John Smith extols New England cod fishery. |
| 1610 | Jamestown colony boats fish in the Gulf of Maine. |
| 1610 | Cupid's Cove settlement in Newfoundland. |
| 1607–1608 | Sagadohoc settlement fails. |
| 1606 | King James I charters the Virginia Company. |
| 1605 | George Waymouth's expedition to New England waters. |
| 1604 | Samuel de Champlain visits Maine waters and debunks the kingdom of Norumbega. |
| 1602 | Bartholemew Gosnold explores the Gulf of Maine, visits Cape Cod and Martha's Vineyard. |
| 1530s | Basque whale hunters in Labrador. |
| 1524 | Giovanni da Verrazzano explores the coasts of New England and Maine, ending in Newfoundland. |
| 1510 | French, possibly Basque, and other fishers inshore fishing at Newfoundland. |
| 1497 | John Cabot voyages to Newfoundland. |
| 1492 | Christopher Columbus sails to the Bahamas. |

| | |
|---|---|
| c. 1480 | Bristol ships sail westward in search of the "Island of Brasil." |
| c. 1450 | Norse abandon Greenland settlements. |
| c. 1420 | Dutch herring fishers adopt the *vleet*, or long drift net. The herring buss comes into use. |
| c. 1412 | English doggers fish off Iceland. |
| Early 1400s | Cod replaces herring as the fish of choice in monasteries. |
| Early 1400s | Skänia herring fishery falters. |
| Mid–1300s | Herring now consumed throughout Europe. |
| 1347–1350 | The Black Death decimates Europe. |
| 1330s | Apogee of herring fishery in southern North Sea, also of Scarborough and Yarmouth herring fairs. Skänia herring fishery expanding. |
| c. 1300 | The Little Ice Age begins. Hanse control of the herring trade tightens. |
| 1066 | William the Conqueror invades England. |
| 1060 | Norse ships sunk in Skuldelev fjord, Roskilde, Denmark. |
| 11th century | Fish farming begins in Loire region and spreads rapidly. Carp introduced to ponds in eastern and central Europe. |
| c. 1000 | Expansion of herring trade begins. Water mills commonplace in Europe. |
| 990s | Leif Eirikson lands in North America and winters over in Newfoundland. |
| 980s | Eirik the Red lands in Greenland. |
| 952–953 | Reconquest of the Danelaw. |
| 10th century | Fishponds well established throughout Europe. |
| 9th century | New herring salting methods used in the Baltic and Low Countries. |
| 900 | Fish well established as part of Lenten diet. |
| 874 | Norse colonize Iceland. Stockfish are part of their seafaring diet. |
| 850 | First Norse invasions of England. Beginnings of the Danelaw. |
| c. 800 | Medieval Warm Period begins. |

| | |
|---|---|
| 793 | Norse raid Lindisfarne, England. |
| 782 | King Charlemagne of the Franks promulgates the Capitulary of Padeborn, which prescribes the death penalty for eating meat during Lent. |
| 625 | Sutton Hoo ship, England. |
| 6th century | Herring fishers said to be active off the River Yare, Norfolk, including some from the Low Countries. |
| 6th century | Benedictine monasteries spread through Europe. |
| c. 530 | St. Benedict's Rule compiled. |
| c. 400 | IXTHEUS symbol vanishes. |
| 4th century | Christianity first spreads to Europe. First monastic communities established. |
| 325 | Council of Nicaea sets rules for fasting, makes dietary recommendations for the faithful. |
| 310 | Nydam ships buried in Denmark. |
| 270 | First recorded Egyptian hermits. |
| 49 | Council of Jerusalem. |
| 1 | Christ fasts in the desert. |

## PART ONE

# THE GREAT ATONEMENT

Let us now consider how great a terror will come upon us created things, in this present time, when the Judgment draws near; and the revelation of that day will be very terrible to all created things. . . . And on that day the earth will be burned to ashes; and in that day the sea will dry up. . . .

Therefore we should now consider the need of our souls while we may and are able, lest we put off this permitted time, and then wish to repent when we cannot.

Blickling Homiliary for Easter[1]

# I

# THE BIG FISH

We being little fishes, as Jesus Christ is our great Fish, begin
our life in the water and only when we abide in the water are
we safe and sound.

Tertullian, *De Baptismo* 1[1]

The IXTHEUS acrostic is as old as Christianity itself, a powerful yet
humble symbol of faith. No one knows where it first appeared, perhaps in
the bustling streets of Roman Alexandria, as a quiet protest against the rule
of pagan emperors.

IXTHEUS stands for Iesous Christos Theou Yios Soter—Jesus Christ,
Son of God, Savior. The first letters of the Greek words become the sacred fish, associated inextricably with the Savior.

The IXTHEUS symbol as commonly depicted today.

For early Christians, the fish symbol was a code word, a profession of
faith in the divinity of Christ, humankind's redeemer. Christ was the Big
Fish and the faithful were little fish. The Roman author Quintus Septimus
Florens Tertullianus (Tertullian), writing in the early third century, proclaimed in *De Baptismo* that Christians were the little fish, who found security only in water inhabited by the Big Fish. The image came from the

apostles themselves: "The kingdom of heaven is like unto a net, that cast into the sea, and gathered of every kind: Which, when it was full, they drew to shore and gathered the good into vessels, but cast the bad away. So shall it be at the end of the world: the angels shall come forth, and sever the wicked from the just, and shall cast them into the furnace of fire: there shall be wailing and gnashing of teeth."[2]

The metaphor has obvious biblical roots. Fish and faith became intertwined during Christ's lifetime with the miracle of the loaves and fishes that fed 5,000, and with the Last Supper, a meal of bread, fish, and wine. And the Gospels tell us that the apostles were fisherfolk who worked their boats at Galilee, far from the emperors' palaces and lavish villas of the Roman nobility, and then became "fishers of men."

Although the fish metaphors of early Christianity clearly spring from the prosaic occupation of the apostles, there is more to it than merely fishing for converts. Fish and sea mammals had profound symbolic importance going back to Homer's time. Many species, especially dolphins, had an association with the dead, carrying such mythic heroes as Achilles on their backs. In *Halieutica,* a five-book didactic poem on sea creatures and how to catch them, Oppian of Cilicia (second century A.D.) wrote of dolphins:

> the hunting of dolphins is immoral . . .
> for equally with human slaughter the gods abhor the deathly doom
>     of the monarchs of the deep;
> for like thoughts with men have the attendants of the god of the
>     blooming sea;
> wherefore they practice love of their offspring and are friendly
>     one to another.[3]

Oppian noted that dolphins, to help humans, actually chased shoals of fish at night into the flickering light thrown by fisherfolks' brands.

There was ample historical precedent and an easy logic in associating large fish with the sacred. In this, as in many other spiritual tenets, Christians borrowed freely from Greek and Roman practices and Judaism.

ᘏ

The fish metaphor came naturally to people who prized fish as a staple. The aristocracy and the wealthy feasted on seafood at elaborate banquets. Humbler folk lived on bread and vegetables. Meat rarely touched most people's lips, being beyond their means, but fish was an occasional treat. Markets in coastal villages and towns sold small fish such as sprats, netted by the thousands close inshore. When dried and salted, the catch traveled inland as food for the poor. Long before Christianity, smaller fish like mackerel and sprats were an inconspicuous staple.

Then there was *garum*, sauce fermented from the viscera of rotting fish and used as a condiment by virtually all Romans, rich and poor, who poured it on fish, meat, and vegetables (see recipe on page 21).[4] The sauce originated in the eastern Mediterranean as early as the fifth century B.C. and spread throughout the Roman world and into northern Europe. Garum factories abounded from Egypt to Spain. Fish sauce merchants carried the stuff as far north as Brittany, Britain, and the Low Countries, supplying army garrisons, markets, and towns. The ubiquitous sauce came in many grades, different vintages if you will, some as expensive as perfume but most affordable even for the poor. Usually the processors used large quantities of smaller fish such as mackerel or sprats, or herring and pilchard in Brittany and the Low Countries.

Fish permeated daily life in the classical world. Almost every kind of food and many medicines tasted and smelled of fish because of garum. Fish symbolism must have emerged in part from this culinary context; the essence of fish, like God, was everywhere. As Laurence Harold Kant remarks in his memorable study of early Christian fish symbolism, "In the air of a typical ancient city street, one would have smelled the odor of fish wafting from the fish markets, . . . from the smoke of fish (especially small fish) grilled on open fires outside buildings, from the factories in which rotting fish were laid out in the sun for the preparation of fish sauce, and from the fish that were set out on altars as offerings."[5]

IXTHEUS was the Big Fish. Two thousand years ago, much of the Mediterranean was already overfished. Large fish were increasingly rare trophies,

Map showing locations referred to in Chapters 1–2.

often caught with difficulty at great depths. Roman emperors, nobles, and the newly rich spent enormous sums on magnificent repasts. Large fish adorned huge platters and were sometimes decorated with jewels, even paraded triumphantly to dinner with flutes and pipes. The larger the fish, the more valued it was; the largest were reserved for emperors and kings. The tradition went back centuries. Herodotus, the inveterate Greek traveler of the fifth century B.C., tells the story of an Aegean fisherman who caught a fish so large and beautiful that instead of taking it to market, he gave it to King Polycrates of Samos, because "it seemed to me to be good enough for you and your rule."[6] When the fish was gutted, the king's long-lost seal ring was found in its stomach. Tales of treasure hidden in fish bellies are commonplace in the folklore of many cultures. Another fisherman caught a "turbot of such astonishing size" in the Adriatic that he gave it to Emperor Domitian (A.D. 238–255), to whom "every remarkable and rare thing in the sea belonged."[7] The court had no platters large enough to hold the fish, so a special one was made for it.

The banquets thrown by Roman emperors leave no doubt of fishy prestige. At a repast in A.D. 69, the brother of the Emperor Vitellius served 2,000 of the choicest fish. The ostentatious feasts of the Emperor Elagabalus (A.D. 218–222) consumed so many fish that oxen were needed to transport them. The historian Fenestella of the first century B.C. tells us that the finest banquets comprised three courses, each served with fish.[8] Pliny quotes him as saying that the "service of three dishes" consisted of first lampreys, followed by pike, and finally a "mixture of fish." The importance of large fish such as sturgeon or turbot inspired the writer Martial to an epigram: "Although a large dish bears the turbot, the turbot is always wider than the dish."[9]

The keen demand for large fish stimulated a boom in pisciculture, especially along the shores of the Bay of Naples. Large surmullets, cultivated in carefully tended and well-drained coastal fish ponds, were so highly prized that Martial records the case of the wealthy Calliodorus, who sold a slave for 4,000 sesterces and used the money to buy a 1.8 kilogram (4 pound) fish.* The most desirable surmullets covered an entire platter. Ponds teeming with carefully tended fish exchanged hands for enormous prices.

Surmullets were farmed fish. Sturgeon, which needed deep water and could not be grown in ponds, were harder to catch and thus of greater value. Writers such as Juvenal complained of fish that cost more than a cow, an estate, or a racehorse. In the second century B.C., a cask of smoked fish sold for more than 100 sheep and an ox.

---

*Surmullets *(Millus surmulletus)* are brightly colored members of the mullet family with chin barbels. They are bottom-feeders that are still highly prized as food. Four thousand sesterces is hard to convert into today's dollars, but it was around $2,200.

## ROMAN SEAFOOD STEW

Roman cookery combined staples like grain with all manner of tasty spices and condiments. The elaboration of meals was a barometer of social standing as fine cooking became an art, particularly in regard to sauces using ingenious combinations of ingredients and the cooking juices of fish and meat. Haute cuisine was alive and well in Roman society, with its lavish banquets and magnificent displays of exotic foods, many of them from specific places of origin.

Much of this highly varied cuisine eludes us, for the surviving literature is largely anecdotal or comic, some of it railing against unbridled excess and luxury. One name stands out—M. Glavius Apicius (c. 25 B.C.–A.D. 35), a connoisseur of food and luxury, who lived in the shipbuilding center and fashionable resort of Minturnae on the Via Appia near the mouth of the Liris River. He is said to have committed suicide when he realized that he could no longer maintain his lavish way of living. Apicius wrote on sauces and claimed to have created an "eating house" cuisine. His name became a byword for gourmet cookery. A collection of recipes, *De re coqinaria,* appeared under his name in the fourth century, a compliment to his reputation, although he had nothing to do with the dishes in its pages. The book survived the collapse of the Roman Empire and was faithfully transcribed by medieval scribes, but its influence on later cuisine is unknown.

This recipe epitomizes the care lavished on flavors in Roman cuisine and offers endless opportunities for improvisation, the ingredients being suggestions rather than requirements.

### ✄ *Roman Seafood Stew*

SERVES 6

1¼ lbs/610 g fish fillet in bite-size pieces—ideally halibut or salmon
8 oz/250 ml white wine, preferably a flowery tasting sauvignon blanc
   (Roman white wines are frequently described as "flowery.")
17 oz/525 ml beef broth
3 finely chopped leeks, including the green portion, well washed before
   chopping. If the leeks are large, use only two.
3½ oz/105 ml olive oil
1¾ oz/55 ml fish sauce/garum/liquamen. A modern substitute is Thai Kitchen
   Premium Fish Sauce, which is widely available, but anchovy sauce or other
   Thai or Vietnamese fish sauces would also work. Adjust the amount to taste.
1 handful finely chopped fresh coriander or cilantro
1 handful finely chopped loveage (liebstoecki) or celery hearts and leaves
Dried or fresh oregano to taste. Rigani (a wild Greek oregano) works well with
   this recipe.

*(continues)*

*Roman Seafood Stew (continued)* _____

> Pepper and salt to taste. Remember that the liquamen/fish sauce substitute is salty.
>
> Combine all the liquid ingredients and bring to a slow simmer. Add the fish and simmer for about 10 minutes, varying the time according to the doneness you prefer.
>
> Remove the fish with a slotted spoon to a warmed serving dish, bring the liquid to a boil until it reduces in volume, add the chopped leeks, cilantro, loveage, and oregano, also salt and pepper to taste. Adjust the seasoning and add to the fish.

The less fortunate scorned the indulgent habits of fish eaters. Many writers linked gluttony and fish consumption, but others considered fish eating a refined custom. According to the writer Claudius Aelian, people on the island of Rhodes "marvel at fish when they see them and . . . enjoy fish more than other foods. . . . The Rhodians scorn those who have a predilection for meat as vain and gluttonous."[10] Many people in the Greco-Roman world thought of fish as an essential part of good eating and as preferable to meat, which was often slightly rotten.

Fish rapidly became a favorite among early Christians, especially on special occasions. The greatest fish of all was IXTHEUS himself. When Avercius of Hieropolis in Turkey, a Phrygian, wrote in his funerary inscription of this huge fish, he clearly associated it with the magnificent catches consumed by the newly wealthy and the aristocracy: "And Faith led the way [as guide] and in all places set before me a fish as food from the spring, gigantic, pure, which a holy virgin had caught."[11]

Such a huge fish, bigger than anything available to emperors, nobles, and the very wealthy, was now accessible to common people in the form of the Christian faith. The Avercius inscription makes it clear that fish eating symbolized the most intimate link between Christ and the faithful, the early Christian Eucharist.

Another epitaph, that of Pectorius of Autun, dates to between A.D. 200 and 400. The inscription tells of Pectorius's journey from Asia to Rome.

As he journeyed, he received as food "Fish from the spring, the great, the pure," a spiritual nurture supplied by the "Savior of the Saints."[12]

Long before Christianity, fish figured in sacred meals; they were the food of deities and, living at the lowest depths close to the nether regions, had associations with the underworld.[13] They served as offerings to the dead and were consumed at Greco-Roman funerary feasts, often by the tomb or at the graveside. Numerous pagan paintings and sarcophagi depict diners sitting at tables bearing fish, which presumably were a symbolic way of communicating with the dead, as well as a preferred food in the afterlife. The association of fish with death had a strong influence on early Christians. Christ appeared before the apostles as they were fishing after his death and resurrection, and caused their empty net to bulge with 150 large fish. "Jesus now cometh, and taketh bread, and giveth them, and fish likewise." He adjured them, "Feed my lambs." Laurence Kant believes this may have been a form of funerary meal, for cults of the dead and graveside funerary feasts were very popular among all kinds of people and groups, including early Christians. Tombs in Rome's catacombs depict funerary banquets, with bread and fish served in separate baskets.[14]

But the sacred meal signified far more than an offering that honored the dead. Fish were linked in meals on holy days with other contexts—with the Eucharist and the *agape*, the heavenly banquet to come in the afterlife, and with the New Testament repast of loaves and fishes. Some early Christian texts identify Christ as a fish roasted on the cross, an association that linked fish eating with both Jesus and death. As pagan symbols of death, fish became an appropriate meal to represent Christ and his suffering.

The journey from fish to deity was a short one for pagan Greeks and Romans; some fish, such as the striped sea bream, were sacred and prohibited as food, while others featured prominently in religious feasts. Thus Christians' sacred associations with fish would seem natural to any Greek or Roman. By the same token, it made eminent sense to early Christians that one of their most potent symbols was understandable in

Conrad Witz (c. 1400–1445/6), *The Calling of St. Peter, or The Miraculous Draught of Fishes*. Altarpiece, c. 1444. COURTESY: GIRAUDON/ ART RESOURCE, NEW YORK, N.Y.

the wider world of which they were members. Non-Christians might not understand the IXTHEUS acronym or the meaning of fish symbols on early Christian monuments, but they would certainly have appreciated the sacred importance of fish.

The IXTHEUS acrostic remained in common use until the fourth century, when it gradually vanished. By then there was no need for symbols of resistance or secret identification. But fish remained an important part of an expanding religion that celebrated its faith with feast and fast, and carried as a central element atonement through Christ's suffering on the cross.

## 2

# MORTIFICATION
# OF THE FLESH

We [Christians], frugal from fasting, squeezed dry with self-denial, abstaining from the ordinary enjoyments of life, are forever rolling in sackcloth and ashes.

Tertullian, *Apologeticum*[1]

The moment Adam and Eve ate the forbidden fruit in the Garden of Eden, humanity's debt to the Creator increased exponentially.[2] Their transgression made it necessary for humans to satisfy God's justice in order to avoid punishment, to atone for original and later sin.

God's first command to abstain came during the Creation, when the Lord recognized that humans depended on him for food from the soil. Ancient religious laws laid down how the devout could meet this obligation, many of them summarized in the book of Leviticus. For instance, on the tenth day of the seventh month no one worked as priests made atonement and cleansed sin while "ye afflict your souls. . . . And this shall be an everlasting statute unto you, to make an atonement for the children of Israel for all their sins once a year."[3] The Old Testament shows how adversity moved Jews to assume the burden of fasting and abstinence in a spirit of penance.

With abstinence came ancient dietary guidelines. In Genesis God tells Noah that "everything that moveth on the earth shall be a meat for you . . . saving that flesh with blood you shall not eat."[4] Leviticus contains detailed instructions on what animals, birds, and other creatures were unclean for the Israelites to eat. The Lord approved of scaled fish: "These shall ye eat of all that are in the waters; whatsoever hath fins and scales in the waters, in the seas, and in the rivers, them shall ye eat."[5] Many of these rules washed over into Christianity.

The Christian tradition of fasting began with Christ's epochal desert fast of forty days and forty nights in the wilderness. He was tempted by the devil and prevailed, whereupon "angels ministered unto him." Christ's fast was not an act of penance but an austere example for his followers. The Savior did not define the days or weeks when his followers were to fast and abstain, but he made it clear that the faithful would be subjected to regulations for fasting after his death, or "after the bridegroom has been taken away," as he put it.

"Everyone striving for the mastery must abstain from all things," wrote St. Paul in his first epistle to the Corinthians. "Let us exhibit ourselves as the ministers of Christ in labors, watchings, and fastings."[6] He advised his correspondents to prepare themselves for the coming end-time by disciplining their bodies and dispositions just as athletes train for competition. This discipline involved avoiding meat. At the Council of Jerusalem, convened in A.D. 49, the apostles prescribed "abstinence from things sacrificed to idols, and from blood, and from things strangled."[7]

Christ proclaimed, "The bread which I shall give for the life of the world is my flesh."[8] From the dawn of Christianity, Friday was a day of abstinence, atonement for the Savior's suffering and commemoration of his death on the cross on that day. The Didache (Teachings of the Twelve Apostles), set down as early as A.D. 50, instructed the faithful "not to fast with the hypocrites, for they fast on the second and fifth day of the week. Rather, fast on the fourth day and the Preparation [Wednesday and Friday]."[9] Many early teachings, among them those of the early Christian theologian

Clement of Alexandria (died A.D. 215) and Tertullian, make explicit mention of this practice.

As early as Tertullian's time, churches occasionally prolonged Friday abstinence and fasting into Saturday. Such penitence was commonplace for hundreds of years, perhaps to commemorate the burial of Christ on Saturday or to imitate the disciples, who mourned the death of Christ even on the seventh day.

At about the same time, a purifying fast of several days before Easter developed as mourning and penance for the time "when the bridegroom was taken away." A short period of abstinence and fasting, with no eating of what is still called "flesh meat," lasted for no more than one or two days during the time of St. Irenaeus (A.D. 177–202).[10] The earliest mention of a formal period of purification known as Lent (or Quadragesima) comes from the deliberations of the Council of Nicaea in 325, which included intense debate about doctrinal schism, appropriate Christian behavior, and the date of Easter. At first, Lent lasted thirty-six days. By the seventh century, the Church had settled on a forty-day Lent over and above Sundays, a duration that coincided with Christ's epochal fast.

For 2,000 years, Fridays have been obligatory days of abstinence from meat on pain of mortal sin, at first for all Christians and then for the Catholic faithful. As recently as February 17, 1966, Pope Paul VI promulgated *Paenitemini*, the Apostolic Constitution on Penance, providing for abstinence from meat for all the faithful over four years of age: "The time of Lent preserves its penitential character. The days of penitence to be observed under obligation throughout the Church are all Fridays and Ash Wednesday. . . . Their substantial observance binds gravely. . . . Abstinence is to be observed on every Friday which does not fall on a day of obligation, while abstinence and fast are to be observed on Ash Wednesday . . . on the first day of 'Great Lent' and on Good Friday."[11]

Canon law flatly states that all Christ's faithful are obliged by divine law, each in his own way, to do penance. And penance the faithful have done for centuries—by eating grains, vegetables, and later fish on Fridays, on holy days, and during Lent.

∞

Early Christian teachings were unanimous: fasting made the body more obedient and the soul lighter. It quieted the restless mind, inhibited sexual desire, and limited nocturnal emissions of semen. Fasting was redress for Adam and Eve's gluttony, a path to paradise, and a foundation for virtue, helped by prayer and penitence. Long-term fasts caused changes in the body. For instance, celibate female ascetics who became emaciated made their bodies more attractive to Christ, the virgin's bridegroom. But for all the competitiveness of the fanatics, fasting brought Christians together in gratitude for God's gift of the harvest, in obedience to divine calls to abstinence—violated in the Garden of Eden but fulfilled on the cross—and in charity toward the less fortunate. St. Augustine of Hippo (354–430) preached that fasting begets a "humble and contrite heart . . . extinguishes the fire of lust and enkindles the true light of chastity."[12] The Mass Preface, used during Lent, declares the Church's conviction that a person "who by bodily fasting suppresses vice, ennobles the mind, grants virtues and rewards."*

A philosophical underpinning for fasting connected it to the health of the soul. The first-century Roman philosopher Musonius Rufus urged people to avoid meat because it was better suited to wild beasts, a heavy food that dulled the intellect and slowed logical reasoning. Another well-known author, Plutarch (A.D. 45–125), recommended eating less food and taking frequent baths. One should consume light foods, he wrote, not "heavy" meat but vegetables, fish, and some birds. The early Christian theologian Basil of Caesarea (c. 329–c. 379) contrasted the simple eating of "paradise" with worldly eating habits: "If you subdue your belly, you will live in paradise, but if you do not subdue [it], you will be a victim of death." He said that God had forbidden Adam and Eve to eat from the Tree of Knowledge as a way of legislating fasting and abstinence. "If Eve had fasted from the tree, we would not have the need to fast now." Fasting was repentance: "Because we did not fast we fell from paradise, let us fast now, in order that we may return to it."[13]

---

*The Mass Preface is the first part of the eucharistic prayers, separated from the rest of the rite by the singing of the Sanctus. There are now eleven in the Roman missal.

Then there was the issue of the "hot surge" of carnal lust. Early Christian writings preached that meat eating inflamed passions that were far from spiritual. "The flesh lusteth against the spirit, and the spirit against the flesh," wrote St. Paul in his epistle to the Galatians.[14] Over a millennium later, St. Thomas Aquinas proclaimed that abstinence from food and drink dampened lust. Abstinence from meat, "hot" and moist, blood and semen-producing food from animals that reproduced by copulating, purified the soul, elevated the mind, and subordinated the flesh to the spirit. These beliefs stemmed from medical doctrine of the time. According to the influential Roman physician and philosopher Galen (A.D. 129–c. 210), the production of abundant and warm semen was the "most miserable" human condition. If the patient did not indulge in frequent sexual intercourse, he would become emaciated and hollow eyed, plagued with headaches and stomach upsets. Galen recommended avoidance of semen-producing foods, the moderate consumption of vegetables, fish, and birds. Such "cold" foods were "not very nutritious" and would not enflame lust.[15]

The austere St. Jerome (340–420), following Galen's ideas, proclaimed that "the eating of flesh, and drinking of wine, and fullness of stomach, is the seed-plot of lust." In a letter to a widow, he urged chastity: "Let them eat meat who serve the flesh, whose seething passion erupts in sex, who are tied to husbands, and whose work is procreation and children."[16]

Oddly enough, there is some scientific basis for these perceived benefits of fasting. Twentieth-century experiments with semistarved control groups on diets of 1,500 to 1,600 calories a day and with famine victims show a marked reduction in sexual desire over weeks and months of food deprivation.[17]

Fasting produced extremes of behavior in the faithful, ranging from backsliding to outright obsession. During the late fourth century, John Chrysostom (c. 349–407), a priest of Antioch who later became bishop of Constantinople, was one of many who urged their congregations to show more discipline in observing fast days on Wednesdays and Fridays, and during Lent. He condemned gluttony and luxurious foods: "The increase in luxury is nothing but the increase in excrement," he remarked in a graphic homily. He spoke approvingly of Christians who put on the

"garment" of righteousness and virtue by renouncing luxury for a more
ascetic life.[18] Those who lived immoderate lifestyles were victims of their
uncontrollable flesh. "Incontinence of the stomach" drove Adam out of
the Garden of Eden. So the Christian, like Adam and Eve, was free to
choose obedience and life in paradise through fasting. "If you subdue your
belly, you will live in paradise," wrote Basil of Caesarea with stark blunt-
ness. The fasting person imitated or returned to the state of humanity before the Fall. Basil pointed out that wine and meat were introduced to the
human menu *after* the Flood—only because God realized the greed and
wickedness of humanity. St. Jerome (340–420), who spent much of his
life in asceticism and quiet study, summed it all up: Christ was "Alpha and
Omega, the beginning and the end."[19] Now that Christ had risen, humanity should return to the ways of the beginning and avoid meat eating.

From fasting it was a short step to asceticism. Ascetic texts set out a vision
of the exemplary individual in great detail, with recommendations on how
to achieve such a goal by fasting. Many tracts recommended a light meal
once daily and avoiding meat, wine, and other delicacies.

Asceticism soon became fashionable, sometimes to the point of ab-
surdity. Early Church councils condemned enthusiastic ascetics who went
to ludicrous extremes and never ceased to discipline themselves. Yet these
fanatics always had admirers, among them St. Jerome, a celibate monk
who praised obsessed fasters like a twelve-year-old girl, Asella, who consumed only bread, salt, and water every two or three days, a diet that kept
her perennially hungry. He told his followers that a full stomach was the
"seed plot of lust," a teaching that endured long in Christian doctrine.

The most ardent ascetics were the Egyptian hermits. In about 270, a
young Egyptian Christian named Anthony gave away all his possessions
and went to live in the desert. He remained in solitude for the rest of his
life and supported himself by manual labor, becoming famous for his ascetic life and holiness. Others soon emulated his solitary existence. Egyptian
monks living in remote caves in the desert became the symbol of ascetic

living. The fourth-century church historian Salminius Hermias Sozomen believed that Syrian monks near Antioch, whom he called *boskoi* (grazers), were the first to copy the Egyptians. They had no homes and "dwelt constantly in the mountains, continually praising God with prayers and hymns according to the law of the Church."[20] The boskoi wandered in the hills with sickles, living off wild plants, their matted hair making them look like eagles with outstretched wings. This wandering lifestyle became popular with counterculture monks from Mesopotamia to Syria, Palestine, and the Nile.

Sozomen's boskoi were the successors of earlier nomadic ascetics whose movements were guided by the Holy Spirit. As late as the sixth century, they could be seen wandering along the Dead Sea or in the desert, or as Abbot Daniel wrote admiringly, "like animals, . . . no longer human in the way they thought. . . . As the body grows, the soul becomes weak; the more the body becomes emaciated, the more the soul grows."[21] The monk and ascetic writer John Cassian (c. 360–c. 435) described their austere diet down to the number of dry biscuits and drops of oil the monks consumed. Only on Saturdays and Sundays did the monks eat slightly more—some legumes, vegetables, fish sauce, and small dried fish. Modern researchers estimate that they lived on a diet of about 930 calories a day.[22] If the starvation research mentioned above is correct, this meager diet of bread, brine, and oil would have brought the Egyptians to their goal of complete chastity in about six months.

Some monks went to great extremes. The fourth-century hermit John, who prayed while standing for three years, ate only the Eucharist brought to him on Sundays. Neither John nor his fellow monks ate meat or drank wine, except when they were sick. Bread, salt, and water were the most common fasting diet—the simplest and most basic observance. They subsisted off small loaves or biscuits that could be soaked in water for easier consumption, and ate this hardtack without embellishment or with some oil and vegetables. Fruit, fish, and vegetable or grain gruels sometimes accompanied the bread.

By the fourth century, abstinence, fasting, and penance had become a defining facet of a faith concerned with atoning for human sins. Inevitably elitist groups of early Christians, men and women remarkable for their discipline and renunciation, took up the challenge of atonement, either individually or, more often, in cloistered communities. But fasting and penance were far more than a basis for group identification. They were part of a practice of atonement debated by the apostles and their successors that became a defining feature of the numerous monastic communities that took Christianity to western Europe and beyond.

During the fourth century a desert hermit, Pachomius, experienced a divine vision and organized his followers into a community and drew up the first monastic rule for them. They were to practice chastity, poverty, and obedience to a spiritual father, or abbot. Pachomius was critical of solitary anchorites, whose self-imposed fasting and mortification of the flesh sometimes led to unnecessary starvation. Religious communities offered psychological support as well as a better way of feeding the devout. No one could go on a fast without the community leader's permission, and then only after being issued specially made loaves of bread.*

Communal monasticism gained a strong following in the west after the fourth century, but at first the various religious communities had little in common. The proliferation of monasteries led to the first attempts to formalize monks' conduct. The anonymous author of *Regula Magistri* (the Rule of the Master), probably set down in the sixth century, proclaimed that monks who ate no meat between Easter and Pentecost and between Christmas and Epiphany must be seated apart from the others: "Let these abstainers . . . be directed to sit together . . . so that the voracious, through sharing the same nature, may blush for not being able in like manner to restrain the cravings of their appetites."[23]

---

*St. Pachomius (c. 292–346) was a former soldier who organized his monastic community on basically military lines, headed by a provost, the abbot of later times. The provost imposed discipline and restrained excessive fasting.

## GARUM: ROMAN FISH SAUCE

Roman cooks placed great emphasis on sauces and flavors, but none was more ubiquitous than garum—fish sauce. The modern equivalent would be tomato ketchup or Tabasco sauce, utilitarian products used to enhance all manner of dishes, both lavish and prosaic. For authentic-minded cooks, today's global cuisine provides an equivalent to garum in readily available Asian fish sauces. There were many garums (also known as liquamen), so there was no universal recipe, much depending on the catch at hand. Highly exotic, even vintage sauces satisfied gourmets at one end of the spectrum. At the other, Egyptian monks, obsessed as they were with penance, considered fish sauce a luxury, but we can be sure it was a very poor variety of what most Romans considered a staple. For most people, garum was a flavoring for the bread and vegetables that composed most of the diet, a sauce as common as salt is today, traded the length and breadth of the empire and manufactured in many places, among them what are now Brittany and Belgium.

There were hundreds of recipes for garum, few of which survive, for each manufacturer—each fishing family—had its own favorite blend. The third-century writer Gargilius Martialis gives an example in his *De medicine et virtute herbarum*:

> Use fatty fish, for example, sardines, and a container, whose inside is sealed with pitch, with a 26–35 quart capacity. Add dried, aromatic herbs possessing a strong flavor, such as dill, coriander, fennel, celery, mint, oregano, and others in a layer on the bottom of the container; then put down a layer of fish (if small, leave them whole, if large, use pieces) and over this, add a layer of salt two fingers high. Repeat the layers until the container is filled. Let it rest for seven days in the sun. Then mix the sauce daily for 20 days. After that, it becomes a liquid.

*We recommend that you don't make this recipe.*

Fish sauce, a type of garum, is still widely used, for example, *nuoc mam* in Vietnam or *nam pla* in Thailand. Most Southeast Asians have their own variations. Like their early Roman counterparts, fish sauces are fermented and very salty. Countless versions exist, some made with whole fish, some with ground fish; many are concocted with anchovies.

Before purchasing a fish sauce, make certain that your version is in a glass bottle. *Never buy it in a plastic container.* All fish sauces are reasonably priced, so you may want to try several. Don't be put off by the aroma, which dissipates during cooking.

In about 530, St. Benedict of Nursia (c. 480–543), founder of the Benedictine Order, set down his famous Rule at the Monte Cassino monastery in Italy. This drew heavily on the longer Rule of the Master and other guidances and soon became the dominant code of monastic conduct in the west. Benedict defined the "instruments of good works," which adjured monks to "love fasting," not to be great eaters, and "never to despair of God's mercy."[24] The "workshop" for the performance of these good works was the enclosed monastic community with its ordered stability. Benedict laid down rules for obedience, silence, humility, and the hours of rising to recite the Divine Office, as well as instructions for performing the "work of God during the day."

His instructions for the monastery diet were explicit: "We believe for the daily meal, both at the sixth and the ninth hour, two kinds of food are sufficient at all meals. . . . Let two kinds of cooked food . . . be sufficient for the brethren. And if there be fruit or fresh vegetables, a third may be added. Let a pound of bread be sufficient for the day." (We know from surviving monastic records that Benedict's loaves weighed 506 grams.)[25] Benedictine houses baked different kinds of bread, one of unsifted flour for fasting and mortification.

The Rule was simple and pragmatic. Monks engaged in especially demanding physical labor might be given extra food, "barring above all things every excess, that a monk be not overtaken by indigestion." Red meat was not on the menu: "Let all except the very weak and the sick abstain altogether from the eating of four-footed beasts. . . . But when they are restored let them all abstain from meat in the usual manner." At first the prohibition included birds, but this soon changed.

For the next 400 years, as Benedictine communities spread through Europe during and after the sixth century, St. Benedict's Rule with its meatless diet governed the lives of religious communities large and small—in or near large towns, in remote country valleys, and in the heart of the vast primordial forests that pressed on Europe's cultivated lands. The prescribed diet was modest indeed for men who spent their days engaged in manual labor. Fast days were so strict that a monk had to draw on considerable willpower to adhere to them. By no means did everyone succeed, even when portions for two monks were served in a single bowl. Instead of the usual two or sometimes three meals a day, a fast day saw just one, usually bread and vegetables, sometimes bread and water alone. As the number of monasteries increased and the need for self-sufficiency demanded hard physical work, monastic diets became more plentiful and varied. By the ninth century, three Benedictine monasteries in France were allowing a daily ration of about 4,000 calories per person. Unfortunately we don't know how the food was divided among monks, guests, servants, and hired men. But the diet was monotonous even though its caloric composition varied daily.

Fish still had powerful sacred associations but were a delicacy, eaten only with the abbot's permission on holidays. Fish soup and garum were not fasting dishes. No fish of any kind became commonplace, either as a celebratory dish or as a fasting food, until after the eighth century, when monasteries acquired land grants and the rights to fish in rivers, lakes, and ponds. Both freshwater and sea fish were only sporadically available, and far too expensive for all but the most princely tables. So monks ate much the same diet as everyone else—bread, legumes, vegetables, and fruit. Exotic foods were effectively inaccessible to most people, devout or otherwise.

Fish were an opportunistic food, still acquired mostly by chance and only eaten by those with fisheries nearby. But as more monasteries came into being and strove toward self-sufficiency, and the diet in both cloister and castle improved, a demand for fish developed throughout Europe.

Part of the reason was the spread of Christianity. From the fall of the Roman Empire to the Black Death of 1343, Lenten and weekly fasting, especially on Fridays, remained a basic mark of Christian observance. By the eleventh and twelfth centuries, a Christian was someone who minimally received yearly Communion, fasted on Fridays and during Lent, paid tithes, and had his or her children baptized. To violate a Friday fast was the most visible way of rejecting the One True Faith. This commitment to fasting and atonement created a huge international fish industry.

# The Fish Industry Is Born

Her only medicine was a temperate diet,
And exercise, and a contented heart.
She was not stopped from dancing by the gout,
No apoplexy ever hurt her head.
She never touched wine, neither white nor red;
Most of the food she ate was white and black—
Milk and brown bread, in which she found no lack,
Grill bacon and an egg or two sometimes:
She was a dairy-woman of a kind.

Geoffrey Chaucer, "The Nun's Priest's Tale"[1]

# "By the Aid of God's Grace"

Thus, it seems to me that hunting and hawking and also fowling are so tiresome and unpleasant that none of them can succeed nor can they be the best way of bringing a man into a happy frame of mind. . . . Doubtless then, it follows that the winner should be the sport of fishing with a hook. For every other kind of fishing is also tiresome and unpleasant, often making folks very wet and cold, which many times has been the cause of great illness. Nothing . . . can upset him, except that some fish may break away after he has been hooked, or else he may catch nothing: these are not serious. . . . And if the angler catches fish, surely then there is no happier man.

Lady Juliana Berners, *A Treatyse of Fysshynge* (1496)[1]

On an early summer afternoon, the roofless cruciform of the great church at Tintern Abbey in south Wales is quiet and still. The sun casts deep shadows across the aisled nave, the choir, and presbytery at the east end. Majestic weathered columns rise from the carpet of grass that now covers the floor. Superb lancet windows frame the green hills beyond. Even today, nearly five centuries after its abandonment, Tintern casts a profound spell on the visitor.

With some effort one may imagine the church dark and cold on a midwinter night, the monks rising at midnight and filing down a stone stair

Maps showing major locations mentioned in Chapters 3–5.

0    200    400 miles
0    200    400 kilometers

from their cells into the frosty presbytery. Dim candlelight from a simple chandelier overhead would have cast deep shadows across the nave, relieved only by the small candles near the monks' stalls so they could read the chants. Every inexperienced novice knew the order of service promulgated by the sainted Benedict: "Let three psalms be said separately, and not under one *Gloria*. Let the hymn for the same hour be said after the verse *Deus in adjutorium* before the psalms are begun. Then, after the completion of three psalms, let one lesson be said, a verse, the *Kyrie eleiso,* and the

collects." The unaccompanied chants and familiar Office echoed toward the church rafters and into the chilly night, as much a part of medieval life as birth, death, and the routine of planting and harvest.

To this day, Benedictine communities follow the same Order: "As the Prophet saith: 'Seven times a day I have given praise to Thee,' this sacred sevenfold number will be fulfilled by us in this wise if we perform the duties of our service at the time of Lauds, Prime, Tierce, Sext, None, Vespers, and Complin. . . . The same prophet saith of the night watches 'At midnight I arose to confess to Thee.' . . . Let us rise at night to praise Him."[2] Day after day, month after month, year after year, the monastery bell marked the passage of the Divine Office in an unchanging litany of adoration, praise, and atonement.

The Benedictines defined the frontiers of European Christianity, partners with God in finalizing creation. As they acquired land, cleared forest, and were given fields or property by wealthy novices or lords anxious to achieve salvation, their communities became nearly self-sustaining.

Like everyone else, the early Benedictines lived at the subsistence level. They met their simple needs from their own fields and pastures; moreover, their monastic routine offered a stability largely unknown in an unpredictable world of sudden crop failure, plunder, and violence.

Their simple monastic diet was more adequate than the 930-calorie regimen of the ultra-austere fourth-century Egyptian monks. Since Benedict had withheld meat from all except the sick, every community subsisted on grains, fruits, legumes, and vegetables. Bread and wine formed the basic diet, sometimes boiled beans flavored with fat. In the early days, fish must have been an unexpected bonus. Oily sea fish like herring could not travel far inland, for they spoiled within hours and did not last long even when subjected to the rudimentary salting methods of the time. For many early monasteries, fish in any quantity was unattainable on Fridays and during Lent. The diet was usually fishless and meatless, except for the ubiquitous eel.

The earlier fish cuisine was largely forgotten. Roman British and Gallic cooking, with its many sauces, had embraced sophisticated fish dishes flavored with pepper, dried onion, honey, and wine thickened with wheat starch. Wealthy citizens in country villas and towns occasionally feasted on imported luxuries such as salt-pickled swordfish and tuna from distant Mediterranean waters. This exotic cuisine flourished in romanized areas such as southeastern Britain but never became universal in a land where most people were subsistence farmers.[3] After the demise of Rome, fish eating reached low ebb in western Europe, except in coastal villages that had subsisted off inshore fisheries and agriculture for thousands of years. These fisherfolk were well aware that their catches could be dried, salted, or smoked, but for the most part they ate their fish fresh, boiling or roasting it as their predecessors had always done.

The religious did not sanction fish eating at the time. The Irish monks, who first brought Christianity to Britain in the late sixth century, disapproved of the practice. The ancient Celts had associated fish with Venus, the pagan goddess of love, which implied a suspicious level of sinfulness. The situation changed when the rites of the Roman Church were brought to England by the Benedictines and others at the end of the sixth century, when the pagan Anglo-Saxons gradually embraced Christianity. Roman policy was always to replace pagan observances with Christian ones, so if followers of Venus ate fish on Fridays, then Christians would eat it on the same day as atonement. There were also more practical considerations. By the time Lent arrived in a subsistence farming society like that of the Saxons, surplus domestic stock had already been killed off to save precious fodder and people were often hungry. Fish, especially easily taken species like eels, could be a crucial late-winter survival food.

The eel *(Anguilla anguilla)*.

Eels *(Anguilla anguilla)* abounded in ponds and streams and were easily taken with trap or spear. They appeared mysteriously in rivers during spring, running inland by the millions as small elvers, swimming downstream to spawn in fall, swarming by the thousands in pools, lakes, and wetlands, where they could be caught throughout the year. Most importantly, eels could be readily preserved by smoking them over high heat for two hours or more, a process that did not destroy, and could even enhance, their flavor. Eels became a form of currency for rich and poor alike, used for rent and as payment for services rendered.[4]

Eel fisheries were of immense importance throughout Europe, but those in England are probably the best known, thanks to studies of monastic records. In the fens of East Anglia in eastern England, and in the Somerset Levels of the southwest, eel crops were so valuable that local monasteries tried to monopolize the supply. Peterborough abbey boldly claimed "all of the meres and fens in Huntingdonshire" for itself. Ely abbey's foundation, confirmed in 970, included a gift of 10,000 eels annually from the villages of Outwell and Upwell, a gift which had previously been paid to the king in lieu of military service. The same abbey received 1,500 eels a year from the nearby town of Wisbech. Ely, surrounded on all sides by wetlands, also received tolls of various amounts from people fishing its fens. Two fishermen alone paid the abbot about 14,000 eels and 13s 4d annually for fishing rights. Farther west, the Benedictine abbey at Glastonbury in Somerset owned an entire local fishery, a third of it the gift of the abbot himself. Fisheries along the nearby Axe River yielded as many as 16,000 eels annually for the abbey's cellarer.[5] We can imagine a bell ringing, the monks filing into the refectory on a day in Lent, the prayers and a psalm being recited as everyone stood by his designated place. Then the food was passed out— trenchers comprising large slices of heavy rye bread, for plates were not yet used. On the trenchers lay dinner for two—some vegetables, perhaps some coarse porridge, and sticklike dried and smoked eels, softened by boiling. Everyone ate in silence as they listened to the reading of the day or some devout tome. A few kilometers away, an iron cauldron would be boiling over a hot fire, filled with vegetables and fresh-caught eels. As the fatty stew simmered for hours, dozens of eel carcasses would dry high above the hearth, their fat hissing as it dripped into the flames.

With much of Europe living from harvest to harvest, most people faced the constant specter of hunger—which is why monasteries carefully safeguarded their eel stocks.

## SMOKED EEL, BACON, AND MASH

The tribes that broke across Rome's frontiers into Gaul adopted some dietary practices from the Romans at a time when the best advice about food and food preparation came from physicians. Medical men like Galen were deeply involved in issues such as fasting and penitence, which also were related to carnality. Between the fourth and tenth centuries, food was increasingly linked to rank. Meat, which medical authorities considered the source of bodily strength, became the symbol of power and command, of strength in battle. Meat and power went together in feudal societies, where the nobility spent time fighting and hunting. Meanwhile, the religious and common folk ate a predominantly meatless diet as St. Benedict's Rule held sway in the cloister. Except in coastal villages and monasteries, fish was rare. The ubiquitous eel, however, was so common that it became a form of currency for paying rent. Even in great castles and palaces, cuisine lacked any sophistication, with the exception of the widespread use of aromatic herbs as flavorings.

Eels could be dried like beef jerky, stewed or boiled, or made into pies. Eel pie was a favorite dish for centuries, especially in growing towns and cities. The New England Pilgrims also consumed eel pie, once the Indians taught them how to catch eels in muddy shallows. William Wood visited the colony in 1634, where he found a "great store" of saltwater eels, not as delicious as those in England, perhaps, but "wholesome for the body and delightfull for the taste."

Today the eel is out of fashion in North America except for sushi bars; Germany and northern European countries import millions of eels from North America. They almost never appear on American restaurant menus, which is a pity, for they are succulent. British chef Fergus Henderson is widely acknowledged as an expert on *Anguilla*, that now-ignored staple. Here is one of his eel dishes, presented in the hope it will prompt some readers to try this most delectable fish.

### ✂ *Smoked Eel, Bacon, and Mash*

SERVES 3; 6 AS AN APPETIZER OR LIGHT SUPPER

1 large whole smoked eel
4.4 lbs/2 kg floury potatoes
20 oz/600 ml milk; more may be needed
5 oz/150 g unsalted butter
Sea salt and pepper to taste
6 thick rashers of good-quality smoked streaky bacon

To prepare your eel, first lay it down with its back facing you. With a sharp knife cut behind its head until you feel the backbone, then run your knife along the bone to the tail. Turn over and repeat. To remove the skin, simply

*(continues)*

*Smoked Eel, Bacon, and Mash (continued)*

ease your fingers under it and run gently along the fillet. Cut both fillets into three pieces. Smoked eel is also available packaged in fillets.

Peel and halve potatoes, and then boil until tender in salted water. Heat the milk and butter, add to the drained potatoes, and mash. Season to taste, remembering that the bacon is quite salty.

Heat a frying pan and add a knob of butter. Place your bacon slices in the pan and cook. Remove the bacon and keep warm. Place the eel fillets in the pan, cooking them for a few moments in the butter and bacon fat.

Serve the eel on a mound of mashed potatoes, topped with two slices of bacon. Pour the remaining bacon and eel fat from the frying pan over the eel and potatoes.

Recipe by Fergus Henderson, St. John Restaurant, London, author of *The Whole Beast: Nose to Tail Eating: A Kind of British Cooking* (London: Ecco, 2004).

While eels were commonplace, fresh- and seawater fishing was another matter. The Venerable Bede (672–735), the most learned man of his time and a compassionate observer of his fellow man, told a weird tale involving Wilfrid, bishop of Colchester, who "found so much misery from hunger, he taught the people to get food by fishing; for, although fish were plentiful in the sea and rivers, the people had no knowledge of fishing and caught only eels." Wilfrid solved the problem by casting his flock's eel nets into the sea: "By the aid of God's grace, they quickly caught three hundred fish of various kinds."[6] An apocryphal story perhaps, but it reminds us that the population of seventh-century Europe put considerably less pressure on its food supply than later populations would. Bede lived during a cool, damp period, when cereal agriculture was riskier than it would be a few centuries later during the Medieval Warm Period. Every farmer expected crop failures, months when families had to fall back on hunting, eels, and wild plant foods for their sustenance. But other kinds of fish were largely an untapped resource. After Bede's time this changed quickly.

Coastal villages were lucky to have fish close to shore. They caught them for their own use as well as for monasteries and towns located on estuaries or easily reached by water. The herring market was large enough by the sixth century to attract the attention of Anglo-Saxon chroniclers. We learn

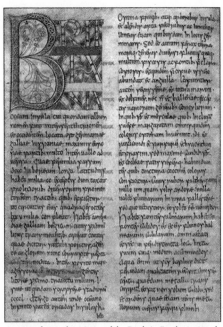

A page from the Venerable Bede's *Ecclesiastical History of the English Nation,* Northumbria, 746.

from them that "Piscatores Angliae, Galli, and Belgae" were active off the mouth of the River Yare in present-day Norfolk. Felix, bishop of the East Angles, built a church near Yarmouth with "godly men placed in it to pray for the health and success of fishermen that came to Yarmouth in the herring season in 647."[7] Even at this early date, boats from modern-day Holland and Belgium fished the English side of the North Sea, a couple of days' sail from their homes. Preservation methods were so rudimentary that most of the herring catch had to be eaten near the coast.

Most people fished near land in open boats, perhaps in hide vessels or crude planked boats little more than dugout canoes with built-up sides. An observer would see bright torches flaring a kilometer or so offshore, the dark water shimmering with silvery herring cascading to the surface to feed. The laden hulls of the boats are black shadows, heeling under the weight of bulging nets as the crew guides a mass of wriggling fish aboard.

Coastal fishers also took cod, haddock, pilchard (related to herring), and salmon. Large fish were especially prized. Nobles in castles and palaces near the coast sometimes dined on fresh porpoise. Stranded whales always attracted busy crowds of scavengers. Under English and Welsh law, such beasts were Crown property, although often granted to the landowner in exchange for the head with the tongue, a prized delicacy.[8] Shellfish, popular in Roman times, subsequently fell into disfavor until the eighth century, when the Venerable Bede listed it as one of Britain's great natural resources. Thetford in eastern England was a prosperous Anglo-Danish town where the people ate numerous cockles, mussels, oysters, and winkles imported from the North Sea coast some sixty kilometers away.

The lakes and rivers of northern and western Europe supported a relatively limited range of freshwater fish compared with the warmer waters of the Balkans and the Danube River far to the southeast. Barbel, bream, pike, and salmon thrived in slow-moving streams. People harvested the annual runs that brought eels, salmon, sturgeon, and trout into estuaries and freshwater streams to spawn. They did so with fishing methods that were little changed from prehistoric times. Success required local knowledge, not only of good fishing spots but of the seasons when salmon runs would occur or when fat mature eels would be hiding in the mud for the taking. Not technology but experience, infinite patience, and close observation were the keys.[9]

The simplest fishing methods required no equipment. I fished this way in my youth, my right elbow deep in the slow-running water of an English stream, moving my fingers gently as I carefully approached a stationary trout clearly visible near the bottom. Time and time again, the fish moved as my hand grazed its body. Then success! The trout remained still as my fingers moved ever so slowly up its body. I reached the gills, seized them like lightning, and whisked the wriggling, slippery fish onto the bank, almost falling into the water in the process. Some medieval fishers used their hands as bait. They mixed a pungent solution of heron grease, flour, pounded bird bones, and bean oil, then smeared it on their fingers. "When thou wilt fish rub thy hands with the ointment and thy shin bones before and behind and thou shalt see wonders," proclaims a medieval text on angling.[10] Some villagers poisoned still pools with narcotics and harvested the fish as they floated to the surface, a practice that was outlawed in most places, just as the practice of exploding gunpowder underwater is today.

Most medieval fishermen worked inland waters from the shore or waded in shallow water. The weapon of choice was a wooden spear with multiple prongs. Spearing required considerable expertise with different fishing spots and the ability to allow for water refraction, which gave a false impression of the fish's size and position. Pronged spears worked well for salmon runs, as hundreds of fish leaped rapids or waterfalls, and in clear pools, where the weapon could be jabbed, plunged, or thrown into one's prey. The eel was another matter, for its elongated shape made it hard to spear. Eel fishers used spears fitted with many sharp iron tines mounted close together, or a comblike design known as a gleave, with flat tines serrated on their opposing edges. The gleave would wedge an eel between the tines without damaging it.[11]

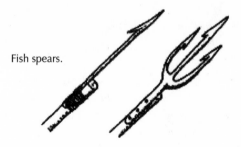

Fish spears.

People also used hand lines, casting a hook and weighted line into the water, then winding it slowly onto a wooden frame, feeling for a bite with the fingers. This was tiring work in deep water, when the unfortunate fisher had to haul in long lengths of line. Sometimes the hooks were little more than gorges (short spines that caught in a fish's mouth) made from thorny twigs, but most medieval hooks were bronze or iron. They were

Medieval fisher.

normally barbed, fabricated in a wide variety of sizes for different kinds of fish. Hemp or bast, even horsehair, formed the line. "If you are fishing for minnows with a lyne of one here. For the troughte, graylynge, barbyll, and the great chevn [chubb] with ix heeres," Lady Juliana Berners advised in *Treatyse of Fysshynge with an Angle*, part of the *Boke of St Albans*, published in 1496.[12] Berners recommended using composite fishing rods made from different woods and a line of pack thread reinforced with wire when seeking pike, lest the fish's sharp teeth sever the line. She also advocated a more drastic method, later endorsed by none other than that maestro of angling, Isaac Walton: tie a line with hook and live bait around "the body or wings of a goose or duck and chase it over the pond." This technique must have worked, since it remained in use for hundreds of years.

To catch larger numbers, freshwater fishers used hemp nets and traps. Once again, the technology was prehistoric. Seine nets, carefully fabricated with a deep center and narrower edges, were highly effective in rivers or

A sea hedge or shore trap, set to catch fish as the tide fell. Fishing technology was remarkably conservative and endured for centuries, so this eighteenth-century drawing probably reflects early methods. FROM DUHAMEL DU MONCEAU, *TRAITÉ GENERAL DES PESCHES ET HISTOIRE DES POISSONS* (PARIS: SAILLANT ET NYON, DESAINT, 1769).

estuaries. The bottom was weighted, the top fitted with floats. The fishers would cast seines in a semicircle either from shore or from boats, then bring the ends together to surround the fish. The vertical wall of the net would herd the fish toward shallow water where they were dragged inshore. Seines were effective for bottom fish, a simple technology that could be used off tidal beaches and in lakes.

Drift nets were invented by medieval herring fishers, a refinement of the seine that was fitted with extra floats so that it could be set in deeper water. Such nets formed a perforated barrier that could be set in the path of dense shoals of herring and other fish. The mesh size was tailor-made, so that the prey would push its head and gill covers through before being trapped.

Trawls, dredge-like nets that began as bags towed along the bottom by two boats, came into use in later medieval times. Subsequently they were modified with a wooden beam across the orifice so they could be maneuvered by a single boat and emptied without coming ashore.

Fish traps became so ubiquitous on rivers and streams that they sometimes posed a hazard to navigation. Most traps included a stationary barrier, a V-shaped weir made of boulders or posts, and wickerwork that

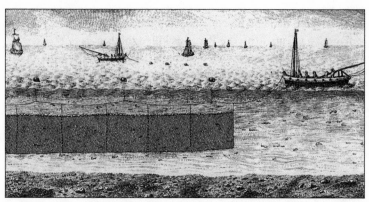

A drift net. From Duhamel du Monceau, *Traité,* 1769.

steered fish toward openings where removable nets lay in wait. Other traps were stand-alone versions, wickerwork or basketry set with posts on a riverbed and weighted at the back end.

The wicker traps used to capture eels were easily constructed from green willow or osier, which survived for considerable periods of time underwater. Fishers would bait the traps with a dead fish. These traps were known by various names, including *kidell*, a late-twelfth-century term that gave rise to the expression "kettle of fish."

As eel demand escalated, so did the intensity of fishing activity. The thirty-five monastery-owned weirs on the Severn River in western England sometimes threatened safe navigation and prompted litigation. Tempers flared when one monastery claimed another was depriving it of fish. A cascade of legislation regulated eel fisheries, often with little success, and forbade the blocking of rivers or streams to the detriment of navigation. In 979, for example, King Otto of Germany settled a dispute between two abbeys by ordering them to maintain an opening between their weirs wide enough for two vessels to pass without touching. The persistence of such legislation over many centuries explains why so many European rivers are now navigational corridors rather than fishing streams.[13]

All of this technology was simple, efficient, and easily made. The village blacksmith would forge fishhooks; fishermen and their wives would weave their own nets, using needles identical to those used today. (Wooden examples have come from medieval excavations in Gloucester, London, and Wölin, Poland.) As late as the ninth century, subsistence fishermen could still work clear lakes and streams that were not yet polluted with human and animal waste or overfished by a rapidly growing population.

But these methods could never yield the growing demand for freshwater fish among monasteries and the nobility. Fish that reached the market were too expensive for most people. Prized catches like mature pike or the highly valued sturgeon became symbols of wealth and prestige, public displays of one's religious devotion. It was no coincidence that technological innovations such as artificial fish ponds came from religious communities, major landowners with ample resources and powerful spiritual incentives to implement them.

"Every man shall . . . serve God," proclaimed King Charlemagne of France, a brutal conqueror who in 782 ordered the defeated pagan Saxons to abstain from meat during Lent or face death.[14] He also attempted, with little success, to reform lax monastic discipline. A half century after the Charlemagne's death, Pope Nicholas I (858–870), one of the greatest pontiffs of the Middle Ages, set out to repair the Church's reputation and forced powerful, independent-minded archbishops to submit to ecclesiastical discipline. A pious, intelligent man of distinguished family, Nicholas was a committed ascetic who actively encouraged missionary activity and the observation of basic Christian doctrine and dietary rules. When Khan Boris of Bulgaria inquired about church discipline in 862, Nicholas adjured him and his subjects to abstain from meat on Fridays and during Lent. The ancient belief that meat provoked carnal lust was never far from Catholic minds.[15]

Papal admonitions had little effect on anyone but the aristocracy and nobility, which already showed its piety through generous gifts of booty and land to monasteries. Most of Europe still lived at the subsistence level in small hamlets and villages. Few people could read or write. Even fewer, including priests, could communicate or even understand the basic beliefs of Christianity. Nearly everyone, including monastic communities, subsisted on a meatless diet year in and year out. Fish was a luxury too rare to satisfy secular demand or religious doctrine.

Fish, prized by abbot and lord alike, were now culled from lake and river fisheries decimated by overfishing and pollution from rapid forest clearance and growing towns. Freshwater fish became a commodity worthy of the attention of the highest lords. Charlemagne instructed the stewards on his royal estates to develop statements of income, including the yields from fish ponds and the number of fishermen. They were to employ good artisans who know how to make nets for hunting, fishing, and fowling.[16]

The king was well aware that expensive fish at table were a mark of devout behavior and social prominence. Prize catches were the right of the rich and powerful, including the abbots and monks of many of Europe's most prosperous monasteries. By the eleventh century, many abbots and priors dined apart, often on much more lavish fare than those in the refectory, even on holy days, often under the fiction that they were entertaining guests. Good food was a mark of a wealthy, powerful host or hostess. A German proverb of the day aptly remarked that "game and fish belong on the table of lords."[17]

Monks were among the dietary aristocracy. By the eleventh century, the monastic diet had grown more varied, partly because of the demands of manual labor. New monastic orders and religious communities also proliferated, some of them austere responses to seemingly more liberal ecclesiastical routines. Some even banned fish. *The Seasons for Fasting*, a late tenth- to eleventh-century poem that reflected efforts at rigorous Benedictine reform, addressed "men of God" (priests) and the faithful: "We have noted how famous ones long ago observed the fast of forty days, and we command through the man of God that every man who lives in the world should equally observe the fast for forty days before the resurrection of our Lord until the ninth hour, and should not partake of flesh or fish, lest he should be proscribed."[18]

Monarchs, the nobility, and monasteries turned to artificial ponds to ensure better fish stocks. At Winchester, successive bishops enjoyed the services of skilled professionals, among them "Master Nicholas the Fisherman," who provided bream and other fish for Advent and Lent from pools fed by small streams; between 1244 to 1262 he traveled constantly from pond to pond.[19]

Fish ponds made economic sense because demand could not keep up with supply. There was a busy local trade. Small river fish like dace and roach cost as little as one quarter pence each—about the same as a salted herring when they became widely available—but the larger and choicer specimens were very expensive. Pike changed hands at two to three shillings each. As historian Christopher Dyer has pointed out, this was as much as a skilled artisan's weekly wage. A sixpenny tench, weighing perhaps eight kilograms, cost as much as twenty-four loaves of bread or six gallons of good ale. At these prices, it was cheaper for a manor or monastery to keep well-stocked ponds than to buy on the open market.[20]

Fresh fish also possessed cachet. Many not particularly tasty varieties, like the chubb, were valued as much for their prestige as their flavor. Gifts of fresh fish reflected royal favor and reinforced social bonds. Thirteenth-century English kings gave bream from the royal ponds as breeding stock to their more important subjects. Churchmen paid respect to one another with "great eels." Towns tried to influence high officials with lavish gifts of pike, salmon, and eels. The rarified social status of fish was reflected in the carefully nurtured and guarded ponds joined to moats or protected behind estate walls that separated nobility from commoner, as well as in the lavish feasts served by the king or his prominent subjects. On October 13, 1257, King Henry III and his court celebrated St. Edward's Day with 250 bream, 15,000 eels, and 300 pike collected from many parts of the realm. The common folk at the occasion, such as artisans and servants, received portions of salted herring.[21]

The earliest ponds probably date to the ninth century, but legal disputes about them proliferated 200 years later. The late twelfth-century abbot Samson of Bury St. Edmonds was fond of fish and zealous in his pond construction. He raised the level of one pond so high "that there is no man, rich or poor, having lands by the waterside . . . but has lost his garden and orchards. . . . The cellarer's meadow is ruined, the informerer's orchard is drowned through the overflow of water, and all neighbors complain of it."[22] When the cellarer remonstrated with the abbot, that worthy responded angrily that he did not intend to lose his fishpond because of a mere meadow.

Fishponds were not a new or difficult technology in an era when peasants regularly constructed timber revetments and intricate earthworks. Their purpose was not to breed fish but to store them to ensure a convenient supply for fast days and Lent. Such facilities also offered a convenient way of enforcing monastic discipline. The tenth-century monastic reformers Abbot Olpert of Gembloux Abbey, in what is now Belgium, and St. Odo of Cluny Abbey, near Paris, are said to have laid out fishponds near their monasteries to reinforce their monks' obedience of the rule with a regular fish supply.

Medieval ponding frequently involved migratory fish, which could be harvested wherever a natural barrier such as a waterfall or rapids restricted their movement.[23] From natural barriers, it was an easy step to creating weirs and other artificial obstacles either to harvest the fish or impound them. Such barriers and traps took many forms. In Hungary, fishers would maintain openings for floodwaters to inundate oxbow lakes of large rivers as artificial ponds. As the water fell, the fishers would use wooden grills to let smaller fish into the main river while holding the larger ones. Some ponds were little more than large fish traps, such as those used on the Oder River in Silesia by the fishermen of Kotowice, who diverted river water into convenient depressions several times a week to provide fish for their lord.

In a world without refrigeration or canning methods, live storage made sense not only for manors and monasteries but also for the increasing numbers of fishmongers who plied their trade in towns large and small. They kept fish alive until the last minute, transporting them in boats with perforated wells that allowed water to circulate around the catch. Such devices carried fish for long distances—up the Thames beyond London and from Burgundy down the Rhone and Saone as far as Avignon. Once at their destination, the fish went into storage tanks. A long row of such "stews" lined the Thames at Southwark near London before the 1360s.

Many fishponds were simple, rectangular ponds, little more than kitchen storage facilities, filled by groundwater and spring seepage. Wooden enclosures or tanks, even netting structures, stored fish for monastery and convent, sometimes for a year or more. Chests fitted with grills dug into the banks of the Loire kept the Counts of Forez in St. Etienne in fish. Royal palaces, major bishoprics, and religious houses built more elaborate storage. Cluny Abbey obtained its fish from rows of tanks set along the nearby Grosne River. The Cistercians at Obazine, at the edge of the Massif Central, built a monastery water system into which they incorporated a sixty-meter fish pond next to the kitchen and refectory. The Benedictines at Battle Abbey in eastern Sussex, England, lived on a ridge. Their rectangular fishponds, each measuring fifty by twenty meters, lay just down the hill. Generally, however, early monastic pools were simple structures, designed to serve the needs of the house, not local markets.

Bream were a staple of fishponds but spawned rapidly, so the waters were soon overstocked. Pike helped control the bream population and was itself a highly desirable fish, said to be "very holesome for seke peple." Tench, on the other hand, "puritifie in the stomach, and bring a man that much eats them to infinite diseases."[24] Worcester Priory stocked its ponds with eels in summer, as many as 6,386 between 1518 and 1524. In winter and early spring, the monks added bream, perch, and roach in smaller numbers.

Despite their exacting construction, medieval fishponds were not intensively managed. Their overall yield was low, even when emptied for cleaning every five to ten years. According to the historian Christopher Currie, a one-hectare pond would support about 227 kilograms of bream without supplementary feeding. But since it took about five years for these fish to grow large enough to be edible, the actual annual yield would have been about forty-five kilograms a year. If ten monks each ate 170 grams of cooked fish per day, they would require about 385 kilograms of fish annually—the yield from 8.5 hectares of ponds—not including the needs of lay brothers, servants, guests, and charitable obligations.[25] Even with rights to nearby river fisheries, very few houses ever came close to self-sufficiency in freshwater fish.

On feast days or for meals hosting important visitors, the finest pike or even a sturgeon might grace the abbot's table as a gesture of celebration, respect, or honor. But fish would not become a dietary staple until more sophisticated means of preservation were developed.

# 4

# Salt upon Salt:
# Preserving the Catch

To make salt white: take one pint of coarse salt, and three pints of water, and put them on the fire until they are all melted together, then pass it all through a cloth . . . then put it on the fire and boil it very hard, skimming it; and let it boil so long that it is almost dry, and the little bubbles which appeared on the water are not seen, then take the salt out of the pan and set it on a cloth in the sun to dry.

Viandier de Paris, fourteenth century[1]

My father's favorite breakfast was bacon, eggs, toast, and a perfectly cooked kipper.* He would sit contentedly at table, the newspaper straight ahead, a strong cup of tea on the right, buttering his toast. Then he would carefully dissect the red-brown fish, separating flesh from backbone with unerring skill. He would eat only the finest herrings from Craster in Northumberland, carefully soaked in a brine solution, then cured over smoldering oak and white wood shavings for sixteen hours.

---

*A note on herring terminology for uninitiated readers: the kipper is lightly salted and then smoked, the word coming from *kippering*, a 1326 verb that means "to cure a fish by cleaning, salting, and spicing it." Kippers and bloaters were associated with Yarmouth, England, but were produced all along the eastern English coast, especially in Northumberland, where the kippering process was invented in the 1840s.

Kippers were my father's culinary nirvana. They are less fashionable to-day, but few British hotels are without kippers on their breakfast menu.

John Woodger of Seahouses in Northumberland invented the kippering process in the 1840s. A relatively mild cure, it was ideal in an era when rail transportation wafted herrings from smoker to kitchen in a few hours. Such light preservation would have been unthinkable in earlier times, when fish took days, even weeks or months, to reach their destination. The waters of the Baltic, English Channel, and North Sea teemed with aquatic life, but the catch couldn't travel. Only a few kilometers inland, a fresh catch would begin to smell, leaving the seller no option but to throw it away. So sea fish had inseparable partners—drying racks, salt, and smokehouses.

Breakfast kippers are fat herrings, salted and smoked lightly to preserve their delicate flavor and texture. There's a world of difference between the salting and smoking that create fine food and the heavy salting that pre-serves it, as in medieval times, when shelf life was the primary considera-tion and people ate fish intensively at certain times of the year. By the twelfth century, the devout who dined on fish during Lent almost invari-ably consumed a dried, salted, or smoked catch.

Two staples sustained the medieval sea fish eater—herring and cod. Her-ring, and its close relative the pilchard, was the most plentiful fish of all. Witness a herring catch in spawning season and you will never forget it. The boat heaving in short North Sea swells, the night wind blowing in your hair, bright lights on the dark water—a mountain of flickering silver tumbles onto the deck from the net, thousands of fish wriggling help-lessly in the mesh. As you haul on the teeming drift net, your back aches and your hands quickly go numb, even through the thickest gloves.

The Victorians called herrings "silver darlings." Chefs loved dressing them up with sauces that brought contrasts of sharp acidity or sweetness. Though rare on American menus today, herrings are still popular in northern Europe.[2] The meat stands up to robust flavors; you can stuff them with cucumbers, apples, beets, or mushrooms. Most medieval cooking involved boiling fish, but herrings were small enough to be wrapped in leaves and roasted over a fire, or grilled over embers or coals.

Unfortunately, the oily flesh of herrings means that they spoil almost at once, so they require salting or a combination of salting and smoking to remain edible for more than a few hours. The Dutch became adept at salting them in brine, packed tightly in barrels. For centuries they dominated the European trade, developing many varieties of cured herring, including the rich-flavored matjes—young, fat virgin herring cured in salt, sugar, and saltpeter.

Heavily salted medieval herring were disliked by the poor and the sailors and soldiers who received them as rations. The fish were dry, sticklike, and either tasteless or rancid, like a very poor form of modern-day jerky.

Cod and its close relatives like hake, ling, and pollack have bland, white flesh with little fat. The nineteenth-century French chef Auguste Escoffier lamented that cod was so commonplace. Had it been rarer, "it would be held in as high esteem as salmon; for when it is really fresh and of good quality, the delicacy and delicious flavor of its flesh admit of its ranking among the finest of fish."[3] But cod's great historical importance lies in its easy preservation, its resulting suitability as transported stores for mariners and soldiers, and its sheer abundance.

Really fresh cod,* if not overcooked, forms large, creamy flakes and is easily boned. This storied fish has a clean flavor that takes well to sauces or accompaniments from bacon to tomatoes or wine. According to the Victorian cookbook writer Mrs. Beeton, cod tends to be somewhat watery when cooked fresh; she recommended rubbing salt into the flesh a couple of hours beforehand.[4] Cod fried in batter is practically a British national dish, the fish part of the quintessential fish and chips, wrapped in newspaper and doused with vinegar.

Before refrigeration, few people ate fresh cod; wind-dried or salted cod, served day after day with monotonous regularity, were the staples of holy days and Lent. Skillful chefs could work wonders by saucing the fish

---

*The family Gadidae comprises freshwater and marine fish, including numerous forms of cod and haddock. After herring, they are the most frequently landed of all fish.

## GRILLED MACKEREL WITH CAMELINE SAUCE

Salted and dried fish was a staple in the medieval world. Even when soaked and sometimes pounded, the preserved catch was stringy and often tasteless, too dry when eaten without some form of enhancement. Then as now, many people served herring with mustard, still a common recipe in French kitchens, but the flavor did little to disguise what was often a unpalatable product. Generations of palace and monastery cooks experimented with sauces. Pity the poor in Paris, who were often served salt herring like sticks of jerky, with nothing but some bread to accompany it, day in, day out.

Fortunately herring has robust flesh that can stand up to lively flavors, so the cook had considerable latitude in experimentation. It was generally cooked and served whole. Today many people cook herring on the grill, where its oil-rich flesh comes into its own and rivals the luscious grilled sardines of Spain and Portugal.

Medieval cooks often prepared grilled herring served with mustard or entrancing sauces. This recipe, tested with mackerel, works just as well with herring or sardines.

### Grilled Mackerel with Cameline Sauce

SERVES 4 TO 6 (FISH LOVERS MAY WANT MORE THAN ONE SERVING)

4 to 6 medium herring, mackerel, or sardines

Clean the fish, leaving the heads on. Slit them open along the belly and remove intestines. Brush the inside and outside of the fish with a small amount of olive oil.

Grill the fish under the broiler or on the grill at a moderate temperature. Turn the fish at 4 minutes, or when the flesh is flaky, turning again appropriately. The skin will be charred. Serve with warm Cameline sauce on the side.

### Tournai Style Cameline Sauce

*Caution:* Do not attempt this sauce in a food processor. It should be made with a mortar and pestle.

1 slice of very stale artisanal wheat bread. Cut off the crusts and cube the rest.
10 oz/300 ml dry white wine
$\frac{1}{16}$ oz/5 g ground cinnamon
Large pinch/2 g ground ginger
Pinch of ground nutmeg
Sea salt to taste
$\frac{1}{3}$ oz/10 g demerara sugar
A few threads of saffron, ground in a mortar and pestle

*(continues)*

*Grilled Mackerel with Cameline Sauce (continued)*

> Soak the bread in about 8 oz/¼ liter water. Mix the wine and the spices.
> Squeeze excess water from the bread and then pound in mortar and pestle.
> Gradually pound in the wine-spice mixture. You cannot overpound this, and
> it's needed to create a smooth-textured sauce. Heat carefully in a nonreactive
> pan until thickened. You may need to add a bit more wine. Season to taste with
> the salt and sugar and serve warm.
>
> Adapted from Chiquart, *Du fait de cuisine.*

with interesting spices and vegetables, but most people ate bland, boiled
fillets. Stew was a very popular way of serving salt cod on account of the
long desalting process. Wind-dried cod, the stockfish of the far north, requires thirty-six hours of soaking in water before cooking. Salt cod needs
twenty-four to thirty-six hours in fresh water before being boiled and
simmered. Today, Portuguese cuisine boasts hundreds of recipes using
*baccalao*, salted cod.

Many other sea fish turned up on medieval tables, among them the
easily dried and salted salmon, firm-fleshed conger eels, frequently used
in soups, as well as plaice, sole, and other flat fish. But herring and cod of
several kinds were the staples.

After the eleventh century, the doctrines of the Catholic Church and
the insatiable demands of armies for light, easily transported victuals created an enormous trade in sea fish. A rapidly growing international commerce depended entirely on preservation methods little changed from
early prehistory—drying, salting, and smoking.

"Habitually dark, oxidized, rancid, sandy, spoiled, and insect infested"—
the cod expert Charles Cutting describes the quality of traditional fish
curing methods in a few succinct words.[5] Nineteenth-century salting and
smoking were labor-intensive and ineffective by modern standards.

Drying, salting, and smoking, the traditional methods of fish preservation, kill bacteria with varying degrees of efficiency. Acids like sugar and

vinegar, as well as certain herbs and spices, can have the same effect. Fermentation, if carefully controlled, can halt decomposition. Ugandan fishers still dry their catches of Nile perch from Lake Victoria in the sun and wind. As I once found to my disappointment, the result is a visually unattractive, unappetizing breakfast for Western palates.

Drying the catch requires the least investment but depends on the quality and size of the fish, as well as the prevailing weather. Drying is the oldest preservation technology of all, having been used by Stone Age hunters for 100,000 years. It works well in dry, windy climates or in the cold spring breezes and bright sunshine of far northern places, like Norway's Lofoten Islands. Dried meat is as old as hunting itself. Strips of game meat dry quickly in the wind and can then be chewed like jerky, carried around on the hunt, or pounded with fat to make pemmican. Fish dry with equal ease, especially the less oily species such as cod and salmon. The ancient Egyptians split open and gutted Nile catfish before drying them in arid sunlight, turning them into *ukas*, a fixture of workers' rations during the building of the pyramids.

In its simplest form, the method is the same everywhere. You gut and butterfly the whole fish or cut the flesh into strips, laying the carcasses or thin cuts on racks to dry in the sun. Such simple drying methods are still commonplace in places like northern Norway, with its cold, sunny, and windy days in late winter and early spring. Tens of thousands of cod lie on wooden racks in the Lofoten Islands each spring, turning slowly into stockfish—headless cod so dry they have to be hammered and soaked before cooking. Yet the hard, white flesh maintains most of its flavor even after months in storage. Generations of northern seamen relied on stockfish during long voyages. Drying was not generally practicable in the Baltic and North Sea region, where rainfall is abundant and summers are long and often damp.

The North Sea fishers of early medieval times caught almost nothing but herring, perhaps the hardest of all seafood to preserve.[6] As demand from monasteries and towns grew, preserving herring became as important as catching it. Herring is oiliest in the autumn, during spawning season. Numerous microorganisms in fish intestines and skin invade, digest, and spoil the flesh. Enzymes also contribute to dissolution and oxidization. Atmospheric oxygen adds to the additional decay process, especially in the case of natural fats. From long experience, fisherfolk knew that fresh herring begin deteriorating before the end of rigor mortis, which begins between one and seven hours after being caught in warm weather but can last as long as five days in cold conditions. The richest herring fishery was close to the Scottish and English coasts, where there were convenient sandy beaches and sheltered inlets where the catch could be landed and processed at once.

Salt is so common and easy to obtain today that we've forgotten how valuable a commodity it was in the past. Salt's preservative qualities, known to ancient Egyptian embalmers, made it a seemingly magical substance. It became a pervasive symbol of permanence, friendship, and loyalty in Christianity, Islam, and Judaism. Christ called his disciples the "salt of the earth," fighters against corruption.[7] Sal Sapientia (the salt of wisdom) is a Catholic doctrine based on the decontamination of polluted water by the prophet Elisha at Jericho: "He went forth unto the spring of the waters and cast the salt in there, and said: 'Thus saith the Lord, I have healed these waters.'"[8]

Salt was used to preserve fish and meats long before Christ. Prehistoric Europeans worked salt mines in Austria at least 4,000 years ago. The Egyptians, Greeks, and Phoenicians found that their hot, dry climate provided excellent opportunities for evaporating salt on seashores, in marshes, and around brine springs. The Romans paid their soldiers in part with bags of salt, whence the modern word "salary." The soldiers in turn gave it to horses and livestock, and used it to preserve hams and olives, vegetables, and fish.[9]

The demand for salt continued unabated throughout the Mediterranean after Rome's collapse, culminating in a major technological advance between the sixth and ninth centuries, just as the demand for fish in western Europe accelerated. Whereas the Romans had trapped seawater in artificial ponds and allowed the sun to evaporate it, Islamic salt traders in

North Africa developed more elaborate production methods. They used pumps and sluices to move fresh seawater from a large open tank into another pond when it reached a higher salinity level, draining it into yet another as the brine reached the density where salt precipitates out, crystallizes, and drops to the bottom. As one pond was emptied into another, the previous ones were refilled, ensuring a continual supply of salt at a remarkably low cost in human labor.

The new system spread rapidly throughout the Mediterranean, along Atlantic coasts, and wherever climatic conditions were warm, dry, and windy enough to allow evaporation. Basque whale hunters used evaporated or "baie salt" from Portuguese and Spanish estuaries to preserve whale meat for French buyers. By the late eighth century, salt workers on the island of Noirmoutier at the mouth of the Loire River, which flows into the Bay of Biscay downstream of Nantes, were exporting salt far upriver into King Charlemagne's domains. Norse raiders eventually took over the pans and developed a lucrative trade with English Channel ports.

Northern Europe was too cool and wet for successful salt evaporation on any scale. Until the Romans came, local communities extracted salt from marshes and brine springs by boiling it. Their conquerors recovered salt on a large, labor-intensive scale by exploiting brine springs in northern England near Droitwich. They also baked brine in clay vessels at many locations in eastern and southern England. The scale of salt production fell rapidly after Roman times, as most communities acquired only enough for their own needs. In East Anglia, salters extracted brine from sand covered by exceptionally high tides several times a year. On the Continent, most salt came from coastal marshes, extracted by laboriously dissolving peat through grass or salt filters, then boiling and evaporating the resulting liquid. The amount of salt produced by all these crude methods was minuscule compared with the yield from evaporation pans.

Traditional salting relied on either dry methods or brining—immersing the catch in a concentrated salt solution; pickling was a combination of the two. Dry salting involved covering the fish with salt, then turning and moving them regularly to obtain an even cure. Fish liquids drain away as the salt penetrates the flesh. Ninth-century North Sea fisherfolk would heap salted herring in piles on the beach or on racks, sprinkling a layer of salt between each layer. They preferred coarse salt because the large crystals dissolved slowly as they penetrated the fish. Fine salt soaked in rapidly and merely sealed the outer layer of the fish, a phenomenon known as fish burn.[10]

After about fifteen days, the herring were given a "green cure." Dry salting is more effective with cod than with oily herring. The high fat content of autumn herring reduced the salt absorption, curing them only enough for transportation over short distances. This severely limited the usefulness of the final product, which even after salting turned rancid within days. During early medieval times, this was apparently the only way to salt herring.

Brining involved soaking the herring in a solution of 80 to 100 percent salt dissolved in water. As the fish absorbed the salt, the strength of the brine had to be maintained, for it affected the salt content of the fish and thus its longevity. Brining was far more than a matter of soaking the fish in a salt solution. The shape and fat content of the fish, the ratio of skin to brine, and whether the fish was skinned all affected the quality of the result, which was often poor.

No one knows when barrel pickling first came into use, but it likely originated in the Baltic region, where abundant salt was available in the Lubeck area and herring fisheries flourished on a large scale as early as the eleventh century. Pickling combined salting with brining in barrels, a method that had the advantage of maintaining the maximum salt content around the fish. Submerging herring in brine prevents fat from making contact with oxygen and turning rancid. As the fish pickled and absorbed brine, the curer added more brine and as many as twice the original number of fish. Until the fourteenth century, the herring were pickled whole. Thereafter they were gutted before packing, which gave a better cure. Pickling in barrels was an ideal way to store fish like herring infused with a high salt content. Barrelled fish stored at ten to twelve degrees Celsius remained edible for up to ten months, or longer at lower temperatures.

By the late fourteenth century, herring fishers in the Baltic and the North Sea had a more or less standardized brining system, which continued to be used by the early-twentieth-century English fishery. The fresh herrings were "gipped" with short gutting knives that removed the gills and long gut with one neat stroke. Teams of women sorted and gipped the fish—two gutting them, a third packing them in barrels. The gippers "roused" the gutted fish with salt, turning them over to prevent their sticking together, then laid them carefully on their backs in closely packed layers, laying each layer at right angles to the next. Each layer was sprinkled with the precise amount of salt needed to effect a uniform cure. The filled and sealed barrel was left for ten days, allowing chemical changes known as pining to take place between the herring and the salt. Then the "pickle" was drained through the bung hole and the barrel opened. By this time the fish had shrunk, so the barrel was topped up with more fish at the same stage of cure. The curers filled the remaining space with pickle before the barrel was resealed and the bung replaced. Only then was the barrel ready for sale and transportation, the result of a carefully monitored, standardized curing process that produced salted herring of the finest quality that were eaten all over Europe.

Pickling is unnecessary for white fish like cod, whose oil content is low. Because of this, production costs were much lower, especially for imported salt, which was everywhere subject to tariffs.

Smoked fish could not be stored for long. Generally, smoking was used in conjunction with drying or salting, over domestic hearths or later in special smokehouses, with beams from which the fish were hung on poles. By using different woods, the smoker could vary the flavor of the catch. The process took several days, with the fish "resting" between smokings. In Britain, fish were smoked below 29 degrees Celsius, a so-called cold smoke, whereas other northern European countries used greater heat, which partially cooked the fish with temperatures above boiling point. Heavy smoking helped desiccate herrings, as the smoke killed any surviving bacteria. Hard smoked fish could be transported over considerable distances, unlike lighter smoked kippers and finnan haddock, which became popular with the advent of the railroad.[11]

A herring smokehouse used to make red herrings. FROM DUHAMEL DU MONCEAU, *TRAITÉ,* 1769.

For centuries, limited preservation technology, not fishing methods, made fish of all kinds (except the eel) inaccessible to most people. After the tenth century, subtle climate changes, a population explosion, and Catholic dietary practices created an insistent demand for fish that turned a subsistence practice into an international industry. The Atlantic cod, introduced into Europe as stockfish by warrior sailors from the north just a century earlier, was about to come into its own.

# 5

# GADUS MORHUA

Yes, the fish in the sea are our daily bread,
Should we lose them, we will suffer and dread,
Forced to utter our miserable sighs.

Petter Dass, 1690[1]

The afternoon wind kicked strongly through the Golden Gate, raising a steep chop against the outgoing tide in San Francisco Bay. We maneuvered our small double-ended faering carefully away from the launch ramp with one pair of oars. The lapstraked hull seemed heavy and clumsy in the tight waters of a Sausalito marina. We dodged sleek yachts raising their sails, then manned both pairs of oars when clear of the traffic. Sudden gusts from the cliffs moved us to and fro in the water. Our oars dug deep, straining against the thole pins, the strokes longer as we gained speed.* The faering was slow to accelerate, but, once moving, surged ahead smoothly, tracking beautifully in the rougher water. We settled to a comfortable stride, backs leaning against the oars and the wind. A mile passed and we pulled clear of the high ground into the full drift of the westerly wind. Some cold spray broke over the high bow, wetting our backs, but the boat kept moving ahead, rising and falling effortlessly over the steep waves.

---

*Thole pins are a simple form of rowlock, a post in the gunwale with a lashing against which the oars are pulled. They are still used in traditional craft of many kinds today. The Norse often made them of natural crooks from small branches.

An everyday fishing scene, based on the 11.2-meter Skuldelev 6 ship from Roskilde Fjord, Denmark, built in 1030 (see figure on page 83). Similar craft of many different sizes but the same general design were used for inshore fishing throughout Scandinavia and in the Lofotens. COPYRIGHT VIKING SHIP MUSEUM, ROSKILDE, DENMARK. ARTIST: FLEMMING BAU.

Now we discovered the virtues of the Norwegian faering, a rowboat with an ancient pedigree (see figure on page 80).[2] We rowed for two hours in rough water and smooth, against the wind, across it, and with the seas behind us. This most seaworthy of small craft never faltered, always kept moving, never bounced unduly. You could stand upright, move from side to side, change places, even in a swell. And if you were tired you just sat and let the wind carry you where it wished. I imagined cod fishers jigging hand lines over the side, standing to lift wriggling fish onto the bottom boards.

Like everything else devised by the ancient Scandinavians, the faering was strong yet flexible, easy for a man with a fine eye and simple woodworking skills to build, and above all a superb platform for any task afloat in weather of every kind. Faerings were the ultimate working boat, one of many types of practical fishing vessels built by the Norse and their successors. You can still see them lying quietly at Norwegian docks, with their lapped oak planks and high ends, low lying and broad of beam, sometimes weathered, more often beautifully varnished, used for fishing or for pleasure, under oars and under sail, and today under engine as well. They are consummate fishing boats, developed on a rugged, demanding coast to pursue cod. Long before the Norse sailed across the North Sea, faerings and larger open fishing boats would lie year-round, especially in late winter, spring, and early summer when the fishing was best, at the mouths of fjords, close offshore, in open water and sheltered bays, their crews casting lines or nets for *Gadus morhua*, the Atlantic cod, and other fish.

Medieval Norwegians couldn't survive without cod. And they could never have caught them, or changed history, without the humble faering.

The Atlantic cod is one of the world's great food fish. A member of the family Gadidae, which also includes haddock, pollock, and whiting, cod thrive in circumpolar to temperate waters along the continental shelf from Greenland south to Cape Hatteras, North Carolina, and from the Arctic Ocean to the Bay of Biscay.[3] *Gadus morhua* is a heavy-bodied fish with a large head, three dorsal fins on the back, and two anal fins on the belly. Most cod are gray-green, with back and upper sides ranging from black to greenish pearl hues, almost always with speckles. The belly is usually whitish. Cod can grow two meters in length and weigh as much as ninety-six kilograms. Even in these days of depleted ocean stocks a twenty-seven-kilogram fish is not unusual.

*Gadus* are ground fish, usually found within two meters or so of the bottom, but they will rise to the surface to feed off herring.[4] They can live in water 460 meters deep but occur most commonly between 35 and 275

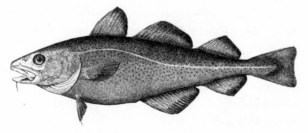

*Gadus morhua*, the Atlantic cod. FROM COLLETTE AND KLEIN-MACPHEE, *FISHES*, P. 228. COURTESY SMITHSONIAN INSTITUTION PRESS.

meters. They surface frequently on the Grand Banks of the eastern North Atlantic and off the eastern coast of Labrador, where they feed off small fish breeding inshore. Adult cod are comfortable in water temperatures between zero and thirteen degrees Celsius; younger cod, less sensitive to warmer conditions, tend to be more common in shoal waters. Their distribution depends on both water temperatures and food supplies, especially a small copopod, *Calanus finmarchicus*, whose abundance depends on the strength of ocean currents and gyrations of the North Atlantic Oscillation, the changing pressure gradient between the arctic regions and the central Atlantic.

A fifty-centimeter female cod can produce 5 million eggs in a single breeding season. Spawning occurs mainly at night in late winter, when the female swims near the surface, the male swimming atop her, then underneath, belly to belly. The few fertilized eggs that survive are buoyant and normally hatch near the surface one or two weeks after spawning. The resulting larvae are four to five millimeters long and metamorphose into juvenile fish by May or June, when they have settled near the bottom, staying there as long as seven years, until they mature. The growth rate varies. A six-year-old cod in the Irish Sea can be ninety centimeters long, whereas those off the Swedish coast grow to only half the size in the same time.

The cod is voracious and easy to catch with hook and line. Twelve hundred years ago it was plentiful in Norwegian waters, especially during late winter and spring, when enormous numbers of them spawned near the surface. Even when fat and ready to spawn, *Gadus* has white, relatively oil-free flesh that is easy to dry in the cool northern springs. It was an ideal food in a society that was subject to long, harsh winters and relied heavily on sea mammals and fish for survival. Unlike other preserved fish of the day, dried, beheaded cod known as stockfish lasted aboard ship on voyages of many months.

In northern Europe, the greatest spawning ground of all was in the Vestfjord, between the northern Norwegian mainland and the Lofoten and Vesterålen islands. This area also happens to be an ideal environment for drying cod to become stockfish.

The Lofotens (and the Vesterålens) form a string of islands, many precipitous, off the northern Norwegian coast.[5] Some of the mountain peaks are so high that glaciers never covered them during the Ice Age. The outer coasts, facing the Norwegian Sea, are battered by fierce winter storms and shrouded by clinging summer fogs. The eastern shores, sometimes called the inner coast, face the mainland and are somewhat less exposed. From at least 3000 B.C., subsistence farmers eked out a living on the narrow coastal hinterland between ocean and mountains, except in the middle of Vestvågoy in central Lofoten, where small farms flourished on tracts of land surrounded by mountains. Even landless peasants kept a few cattle and sheep, which they grazed on almost inaccessible mountain hayfields. But the staple was fish, especially cod. Every farmer combined fishing with agriculture or stock husbandry. The men went fishing; the women stayed at home and managed the animals.

Lofoten is famous for its strong winds and endless rain. Though the islands lie well north of the Arctic Circle, they are surprisingly habitable because the warm waters of the Gulf Stream flow close offshore, making the winters relatively mild. This fortune of geography brings *Gadus* to the archipelago to spawn. The Vestfjord, encircled by the arm of Lofoten, has been called the world's largest maternity ward.

Vestfjord is a perfect environment for spawning cod. The sea temperature is between four and six degrees Celsius, the salinity level just right; the water is the correct depth, and there are abundant krill and other plankton. The young cod thrive in the cold waters of the Barents Sea until they reach sexual maturity at seven or eight years. Every November and December, the mature fish swim back to their place of birth, 800 kilometers to the south. They arrive in Vestfjord in January. For the next four months, the cod harvest continues day and night.

The Lofoten cod fishery has existed since the Stone Age, when people used vegetable fiber lines and hooks made of horn and bone. Sea fishing was a staple of the local economy long before specialized and permanently settled fishing villages catching and processing stockfish developed in about A.D. 1300. These *fiskevaer* did not spring up overnight. We know from recent excavations at the Langenesvaeret site on the northwest coast of Langøya Island, Vesterålen, that at least some of these permanent locations were used occasionally over long periods of time before stock-fish became a nearly industrial commodity in response to the demands of the Hanse and the Christian Church in the fourteenth century. Using radiocarbon dates and thin-section micromorphology, also spectrometry analyses, the archaeologists showed that the early deposits contained little or no animal manure but evidence of fishing in the form of soil features associated with decaying fish bones with a high strontium content.[6]

Langenesvaeret shows that cod fishing was an important activity long before Hanse times. Powerful local chieftains in search of prestige more than profits traded stockfish for grain from communities far to the south when Norse voyaging was at its height, long before a full-scale commercial cod fishery developed between A.D. 1150 and 1200. Thanks to sophisticated analyses of thousands of fish bones from village middens, we know that earlier fishers took not only cod but halibut, saithe, and other species. Such fish counts reflect a subsistence economy, where much of the catch was eaten fresh, although large quantities of stockfish were also produced. For centuries, stockfish underwrote the entire political economy of northern Norway, acting as the truck that provided barley for the beer that was at the core of chiefly feasting. Sober feasting was unacceptable, so Lofoten's chiefs relied not on their unreliable barley crops but on seemingly unlimited cod to buttress their power and prestige.

The Lofoten fishery was the first to acquire an international market. Stockfish production intensified dramatically and spread southward and northward from the Lofotens. Stockfish soon became a vital source of income for both the Crown and the Church. Even before the eleventh century, stockfish featured in state tax policy. So lucrative did the fishery become that most Lofoteners abandoned subsistence farming and concentrated on fishing. The middens of the Vågan settlement on Lofoten tell the story. Cod are the dominant catch, to the virtual exclusion of everything else. The garbage deposits contain almost no cod heads, whereas the articulated portions of backbones are common, a clear indication that stockfish production was all-important. Furthermore, the size of the Vågan fish peaks in an identical window to that for modern stockfish.[7]

The fishery was so productive that boats from far away flocked to the islands each January, their owners sleeping ashore in turf-roofed or wooden huts or under their upturned craft.

Anyone working Vestfjord harvested cod the old-fashioned way with baited iron hooks, hauling up the fish one by one until the boat was in danger of sinking from the catch. The fishing continued in all weather, including blizzards. Long lines carrying rows of hooks did not come into use here until the sixteenth century.

Fishing in January above the Arctic Circle was a hard and perilous life. Sudden storms swamped dozens of boats at a time, drowning a hundred men in a few minutes. Even on a calm day, the men would work for hours in the winter twilight soaked to the skin, enduring frost and dry wind. A bailiff, E. H. Schønnebøl, wrote in 1591, "The wretchedness that these poor people suffer for their daily bread is beyond description. I am quite sure that no-one on earth suffers so much for their meager sustenance as do these poor, destitute people here in Nordland."[8] In his day, Lofoten fishers had lived this way for centuries. The profits others made from their labors were enormous. For hundreds of years, Lofoten and northern Norway produced about 80 percent of the country's exports: skins, furs, walrus tusks, and above all dried cod. Today industrial-scale fishing with gillnets, long lines, and seines has reduced cod stocks to the point that the few remaining small-scale hand liners can barely make a living.

Every day during the season, the boats would land their catches. The fishers would gut the catch, split the cod open, and hang them on racks to dry. They threw the viscera into large oak vats and left them to ferment. The resulting oil floated to the surface and was skimmed off. The Norse called this oil *lysi*, "light," and used it for their lamps, for tanning, and in cooking, unaware of its healthful Vitamin A, D, and unsaturated fatty acid content. As demand rose, the islanders took to boiling the cod livers and other viscera in iron cauldrons to produce more oil.

A powerful smell of rotting fish and cooking oil pervaded even the smallest coastal settlements, most of them little more than clusters of small timber houses surrounded by dozens of wooden racks. The drying continues to this day. Visit Lofoten in May and you'll see tens of thousands of beheaded cod lying or hanging on racks to dry in the cold, dry wind, and Arctic sunshine. The Lofoten climate in late winter and spring is ideal for drying relatively oil-free *Gadus* flesh. A cool wind with a touch of salt from the ocean blows over the islands, keeping temperatures above freezing yet cold enough to discourage black flies and maggots. Temperatures change relatively little from night to day. The fish freezes at night and thaws slightly in daytime, so the flesh dries slowly without spoiling. The slow drying retains the fish's flavor. Even today, by late April the drying racks in Lofoten hold about 11 million kilograms of cod slowly dessicating into stockfish. Large cod rot before they can dry, and small ones have insufficient flesh to be anything more than dog food. The minimum length is about sixty centimeters, with a weight of three to four kilograms.

Stockfish is the ideal preserved food for people without ice or refrigerators —lightweight, easily stacked and carried, and readily stowed aboard a crowded boat. Unlike many other dried or salted fish, it is nutritious. A kilo of properly dried stockfish has the nutritional value of five kilograms of fresh cod. The size of the fish, between about 60 and 110 centimeters, is vital, for smaller fish dry out rapidly and larger ones tend to rot. Drying requires almost no labor, but the temperature must be carefully monitored to make sure it does not rise much above one degree Celsius. If the temperature rises too much, a rare occurrence, the fish has to be removed or covered. By June, the fish is dried and taken off the racks for grading and sale. Properly cured and kept dry, stockfish can last for five years or more. Hammer it to open the fibers, soak it in multiple changes of fresh water, and you have palatable cod that can be turned into all manner of savory dishes. Or you can eat it as a form of hardtack, as the Norse often did.[9] Most commoners ate their cod boiled or in stews, while the nobility dined off delicately seasoned and sauced fresh and salt *Gadus*, often flavored with a green sauce made of parsley ground with vinegar, bread, and salt in infinite variations.

## SALT COD IN PARSNIP GRATIN

*Gadus morhua* arrived on Lenten platters with monotonous regularity, all too often an anemic dish that made people dread the forty days of meatless diets. John Collins, writing *Salt and Fishery* in 1682, provided a basic stockfish recipe that must have been in widespread use at the time:

> Beat it soundly with a Mallet for half an hour or more, and lay it three days a soaking, then Boyl it on a simmering Fire about an hour, with as much water as will cover it till it be soft, then take it up and put in Butter, Eggs, and Mustard champed together, otherwise take six Potatos (which may be had all year at Seed-Shops;) Boyl them very tender, and then Skin them. Chop them, and beat up the Butter thick with them, and put it on the Fish and serve them up. Some use parsnips.

Daphne comments, "This is a very clear and easy recipe to follow." The reference to potatoes is interesting, for they were still regarded as a curiosity at the time, and parsnips were a novelty.

For some reason, salt cod has received a muted reception at table, even when dressed up and flavored with loving care. But the Portuguese have embraced *bacalhau* as virtually a national dish; it's said that there are different recipes for every day of the year for a dish that is part of the fabric of life.

After the revolution in agricultural practices in northern Europe during the seventeenth century, many cooks served salted Lenten cod with a mashed parsnip, a vegetable with sweet winter flavor that was harvested as Lent began. Here's a delicious contemporary recipe for salt cod that uses the ancient tradition of favoring a basically flavorless fish with a green sauce.

### ✂ *Salt Cod in Parsnip Gratin*

SERVES 6

1.7 lb/750 g salted cod
8 oz/250 ml milk
1.7 lb/750 g parsnips
3 medium eggs, hard-boiled
7 oz/20 g unsalted butter
Generous measure of flour
3.5 oz/105 ml heavy cream
1 oz/30 g fresh breadcrumbs
Bunch of parsley
Dijon mustard and pepper to taste

*(continues)*

*Salt Cod in Parsnip Gratin (continued)*

Preheat oven to 425F/220C.

Soak the salted cod for 24 hours, changing water several times. Rinse well and poach it in 50 percent water and milk for 10 minutes. Drain (saving the liquid) and flake the meat into a shallow dish, removing any bones.

Steam the parsnips for 20 to 25 minutes, until tender. Peel away the skins and cut into thin slices. Cut the hard-boiled eggs into quarters. Chop the parsley and mix with the remaining ingredients in the dish.

Make a roux with the butter and flour in a saucepan, stirring well. Use a small amount of the fish liquid to make a smooth mixture before adding the remainder. Wisk constantly as it simmers and becomes a smooth sauce. Add the cream and season with black pepper. Simmer (do not boil) for 10 minutes, then pour over the mixture in the dish.

Bake for 10 minutes; then sprinkle the breadcrumbs over the surface and bake until they are brown (5 to 10 minutes more).

Modified with permission from a recipe by Rowley Leigh, Kensington Place, London.

Thirteen hundred years ago, Norway was a land of isolated, largely self-sufficient communities, many accessible only by sea. Their inhabitants were dairy farmers, for most of them lived in places where the growing season for cereal crops, if it existed at all, was very short. Life centered around the water, where sea mammals, herring, and cod abounded. People traveled from one community to the next in small open boats. This was faering country, a place where seaworthy, double-ended rowboats developed out of necessity. The ancient tradition of Norse seafaring, of venturing out in all weather, grew out of thousands of years of fishing from such boats, vessels that were sturdy platforms and strong enough to transport people and heavy catches. The Viking warship and merchant vessel of the eighth century developed from a cod-fishing tradition that trained expert seamen, to say nothing of shipwrights, literally from birth.

Napoleon Bonaparte famously remarked that an army travels on its stomach. The Norse voyaged on their stockfish. Without it they would never have crossed the North Sea or sailed to Iceland and beyond, however seaworthy their ships. Norse sailors took grain and live animals with them on their voyages, but grain spoiled in the damp and sheep required bulky fodder. Nor was it generally practicable to cast lines over the side and hope to catch cod or other fish far offshore. Stockfish was the fallback, the staple of armies and navies as well as the ideal way to satisfy the requirement to eat fish on Fridays and during Lent. It was no coincidence that every Norse merchant ship carried a faering, not only to ferry cargo and passengers ashore but to catch fish.

The most seaworthy watercraft in the world is useless without expert seamen. Scandinavia encompasses some of the most rugged waters in the world: rocky coasts, deep fjords, narrow waterways, and the shallow Baltic Sea, where vicious waves can swamp a small boat in short order. I vividly remember sailing from the Kiel Canal to the island of Bornholm off southern Sweden in the face of a rising easterly gale. The wind came out of a clear sky at twenty-five to thirty knots. Within minutes, short, steep seas descended on us from every side, cascading against one another chaotically. Despite the strong wind, we hobby-horsed up and down, making almost no progress. In the end, we reduced sail and hove-to to wait out the storm as night fell. Even then the constant thunk of waves against the hull kept us awake. Pity the poor sailor in a lumbering fishing boat, caught out in such conditions with a rocky coast close to leeward. Small wonder the casualty rates among Baltic fisherfolk were always high.

Tough coasts breed fine, careful seamen, and the Norse were consummate sailors from childhood, as comfortable afloat as they were ashore. They were intimately familiar with the convoluted Norwegian shoreline and its 150,000 bays and islands. They noticed local tidal streams and currents and gauged water depth in the Baltic from subtle changes in sea colors and the shapes of waves. The habits of seabirds, migrating geese, of herring and cod, were an open book to them. Every sea captain carried in a mental atlas of the oceans in his head—of fjords and skerries, of offshore cod banks, and of the shallows of the Baltic and southern North Sea. Such skippers could tell their direction from sun and stars, from the light on the horizon at dawn. There was nothing arcane or magical in their uncanny ability to navigate open water. They knew the North Atlantic and North

Sea the way the pious know the Bible. And they had behind them a tradition of coastal voyaging that began before Roman times.

Of many quiet voyages, completed for the most part by illiterate sailors who kept their knowledge in their heads, we can know nothing. But occasionally we are offered a glimpse of this forgotten world. During the 850s, a merchant from northern Norway named Ottar (or Ohthere) visited the court of Anglo-Saxon King Alfred of Wessex in southern England. Ottar was an honored guest. He presented the king with fragments of walrus ivory, northern animals whose hides were "very good for ship-ropes."[10] Alfred's court measured wealth in cattle and land. Ottar had few cattle, but his 600 tame reindeer and his gifts of furs, ivory, and walrus hides ensured him a warm welcome. He regaled the court with accounts of his voyages along the coast of what is now Norway. Whales abounded in Ottar's country. "He said that he, one of six, had killed sixty in two days." The southward voyage from his native Halogaland to a trading station in Viksfjord, west of Oslo Fjord, took more than a month with favorable winds. Like all Norse sailors, Ottar patiently waited out contrary breezes, riding southward on northerly winds. He may have been under way as little as a third of the time. This was classic Norse coastal voyaging, always by day, always close inshore, navigating from headland to headland, landmark to landmark. He would anchor or beach the boat every night in known spots an easy distance apart.

South of Viksfjord, Ottar voyaged for five more days along the western Swedish coast, then through the Danish archipelago to Hedeby, "the town on the heather," at the base of the Danish peninsula in modern-day Jutland. This important commercial center lay close to the modern-day entrance of the Kiel Canal, a sheltered harbor up a long, narrow fjord. Sometime later, in 950, a merchant from Córdoba in Spain, Ibrahim al-Tartushi, wrote that Hedeby was known from Iceland to Baghdad.

The prosperous entrepôt of Hedeby was the outer limit of Ottar's Baltic voyage. Wulfstan, another northern visitor to Alfred's court, described a very different 600-kilometer voyage, eastward from Hedeby along the windswept southern Baltic coast past the island of Rugen to Truso on the Vistula river delta, the boat running under sail the whole way. Wulfstan sailed day and night, within sight of a low-lying coast, without many conspicuous landmarks and certainly none of the powerful lighthouses that today guide mariners in these waters. He reached Estland, a coast where there were numerous fortified settlements and "a great deal of honey and fishing." The sources of the Vistula River lay far inland, close to the Dneiper River and ancient routes to the Black Sea and Byzantium.

The journey from Hedeby to Estland would have been a difficult passage with its few landmarks, but a lead and line would have enabled Wulfstan to maintain a safe distance from the coast along the ten- to twenty-meter depth contour line. The lead and line was a vital part of the Norse seafaring tool kit and is illustrated aboard the Norman ships on the Bayeux tapestry, which describes William the Conqueror's invasion of England in 1066.

Throughout Ottar's Norwegian coasting, the open ocean lay on one side, seemingly limitless, stretching to an empty horizon. A ninth-century sea captain would know of the Faeroes and Scotland, but the Atlantic was one of the boundaries of the known universe. Ottar practiced cautious, conservative seamanship, keeping in touch with the coast and conspicuous landmarks, his route driven by the vagaries of wind and current. We can guess that he and his crew lived mostly from the land but also on fresh fish, caught while they were at anchor. Being from the far north, he must have been familiar with stockfish and carried it with him, if only to trade for wine and other luxuries. Even at this early date, Scandinavian stockfish were highly prized by people who spent much of their lives eating nearly rancid herring.

But by Ottar's time a different tradition had already begun to emerge. Under the more benign climatic conditions of the late ninth and tenth centuries, the Norse had erupted out of their homeland to conduct quickfire raids across the North Sea. They had also begun to sail further offshore in refined vessels capable of transporting large cargoes and surviving bad weather. This burst of voyaging brought the Norse in collision with much of western Europe and eventually took them far over the hitherto unfathomed western horizon.

# 6

# THE NORTHMEN

The number of ships grows: the endless stream of Vikings
never ceases to increase. Everywhere Christians are victims of
massacres, burnings, plunderings: the Vikings conquer all
in their path, and no one resists them: they seize Bordeaux,
Périgueux, Limoges, Angoulême and Toulouse. Anger, Tours
and Orléans are annihilated and an innumerable fleet sails up
the Seine.

Ermentarius of Noirmoutier, c. 860[1]

The portents foretold disaster and a local monk remembered how they
"sorely frightened the people." Thunder sounded; immense lightning
flashes lit up the sky, fiery dragons rode on the wind. "The great famine
followed these signs." People died in the cold of late winter. Then, on June
8, 793, the meaning of the omens was revealed. "The ravages of heathen
men destroyed God's church on Lindisfarne with plunder and slaughter."[2]
Norse longboats from Scandinavia burst over the horizon, intent on plunder. The marauding northmen arrived on Holy Island without warning.
They approached their destination under sail, probably just before dawn,
without the sound of oars to give them away. The dark longboats slid quietly onto the beach in the early morning light. Their crews jumped ashore,
weapons drawn, bent on pillage and plunder.

The Norse had chosen their quarry carefully. Lindisfarne on Holy Island was one of the most sacred Anglo-Saxon sites in England, founded
by an Irish monk named St. Aidan from Iona in Scotland in 633 at the

invitation of King Oswald of Northumbria. Aidan had built a monastery of wooden buildings on Holy Island in the Irish style, where he and his companions lived in austere modesty. The monks served as missionaries in the nearby countryside, while Aidan encouraged book learning, the copying of the Gospels and Psalms. After Aidan died in 651, Lindisfarne continued to prosper as a great center of monastic learning, associated with the saintly hermit St. Cuthbert, whose relics made Holy Island a pilgrimage site. It was here too that the illuminated Lindisfarne Gospels were created in honor of God and St. Cuthbert, eleven years after his death in 698.

The Norse descended on a place of fabled wealth. Generations of pilgrims had brought offerings of gold and silver, in exchange for prayers and the serenity of their souls. The monastery's storerooms were piled with golden crucifixes and shepherd's staves, with silver plate and ivory chests for saintly relics. Delicate tapestries hung in the chapel; illuminated manuscripts filled the scriptorum. With brutal efficiency, the Norse despoiled the chapels and plundered holy valuables. They slaughtered the helpless monks and left them bleeding by their altars. Then they departed as rapidly as they came, with the treasures of Lindisfarne carefully packed in their boats.

A frisson of horror reverberated through England and the Continent as news of the disaster spread. The Northumberland scholar Alcuin, an adviser of King Charlemagne, wrote in a letter that the people had always assumed they were safe from the Norsemen. Why had St. Cuthbert not intervened to protect his monastery? Did the attack result from divine wrath? What assurance was there for the churches of Britain if St. Cuthbert could not defend the faithful?[3]

No one knows why the Norse suddenly burst forth from their homelands in search of plunder and conquest. Merchants from Scandinavia had long been peacefully active throughout northern Europe, deep into the Baltic and along rivers far into Central Asia. Travelers from Byzantium and Islamic lands visited trading centers as far north as southern Norway.

The Viking raids began just as Europe was enjoying somewhat warmer climatic conditions—the Medieval Warm Period—after four centuries of

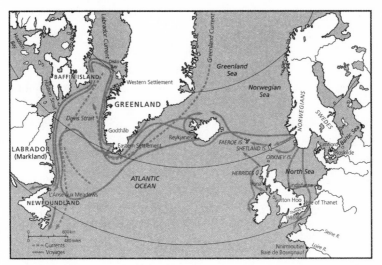

Norse voyages.

cold, wet summers. Milder winters, less severe pack ice in the far north, and a longer growing season for cereals in Scandinavia may have coincided with sudden population growth and not enough land to go around. At the same time, Scandinavians developed (still little studied) navigational skills such as latitude sailing that allowed them to sail out of sight of land. The economic and political changes were especially marked in the far north, in the Lofoten and Vesterålen islands, where powerful chiefs vied with rivals in lesser kingdoms to the south for power and prestige. Norse society was violent and volatile, seething with individuals jockeying for power, seeking followers and wealth. Young men and younger sons, eager for wealth and their own land, sailed from the north to distant shores year after year.[4]

Advances in navigation, ship design, and construction permitted Norse warships and merchant vessels to sail far offshore. With abundant stockfish from the north, their provisioning was secure. Endless opportunities awaited just over the western horizon for a society where opportunism, personal and family honor, and the acquisition of prestige and wealth ruled the day. Economic and political circumstances at home combined with favorable ice and sailing conditions in the North Atlantic to take European sailors far offshore for the first time.

There are scattered records of at least thirty raids on Ireland before Lindisfarne. Afterward and into the ninth century, the *drengir*, crews of fighting ships, returned in search of more easy pickings. They attacked other wealthy religious houses like Iona in Scotland and bled them of their wealth. By the middle of the century, the Norse were setting up huge camps to act as bases for protracted looting and eventually trade. Entire warrior armies landed and campaigned for months on end, relying not only on what they could plunder but also on stockfish as their hardtack, a style of provisioning adopted by armies everywhere in the west in later centuries. In 851 an anonymous writer commented that "the heathens now for the first time remained over the winter in the Isle of Thanet. The same year came three hundred and fifty ships into the mouth of the Thames."[5] In 865 "a great heathen army" invaded England and maintained a continuous presence for fifteen years, overwintering in defensive encampments. By 876 parts of this army had settled in the conquered lands, where they "began to plough and settle themselves." Scandinavian laws and customs known as the Danelaw now prevailed over a huge swath of Britain, putting it beyond the control of Anglo-Saxon King Alfred of Wessex to the southwest. Alfred's heirs eventually reconquered the Danelaw between 952 and 954, creating the kingdom of England. But the Scandinavian influence remained immense and long-lasting, not only culturally but also politically and economically through ancient Norse trade routes that brought ever-larger supplies of stockfish, among other things, to North Sea shores.

The Danish Norse sailed to the mouth of the Seine, where they founded a huge base from which another great army looted the defenseless cities of northern France. They captured Rouen and Nantes, and took control of the salt evaporation pans on the island of Noirmoutier at the mouth of the Loire. Fishers all, the newcomers knew the value of evaporated salt, which they began to trade northward into Channel ports and the North Sea to service the slowly growing herring fishery. By 844 Norse ships had sailed as far as Portugal. A decade later, they were well established in the Balearic Islands of the western Mediterranean.

# BAKED SALT-PACKED TURBOT WITH
# SANDEFJORD BUTTER

Norse subsistence cookery revolved around basic ingredients, among them dried cod. Stockfish played a vital role in Norwegian history and is a virtual icon of Norwegian identity. The Norse used dried cod as hardtack aboard ship in lieu of bread and also traded it for grain, honey, textiles, and wine. This most ancient of Norse foods can be stored for years in tropical heat, moderate temperatures, and extreme cold.

On land and at sea, the Norse would pound a stockfish with a wooden mallet, a convenient stone, or any blunt instrument. The pounding breaks down the coarse fibers so that it can be consumed like beef jerky. Raw stockfish is still a popular snack in many parts of Norway.

The Norse cooked fresh fish directly over hearth embers or boiled them in seawater. They would clean the cod, cut it into pieces, then submerge the fish in an iron pot, where the salt water added flavor. The cook often removed the liver, cut it into small pieces, then set it on top of the fish before cooking. The water was brought to a boil and the vessel then removed from the heat. This allowed the bones to loosen from the flesh. *Fiskemølje*, fish and liver, is still a popular dish in northern Norway, but today the cod is boiled in salted fresh water, the liver cooked separately and combined with the fish at serving. Delicious!

Here's a contemporary Norwegian fish recipe that can also be made with cod:

## ✂ *Baked Salt-Packed Turbot with Sandefjord Butter*

4 SERVINGS

1 whole turbot, 4.4 lb/2 kg, cleaned
Salt and pepper to taste
4.4 lb/2 kg coarse sea salt (kosher salt may also be used)
3.5 oz/100 ml fish stock, white wine, or cream
1 tsp cornstarch
Medium handful finely chopped parsley
9 oz/280 g unsalted butter, room temperature
½ oz/15 ml to 1 oz/30ml lemon juice

### *The Fish*

Preheat oven to 435F/225C.

Cut away the gills and remove the insides. Rinse the fish thoroughly under cold running water. Pat it dry with paper towels. Sprinkle salt and pepper into the

*(continues)*

*Baked Salt-Packed Turbot with Sandefjord Butter (continued)*

body cavity. Make a bed of sea salt in a baking pan. Place the turbot on top of it with the darkest side facing up. Spread a thick coating of sea salt (less than 1 in/2 cm) over the exposed surface until the fish is completely covered. Place the pan in the center of the oven.

Cook for 25–30 minutes. Remove from the oven and set to rest for 5 minutes. Break and peel away the salt after cooked fish has rested. Lift off the skin and fillet it.

Serve with boiled small potatoes, steamed spinach, and the sauce.

### Sandefjord Butter Sauce

Make the sauce while the fish is in the oven. Whisk the fish stock (or substitute liquid), cornstarch, and parsley into a smooth consistency. Pour the mixture into a saucepan and bring to a boil. Reduce the heat and simmer for 3 minutes. Remove from the heat and gradually whisk small pieces of the butter into the mixture. Add the lemon juice and salt to taste. Keep the sauce warm in a double boiler until ready to serve.

By Ingrid Espelid Hovig of Oslo, who is an eminent Norwegian food authority, cookbook author, and television personality.

---

Meanwhile, the Norwegian Norse expanded through the northern islands, occupying the Orkneys and Shetlands in the eighth century, and the Faeroes, Hebrides, and eastern Ireland in the ninth. By 874 they had ventured as far west as Iceland.[6]

The Norse were neither an expanding nation-state nor a band of warriors. They belonged to diverse tribal cultures of farmers and traders, fishers and boatbuilders, a powerful warrior culture in which personal prestige, kin ties, and wealth were of consuming importance. They voyaged to seek wealth and new pasture and to satisfy a profound wanderlust, not to discover new continents or fishing grounds. Having lived off the sea from birth, Norse seamen treated Atlantic cod as both the currency of existence and the fast food of their day—abundant, easy to carry, and reasonably edible. Its significance as a religious food was negligible, except when a profit could be made.

Partnered with the the stockfish were seagoing ships born of an ancient boatbuilding tradition—easily sailed, seaworthy, and capable of standing up to bad weather far from land.

Between 1859 and 1863, Danish archaeologist Conrad Engelhardt uncovered three boats with numerous artifacts that had been buried as sacrificial offerings in a bog at Nydam in southern Denmark.[7] Two boats were more or less intact, the largest an open rowboat built for fifteen pairs of oars, over twenty-one meters long with a beam of 3.9 meters amidships. Tree-ring dates show the hull was built in A.D. 310–320, making it the oldest known clinker-built boat (for clinker construction, see figure on page 84). The other intact ship, probably a sailing vessel of about the same age, was 18.5 meters long and built of pine, which means that it came from either Norway or Sweden.

The largest Nydam ship is lean and mean looking, with raking stem and stern, clearly designed to be rowed fast, its hull built of five overlapping oak strakes on each side fastened with iron clench nails. Stout lashings fastened the internal strengthening frames to the strakes and a flat keel. The keel structure was probably too weak to support a mast and sail, so the boat was probably used in sheltered waters. The pine ship had a stronger keel with a T cross-section and an efficient side rudder.

Nydam's ships are the earliest known examples of Norse-style hull construction. The shipwright laid out the keel, aligned it carefully, then built up the planked sides by eye, overlapping each plank against the one beneath it—what is known as clinker or lapstrake construction. Once the hull was complete, the builders added frames and seats to strengthen the hull. With their high stems and sterns, broad beam, and slight depth, the Nydam ships were perfectly adapted to the shallow waters of the southern North Sea and the Baltic. Strongly built versions of these craft were perfectly capable of crossing the narrower reaches of the English Channel, even the southern North Sea under oars or sail, waters where a tradition of piracy and raiding preceded the Roman conquest.

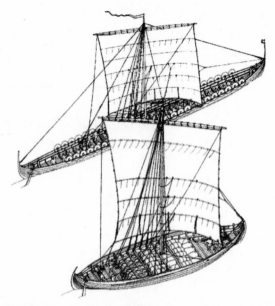

Norse ship types from Hedeby, Denmark, reconstructed from shipwrecks. An artist's impression of the Hedeby 1 long ship and the Hedeby 3 cargo ship under sail. The long ship was 30.90 meters long with between fifty-four and sixty-two oars. The cargo ship was 22.1 meters long and 6.25 meters across. Its carrying capacity was sixty tons. COPYRIGHT THE VIKING SHIP MUSEUM, ROSKILDE, DENMARK. ILLUSTRATOR: SUNE VILLUM-NIELSEN.

One such pirate (or warrior), King Rædwald of East Anglia, voyaged to eternity in 625 aboard a twenty-seven-meter ship laden with his treasures under an imposing tumulus at Sutton Hoo in eastern England.[8] His vessel, known only from the plank impressions and rust stains of iron nails in the sandy soil, was built in the Nordic style with nine narrow strakes each side, the stems rising at least 3.8 meters above the keel. The twenty-eight oarsmen probably sat on sea chests, as they did in later Norse vessels. The hull was strengthened at the stern to bolster it against the strains of maneuvering the steering oar under sail. Experiments with a half-scale model reveal that the Sutton Hoo ship was a highly effective sailing vessel, fast, maneuverable, and, despite its low freeboard, remarkably dry in choppy seas.[9] The Sutton Hoo ship was only slightly inferior to the Norse long ships and knarrs of later times, sailing as fast as ten to twelve knots in moderate winds. More important, the ship could have sailed efficiently in a strong wind, something of vital importance to any vessel heading into open water.

The waters of the southern North Sea and the Baltic required shallow draft vessels capable of maneuvering at close quarters. Such craft had to sit upright when moored alongside piers at low tide or when run aground. Deep-keeled boats find life hard in such waters. I once traversed Denmark's Lijmfjord in a twelve-meter offshore yacht with a 1.8-meter draft. It was a hair-raising experience, navigating tortuous channels under sail with mud banks and sandy shoals on either side. We ran aground at least six times but were able to use the anchor to pull ourselves laboriously into deeper water. Fortunately we didn't spend the night at forty-five degrees on a remote sand spit. But we saw firsthand why the Sutton Hoo ship and the vessels used by the Danish Norse had shallow keels.

Conditions are very different on the Norwegian coast and in the stormy Skaggerak between southern Norway and Denmark—deeply indented coasts battered by unpredictable winds and large ocean swells. Norwegian shipbuilders modified their ships for these challenging waters by fashioning massive keels that gave the hulls greater depth and more stability in heavy swell and strong winds.[10]

The shipwrights were cautious, conservative innovators who based their changes on hard-won experience at sea. They crafted a wide array of vessels, including warships, cargo ships known as knarrs, fishing boats, and thousands of small rowboats. In 1962, in a narrow fjord at Skuldelev near Roskilde Fjord west of Copenhagen, Danish archaeologists investigated five wrecks deliberately sunk in the eleventh century as a defensive barrier. The excavators recovered the ships by driving pilings around them and then pumping out the water. The remains of five ships of different shapes and sizes lay piled one atop the other in a challenging archaeological jigsaw puzzle.[11]

A replica of the Skuldelev 2 ship named *Ottar* during sail trials in 2003. Skuldelev 1 is an oceangoing knarr built in 1030, 16 meters long, 4.5 meters wide, with a carrying capacity of 20 to 25 tons. It drew only 1.6 meters fully loaded, so the knarr could navigate shallow creeks. All the Roskilde replicas are as precise copies as possible, built using traditional methods. Only the sail plans are conjectural and based on the best available information. COPYRIGHT THE VIKING SHIP MUSEUM, ROSKILDE, DENMARK. PHOTOGRAPH: WERNER KARRASCH.

Skuldelev 1 was a knarr, 16.5 meters long and 4.5 meters across at its widest point, a true oceangoing trader, built in about 1030 of Norwegian pine that bore an arrow mark from some long-forgotten attack. The ship had fore and aft decks and an open hold amidships. It could carry about twenty-four tons of cargo and a crew of five to eight people. When the Viking Ship Museum at Roskilde built an exact reconstruction, *Saga Siglar*, with a ninety-square-meter square sail, she averaged five knots in moderate breezes and sailed as fast as ten to twelve knots under gale conditions, a good performance by any standard. Another small coastal trader, Skuldelev 3, was fourteen meters long, with loose plank decks fore and aft and a center hold. This was a byrding, predominantly a sailing vessel used in coastal waters and the Baltic for routine voyages by farmers and others. It was built in Denmark in about 1040. A warship dating to 1030 came from Roskilde

Fjord itself, thirty-six meters long and capable of carrying 100 men, the largest known Norse ship anywhere, perhaps the property of a wealthy chieftain.

The most impressive Skuldelev ship was a warship capable of carrying as many as eighty warriors and sailing well over ten knots under ideal conditions. With sixty men at the oars, it could average five knots over long distances. These vessels were efficient war machines and status symbols for their powerful owners, who kept them in immaculate condition. Carved dragon heads, birds of prey, and snakes adorned the bow and stern, inspiring simultaneous fear and admiration. Tree rings from the Skuldelev warship timbers date it to 1042; the wood came from Ireland. Perhaps she was built in Dublin, an important Norse outpost at the time.

The humblest Roskilde craft is a fishing vessel known as a *ferja*, built in Norway in about 1030 for a crew of ten to fourteen men. At some

A replica of the Skuldelev 6 ship under sail, the smallest of the Roskilde ships. Built in 1030, the original was probably a fishing boat and was 11.2 meters long, 2.5 meters wide, and shipped fourteen oars. COPYRIGHT: VIKING SHIP MUSEUM, ROSKILDE, DENMARK. PHOTOGRAPH: WERNER KARRASCH.

point in its history, the owners added an additional plank, a so-called plank of avidity, on each side to raise it, a common practice when fish were abundant. At the same time, the number of oar stations was reduced, as if the boat was used more for transport than fishing, going to sea with a smaller crew.

Thanks to the program of replica building at Roskilde, we now know a great deal about Norse ship construction. Whereas Roman builders erected a keel, stem, and stern, then a skeletal frame of the hull that they subsequently planked, the Norse built entirely by eye. First they felled the trees for the hull, then split them using hammers and wedges to produce straight-grained planks of surprisingly uniform thickness. Then they set up the keel with a centerline, laying the garboards (keel planks) and hull floor along it before planking alternate sides with lapstraked timbers, bent into

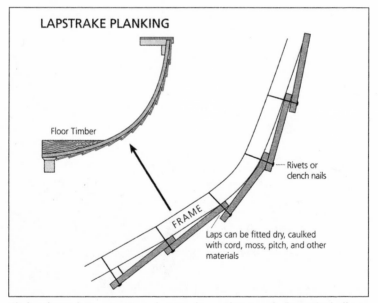

**LAPSTRAKE PLANKING**

Floor Timber

FRAME

Rivets or clench nails

Laps can be fitted dry, caulked with cord, moss, pitch, and other materials

Clinker (lapstrake) contruction, showing the overlapping planking. The hull was planked before frames were added, a construction method that produced flexible, seaworthy hulls.

place with stout thongs. Only when the hull was planked would they add strengthening frames and seats for the oarsmen. The result was an immensely strong but flexible hull fastened with iron and lashings, the upper planks caulked with woolen twine soaked in tar. Norse lapstrake construction was tough, highly adaptable, easily repaired, and, above all, low tech, producing seaworthy hulls that, with suitable bracing and keel, could carry a large sail area. Since the frames and bracing came last, the builder could modify the boat as it was built and take advantage of the timber on hand.

Lapstrake construction depended on a simple technology of axes and adzes, hammers and wedges, tool kits already familiar to fishers and subsistence farmers. Above all, however, it required an ability to envisage hull shapes in three dimensions and an expert eye to judge bevels and angles when fashioning planks for the hull. I once watched an old shipwright in a small Devon fishing village as he planked a small dinghy. He looked at the run of the previously installed plank, chose a suitable length of oak, and then eyed the angles. No tape measures or protractor, just a wooden plane. Unhesitatingly, he cut the plank to approximate length, then beveled the lower edge so that it fit snugly against its predecessor, occasionally holding to the hull as he worked. Within a few minutes, the new plank nested perfectly to the hull, fixed in place with copper rivets, clenched with hammer and rove. A lifetime's experience went into the planking, combined with a three-dimensional eye not given to many of us.

Whatever their size, Norse ships were lightly built, which gave them great speed when sailing across or before the wind. The same lightness made them easier to row against a breeze, even in lumpy seas, at speeds up to three knots. The skippers set a single square sail on a yard, symmetrically distributed on both sides of the mast. The yard could be braced on either side of the mast to facilitate sailing in different directions. Like every other aspect of Norse ships, the rigging was simple. The mast was supported with fore and aft stays, as well as braces to either end of the yard and sheets to the bottom edges of the sail, all running to the stern.

From generations of experience, Norse skippers knew the art of sail trimming, flattening the sail in strong winds to produce an efficient shape. They added additional ropes to help sheet the sail in tight when sailing closer to the wind. In the hands of an expert seaman, a square-rigged warship or small knarr could work to windward surprisingly well, perhaps within sixty degrees of the true wind in calm waters. But progress was never fast. The skippers kept the sail plan low, its heeling force counteracted by stone ballast, trimmed with great care to achieve maximum speed and stability.[12]

The simple, controlled Norse rig was ideal for northern waters with their strong and changeable winds. In the Mediterranean, where lighter winds and calmer seas prevailed, the tall lateen sail, with its long yard and ability to sail close to the wind in light weather, was a better choice.* But the square rig gave the Norse navigator greater flexibility and control in waters where the wind could rise from ten to forty-five knots in minutes.

Ships were a pinnacle of Norse material culture, to some owners a greater object of delight than their wives. By the time the Roskilde ships went to sea, Norse shipwrights were building ships with well-developed keels, often with a narrow T cross-section. They knew how to strengthen the hulls with a girderlike network of frames notched over the iron-fastened planks. Stout beams braced the hull, set on the frames and strengthened with knees to counter flexing. The mast step was locked into the beams, the mast itself lashed or set into a crossbeam. A side rudder hung off the starboard quarter, attached with withies or a leather strap to the hull, with the tiller set at right angles to the blade.

Unlike the famous and widely illustrated Viking warships, Norse knarrs had fuller lines and were designed for heavy loads. The Roskilde knarr has a deeper hull and a wider beam, also more height above the water, features that made it more of a sailing boat than the long ship. Knarrs had few oars, which were used only to help the ship turn from one tack to another.

---

*A lateen sail has a long spar, which acts as the leading edge, and is set on a short mast. This configuration makes for efficient progress sailing close to the wind and with the breeze on the beam. Excellent in light airs, lateens can be difficult to manage in rough weather. They also require a large number of people to "dip" the yard— to pass it from one side of the mast to the other when changing direction through the wind, "tacking."

Many such vessels were larger than the Roskilde example. A later one from Bergen, dating to before 1248, was over twenty-nine meters long and nine meters wide. Though their capacity was modest by later standards, knarrs were still capable of carrying three or four dozen men, cattle and their feed, and the entire furnishings of a farmstead across the open North Atlantic. All this cargo lay amidships, covered with ox hides, with a faering lashed atop.[13] Like merchant vessels of every age, knarrs were workhorses— tough, utterly practical ships developed over many centuries of harsh experience, but capable of venturing into offshore waters that no earlier sailor would contemplate.

The secret of Norse ships lay in their lapstrake construction, which was tough yet pliant enough to survive extremely severe weather. When Captain Magnus Anderson sailed a replica of the twenty-three-meter Gokstad ship across the Atlantic to the 1893 Columbian Exposition in Chicago, he found that she exceeded every expectation for speed and seaworthiness. The ship rode as gracefully as a swan, flexing as much as three-tenths of a meter when rising to steep Atlantic swells. This inherent flexibility was one of the secrets of Norse long-distance voyaging. The ship twisted easily in the waves, offering them a more flexible target than a rigid hull would.[14]

As parties of young Norsemen descended on monasteries and villages along North Sea coasts, other adventurous crews sailed west into unknown waters. Each ship was self-sustaining, capable of repairing damage at sea or on a remote beach, with enough stockfish aboard to support the crew for many weeks at sea. The dried cod were insurance against stormy weather, delays, even shipwreck on a remote island. So was the faering, lashed over the cargo and used as a lifeboat and a fishing vessel as well as a tender to ferry passengers and crew. Experienced skippers, the Norse sailed south and west into waters unknown to any except a few Irish monks, who had ventured as far afield as Iceland in their hide boats sometime earlier.

We know little of the early Norse voyages. Many of them, unrecorded in epics, ended in fatal storms far offshore or in shipwreck on rocky lee shores.* The casualties must have been enormous, but the journeys continued. Norse colonists settled in the Orkneys and Shetlands off northern Scotland soon after 800, and on the Faeroe Islands shortly thereafter. Around 874, a Norseman named Ingólf landed in Iceland, a land "covered with forests between mountains and shore. . . . Christian men whom the Northmen called Popes (*papar*) were here; but afterwards they went away, because they did not wish to live here together with heathen men." At first only a trickle of immigrants followed, but by 900 seafarers from coastal districts of Norway, the Scottish isles, and Ireland arrived in larger numbers. The newcomers gave the exposed south coast a wide berth, following the prevailing current around Reykjanes and up the western shore. A few bold captains sailed the ice-strewn north coast instead. Although most voyages apparently were uneventful, the Norse sagas refer to ships blown far off course by savage gales and head winds, and of shipwrecks on the south coast, said by the author of *Olaf's Saga* to be "nothing but sands and vast deserts, and a harborless coast, and, outside the skerries, a heavy surf."[15]

The Norse arrived in Iceland during the Medieval Warm Period, when winters were milder than they had been for centuries. Today, in average years, the January-to-April pack ice edge lies about ninety to one hundred kilometers off Iceland's northern shores.[16] When the first Norse settlers arrived, the pack was at least twice that distance away. They would never have survived the severe winters of the subsequent Little Ice Age. Even in these good times, life in Iceland was a struggle. In bad ice years, people starved, especially when several cold winters followed in succession.

The Norse brought with them a medieval dairying economy like that at home, which they combined with seal hunting and inshore cod fishing. At the time, milder summers allowed them to grow hay as winter

---

*A lee shore is one onto which the wind blows from open water. It is extremely dangerous in rough weather, especially for sailing vessels and fishing craft.

fodder and plant barley. After the twelfth century and the onset of the Little Ice Age, barley didn't grow in Iceland again until the early 1900s.

The voyages continued. The quarrelsome Eirik the Red, exiled after some killings in about 985, sailed west from Iceland and settled in south-western Greenland, where he and his men found better grazing than at home. One Norse colony flourished in the sheltered waters of the south-west, another further north in the modern-day Godthåb district, at the head of the sheltered Ameralik Fjord. The Greenlanders who sailed northward were soon aware of snow-clad lands to the west across what is now the Davis Strait, and eventually a voyager named Bjarni Herjolfsson, blown far off course while sailing from Iceland to Greenland, sighted the forested coast of southern Labrador. He sailed back to Greenland without landing, a lapse for which he was heavily criticized. In the 990s, Leif Eirikson, son of Eirik the Red, crossed to the western side of the Davis Strait and sailed southward along an increasingly forested coast until he was well south of the latitude of southern Greenland. He and his thirty-five men overwintered in northern Newfoundland, at a place now known as L'Anse aux Meadows, surviving an unusually mild winter.[17] They explored the surrounding country, loaded up with timber, and then returned home on the prevailing westerlies.

Eirikson never returned to the lands he called Markland and Vinland, the latter named for the wild grapes found there.[18] His brother Thorvald followed in his footsteps, mounting an expedition that lasted two years, but was killed in a skirmish with local people. More sporadic and unrecorded voyages ensued, many of them in search of timber for treeless Greenland, but the Norse kept their discoveries to themselves for centuries.

Human and natural disasters wracked the Greenland voyages: sudden storms far offshore with waves that could swamp a laboring ship before the steersman could alter course, icebergs invisible in dense fog, freezing temperatures loading a knarr with ice. In adverse weather, the ship would try to maintain position or even attempt to beat against the wind to gain some ground while waiting for it to shift astern. A voyage from Norway to Greenland could take anything from two weeks to most of the summer, depending on the skipper's luck. I've been aboard a 250-meter ship sailing at eighteen knots into a forty-knot wind and ice-strewn sea close off the shore of southern Greenland in late summer. We traversed the rising wind waves effortlessly, our powerful radar detecting icebergs long before we could see them. I thought of a heavily laden Norse knarr, her square sail solidly reefed, lying to in such conditions, completely at the mercy of the savage ocean and dependent on the skill of her weather-beaten steersman. Then I realized the magnitude of the Norse achievement and fully appreciated their remarkable ships and consummate seamanship, and began to appreciate as well their intimate familiarity with quick nautical death. Norse shipwrights and seamen traversed the western ocean centuries before North Sea fishers ventured offshore to Iceland and beyond in search of fish for Lent.

The Norse were the first to treat fish as a commodity. Their stockfish was of standard size, carefully beheaded and trimmed, then dried under close supervision to ensure a long shelf life. They used it as currency to pay debts, offer tribute, and obtain prestigious luxuries. But much of it they consumed themselves. Tightly packed in their knarrs' holds lay stacks of sun and wind-dried stockfish from Norway's coasts and islands, without which their skippers would never have been able to sail far from land. And their armies could not have terrorized Europe and the British Isles. The Atlantic cod was as important a player in the Norse world as the men and ships that sailed to North America centuries before Cabot or Columbus.

For millennia, fishers in the Baltic and North Sea harvested a different catch—the huge herring shoals that swarmed southward to spawn in late summer and autumn. But because it spoiled when brought ashore, herring was limited to satisfying the needs of coastal fishing communities. Then, sometime before the tenth century, Baltic fishers developed new salting methods that cured herring in brine-filled barrels. Within a century, herring had become big business in the growing towns of an increasingly Christian Europe.

# 7

# THE ANT OF THE SEA

Herring can be purchased very cheaply for the supply is copi-
ous. They present themselves in such large numbers off shore
that they not only burst the fishermens' nets, but, when they
arrive in their shoals, an axe or halberd thrust into their midst
sticks firmly upright.

Olaus Magnus[1]

Cromer, eastern England, at the September equinox. The southeasterly
gale flung spray at us as we walked along the low cliffs, leaning into the
wind under low, gray clouds. Heavy rain drove horizontally on the wind,
stinging our faces. Below us, the gray-brown North Sea held a froth of
whitecaps. The steady roar of the waves breaking on the beach with the
harsh rasp of shifting gravel drowned out even the sound of the wind. Under the cliffs, well above the high-water mark, we could see the pointed
ends and overlapping planks of the open crab boats, their design unchanged from centuries ago despite the advent of the internal combustion
engine. Then as now, in fair weather and foul, tough fishermen launched
their boats off this beach for crabs and herring when they ran close inshore.

I imagined a similar set of boats 1,300 years ago, when fishing was vital
to survival—a row of them drawn up ashore during late afternoon on a fine
September day. Crude thatched dwellings stand in a cluster behind the
beach, where a rough cart track leads inland. Wooden racks support rows of
gutted herring drying in the sun and wind; there's a pervasive smell of rotting fish and wood smoke. A few women mend nets at the foot of the cliffs.

The endless cadence of the breakers overwhelms the soft murmur of voices, everything except the endless mewling of seagulls high overhead.

The same routine unfolds each autumn day. Three or four men and boys cluster around each boat, loading light nets and kindling pine torches set in the bows. They fish at night, when the herring feed near the surface. The crews haul the lightly constructed boats into the breakers. Two oarsmen jump aboard while the skipper and two boys wait at the stern, watching the steep breakers, keeping the light craft steady. A quick shout, a few hard strokes, and the boat surges ahead. Skipper and crew jump nimbly aboard, soaked to the waist, oblivious to the chilly wind. They grab more oars and row vigorously until the breakers are astern, digging in their strokes as the boat rises sharply on an incoming wave. Beyond the breakers, they pause for a moment, then row slowly offshore to where the spawning herring will rise with nightfall.

The sea is dark in the small hours, with only a new moon high in the heavens. Everyone ashore is asleep, but a few kilometers offshore, bright flares bob up and down in the darkness. Coming closer, you see bright flashes of silver—hundreds of fish trapped in fine-textured dip nets in a scene that has repeated itself for centuries, if not millennia. Each fall, spawning herring swim southward along the English coast. And here, each autumn, the fishermen wait for them as they come to the surface at night to feed.

As dawn breaks, the herring return to the bottom. The laden boats return to the beach and are rapidly unloaded. Men and women alike grab the fresh fish, gut them, and place them on drying racks. Some they cast onto piles of coarse, dirty salt on the beach, covering them roughly, in an effort to preserve them before they rot. After a day or so, the women will uncover the now partially cured fish and load them into baskets.

The fishers are laconic, weather-beaten folk who fish in autumn and winter and farm inland during the rest of the year. They live only a short distance from the sea and carry their catch on their backs to eat at home or sell to a nearby monastery or in a village market. An occasional oxcart heaves a load inshore for the lord of the local manor. But the villagers catch fish largely for themselves. Every day during the fishing season, they dry (and sometimes salt or smoke) their catch, using technology as old as fishing itself. If the wind is calm or it is raining, as it often is, or it's cloudy, most of the catch rots on the beach or is good only for fertilizer. Fresh herring is a rarity at any meal away from the beach; salted or dried fish are as hard as nails and usually spoil within a few days anyway.

The herring trade began along Baltic shores, in the Low Countries, and in eastern England, where sheltered estuaries and creeks linked to communities far inland. A Dutch mercantile record of A.D. 880 speaks of enormous quantities of herring taken near the island of Helgeland for "English needs." We know little about its beginnings, for, as always, fishers were silent folk who avoided port officials and tithe collectors, quietly selling their catch and then returning to sea. We know that commercial vessels operated drift nets known as "flews" in late medieval and early modern times. The meshes were about 6.4 centimeters square and about 18 meters long, of varying depths depending on the water. Each net comprised four or six separate sections laced together, with thicker line at the top and bottom. To work properly, the nets were attached to a separate "cork" line, with flat corks that provided buoyancy. Before being cast from a boat, the nets were bent onto a thick master rope or warp, from which they hung below the surface of the water. Small barrels set at intervals along the warp kept the warp near the surface. Some larger boats operated nets up to 1.6 kilometers long.

Fishers usually cast their nets at sunset, when herring rise from the bottom to feed near the surface. The fish became caught by their gills in the mesh and remained there until the net was hauled, usually after about six hours, the duration of a tide, or when the skipper perceived the net was full. The crew then hauled the heavy net in with a hand capstan, detaching each net as it came aboard, then shaking the herring from the mesh down chutes into the hold. Depending on the yield, a boat might acquire a full cargo of several lasts in a single night, but more often a full catch took two or three nights.* The fishers rarely worked more than fifty kilometers from shore.

---

*A last was ten, twelve, or sometimes fourteen barrels of salted herring, nominally about 10,000 fish, but usually 12,300 to 13,000.

Almost all the catch remained at home on the coast, since there was no way of preserving oily-fleshed herring for transport inland. Until about 1000, most people met their fasting obligations by eating freshwater fish, especially eels. Then herring suddenly appeared in large numbers in towns far from the ocean.

Dozens of archaeological excavations in monasteries and secular buildings, as well as growing towns, chronicle a profound change in fish-eating habits virtually ignored in historical records.[2] Between the seventh and tenth centuries, seafish appear only near coasts or estuaries. Fish markets at growing towns like York, Ispwich, London, and Hamwic (modern-day Southampton) sold herring during those centuries, but freshwater fish far outnumbered them in the marketplace. Cod, frequently caught inshore in the North Sea, was virtually unknown away from the coast. Incredible although it may seem to us now, there was no word for "cod" in Anglo-Saxon English. Norse stockfish were apparently still seafarers' food, confined mainly to ships. The only fish that could be harvested on a large scale were herring and pilchard. But until someone developed a way of salting them effectively, these most abundant of fish could not travel.

The small, streamlined Atlantic herring, *Clupea harengus harengus,* is the ant of the ocean, so abundant that the eighteenth-century maestro of taxonomy, Karl Linnaeus, described it as *copiosissiumus piscis,* "the most prolific of fish." Herring was a staple for North Sea coastal communities long before Christian abstinence and military demand brought it inland. Bronze Age villagers netted *Clupea* from canoes over 3,500 years ago. Roman garrisons on the Thames devoured herrings by the thousand. Roman fish merchants at Utrecht sold pickled herring preserved in vinegar, as well as fish sauce, and prospered mightily. But salted herring didn't travel far until the tenth century. There was no way of preserving them in barrels, and not enough high-quality salt to do so. Even when they could be salted efficiently, the tightly packed containers required large amounts of cargo space. *Clupea* was a bulk product that could not be sold or shipped cost-effectively except in large, standardized units. Cargo ship capacity before the eleventh century rarely exceeded twenty tons. Then the bulk carrier was introduced to transport sixty tons or more of loaded barrels. Herring was one of the commodities that stimulated the development of such vessels.

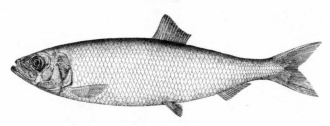

*Clupea harengus,* the Atlantic herring. FROM COLLETTE AND KLEIN-MACPHEE, *FISHES,* P. 141. COURTESY SMITHSONIAN INSTITUTION PRESS.

Like any other fish, herring was unpredictable.[3] In good years herring arrived by the millions in the Baltic and North Seas in the summer to spawn, congregating in shoals that could cover four cubic kilometers of ocean. In bad years the fish might appear in one place but not another. Most years, they would swarm off the Shetland Islands and Scotland between February and April. During the summer months they made their way east and south, into the Skagerrak and the Baltic, and into the Irish and North Seas. By September and October, they swarmed off England's East Anglian coast, where they laid eggs on shallow, gravelly parts of the seabed close to land and in a huge nursery area on the Dogger Bank in the central North Sea.* The sticky egg masses adhered to stones and weeds on the bottom, hatching in about eight to ten days. After spawning, the exhausted fish drifted northward during the winter along the low-lying coasts to the east until the entire cycle began all over again.

Harvesting the North Sea fish was simplicity itself; preserving them was another matter. Wind drying did not work for herring as it did for cod, even if the climate had been sunny and cold enough to allow it—which it was not. Such a procedure only worked in the far north, along parts of the

---

*The Dogger Bank covers about 17,610 square kilometers of the central North Sea, an extensive sand bank with depths of seventeen to thirty-six meters.

Maps showing locations in Chapters 7–10.

Norwegian coast and in the northern Baltic, where cold winds and bright sunshine in spring and early summer allowed gradual, predictable drying. Smoking required salting, which at the time consisted of little more than throwing the gutted fish into a weak solution of salt and water or layering them between piles of salt on the beach. Until the salting problem was solved, herring could not be transported.[4]

Northern Europe was a cloudy, rainy world, without the long days of bright sunlight needed to evaporate salt in shallow ponds. Some villages

tried using wood fires, but this process was slow and costly. Farmers in the Low Countries burned peat impregnated with seawater, digging it out of marsh flats, drying and burning it to produce ashes and salt that were then placed in seawater to create brine. The resulting *zelle* was scarce and expensive. As the demand increased and supplies of salt-laden peat diminished, the unscrupulous risked savage punishment by raiding sea defenses for suitable raw material. Some Scandinavian communities produced salt by evaporating seawater to a denser brine and then boiling it. This process was expensive but economically feasible if conducted on a sufficient scale, and it made Oslo a salt trading center as early as the ninth century.

The solution to the salt problem came from two sources. During the ninth century, the Norse raided deep into Normandy and Brittany, where they attempted to evaporate salt in the summer sun. They hoped to produce salt herring and cod to feed their raiding parties and merchants, but their efforts failed. In 819 their ships reached Noirmoutier Island, north of modern-day La Rochelle in the Bay of Biscay. After vicious fighting with the resident monks, they took over the salt pans and also gained control over the salt marshes on the mainland at the mouth of the Loire. In a single stroke, raiders became salt traders; Biscay salt now reached English Channel and North Sea ports in the holds of Norse knarrs and later Hanse ships. Every year, dozens of merchant ships would coast slowly down the Channel and creep past the stormy rocks of Ushant into the Bay of Biscay. Many heavily laden vessels met their doom at the hands of pirates or among the sharp rocks and fast tides of the French coast, but the risk was justified by the profits. Coarse Noirmoutier salt became a staple commodity for the Dutch and English herring fisheries.

In Stockholm during the winter, the inhabitants ate fresh fish, carried there frozen from the fisheries. But dried and salted pike, perch, and other freshwater fish were commercially more important to the Swedish monarchy. Long before Christianity, Baltic herring provided sustenance for thousands of people. Drying was practical in cold and windy but sunny months of spring and early summer, especially in the far north. The sixteenth-century Swedish chronicler Olaus Magnus remarked that the smell of drying fish on the island of Bjuröklubb off Vasterbötten in northeastern Sweden was so strong that it was a navigational aid far offshore, warning mariners of the danger of shipwreck. Bjuröklubb had dried fish for centuries before Magnus's time.[5]

Herring spawned in the southern Baltic each summer, especially off the Skänian coast of southwestern Sweden. A prolific fishery developed, thanks to locally abundant salt, which was better for herring curing than baie salt from the south. The coarse salt crystals came from mines in the Luneburg region of northern Germany, exploited since prehistoric times. The narrow Skanör-Falsterbo peninsula became the epicenter of an international market for Baltic herring.[6] The shoals here, crossed by strong currents, extend almost due south for sixteen kilometers, making the place a deathtrap for sailing ships in rough weather. I once sailed by on a fine day with a strong following wind and excellent visibility, and the shallows were a mass of white breakers. I was thankful not to be caught there in a gale. The water shoals so rapidly that even that standby of the Norse sailor, the lead and line, would have been virtually useless here in a fog—and fogs can persist for days. But here is where the herring congregated to spawn, and so here the fishing boats worked. By the fourteenth century, as many as 5,000 people labored seasonally in what had become a highly regulated fishery.

Sometime around the tenth century—presumably not long before the fish began to enter the archaeological record at future inland sites—Skänia herring fishers developed a new curing method that involved laying gutted fish between layers of salt in wooden casks, allowing the salt to suck the moisture out of the fish, then repacking them in fresh brine. Unless carefully regulated, the quality was irregular. But when it worked, the new process preserved fish for up to a year, far longer than English and Dutch methods at the time. Mass production of salted herring became a reality for the first time. Within generations, large segments of the coastal population, as well as people far inland, were consuming Baltic catches.

Herring as a solution for Lent probably took hold first in almshouses and urban hospitals, where religious doctrine and cheap rations went hand in hand. Cured herring was a lowly food, far less palatable than cod. Many of the poor hated their enforced herring diet on holy days. But the fish were easy to catch, and the sticklike preserved carcasses now survived the journey inland. The French soldier and traveler Philippe de Mézières remarked in 1390 that anyone "can have a herring who cannot afford a big fish."[7]

## A Jellie of Fysshe

The history of cooking, to a large extent, belongs to the elite—monarchs, nobles, the wealthy, and the religious, who increasingly were aligned with the influential and rich. Commoners' diets are off the historical radar screen, most cooking being done over open fires in earthen ovens and iron cooking pots. Soup, made from a stockpot almost continually on the hearth, was a staple for farmer and fisher alike, the ingredients depending on what was thrown into the vessel. The diet of the more privileged was another matter. As early as 520, we find the Greek physician Anthimus inventorying the foods eaten by Frankish chieftains, among them plaice, a flat fish "good and agreeable boiled in salt and oil." He recommended them for the sick. Anthimus advocated well-prepared food and moderate helpings for everyone. His advice, and that of other physicians, proclaimed that everything was a careful balance of heat and cold, moisture and dryness. An imbalance could also affect a person's temperament, engendering choler (anger and ill humor), melancholy, or passion. These beliefs tie in with early Christian attitudes to fasting and diet. To produce finely balanced dishes, a cook heated or chilled them but also used spices, sweeteners like sugar, and coloring like saffron and parsley.

For centuries, culinary practices passed from cook to cook by word of mouth, forming a body of carefully guarded knowledge that was never set down in writing. There were no formal recipes, just general descriptions of dishes of all kinds.

The "jellie of fysshe" that follows is an example of a dish that would have graced a noble table during a formal Lenten meal, made using lore passed through the generations.

### ✄ A Jellie of Fysshe

SERVES 6

*We recommend making this a day ahead and unmolding it before serving.*

8 oz/250 g hake, cod, haddock, or other flavorful white fish
3 scallops
3 oz/90 g shrimp
2 onions, coarsely sliced
½ oz/15 ml white wine vinegar
1 oz/30 g ginger root, peeled and finely chopped
Large pinch of sea salt
Small pinch of white pepper
15 oz/450 ml each white wine and water
¾ oz/20 g gelatin

*(continues)*

*A Jellie of Fysshe (continued)*

Place the fish in a pan with the onions, vinegar, ginger root, salt, pepper, wine, and water. Bring it gently to the boil and simmer for 5 minutes, as we did, or at the most 10.

Add the scallops and prawns and cook for another 3 minutes.

Remove the fish; bone and skin it. Peel the shrimp and set aside. Strain the cooking liquid into a bowl and leave to cool for several hours. This will allow much of the sediment to settle to the bottom.

Carefully pour off the liquid, leaving the sediment, and then strain several times more through a clean cheesecloth. You should have approximately 25 oz/750 ml of liquid remaining. Melt ¾ oz/20 g of gelatin in a small quantity of the liquid, cool to room temperature, and then stir it into the remaining liquid.

Pour ½ in/1 cm of the juice into the bottom of a 2 pint/1.2 liter/5 cup soufflé dish or fish mold and put it in the refrigerator to set.

Flake the white fish into smallish flakes; remove the coral from the scallops (if present) and cut the white flesh into three or four pieces. Once the jelly is firm, arrange the most decorative parts of the fish in the bottom of the dish— some scallop coral in the middle, shrimps around the outside, flakes of white fish in between or however you feel inspired. Spoon a little more of the liquid into the dish and return it to the fridge to set. Continue to layer the fish in the mold, setting each layer with a covering of liquid until you have used up all the fish and juices.

Leave the jelly to set for at least 4 hours, preferably longer, in the refrigerator. Unmold and decorate with fresh herbs.

Adapted from Michelle Berriedale-Johnson, *The British Museum Cookbook* (London: British Museum Publications, 1987). Reprinted by permission of the Trustees of the British Museum.

The warmer temperatures of the Medieval Warm Period caused the sea level to rise significantly, making the configuration of North Sea coasts somewhat different from today. Towns now inland thrived off herring. Beccles in Norfolk, now far from the sea, was a flourishing herring port. In Edward the Confessor's time (1042–1065), the town supplied 30,000 herring a year to the nearby Abbey of St. Edmund. William the Conqueror doubled the assessment. Like eels, herring became a form of currency used to pay rent and taxes. Dunwich paid 6,000 annually to the Crown; Kessington, also in Suffolk, 22,000; Brighton on the south coast 4,000. Almost all this traffic was in lightly salted herring taken close to shore. These *sapoudre* or *korfharing* sometimes traveled as far as London and even Paris.[8]

By the new millennium, the herring trade was expanding rapidly to satisfy a growing demand from urban populations, especially during fasting months. The historical literature abounds with accounts of fish catches, of customs and toll records of lasts of fish shipped from Yarmouth and other ports, with tribute in eels paid to the religious, and later with details of cargoes of salted cod destined for Mediterranean lands. Thanks to a number of contemporary accounts, we participate, albeit at a distance, in lavish royal feasts and diplomatic banquets. But only occasional snapshots of the actual consumption of the catch survive for us to assess. What happened to the millions of herring that passed through fishers' hands? We can but speculate from literary fragments that commemorate a world where fish was a daily staple for millions, and an essential for everyone on holy days and during Lent. What happened to the estimated 3,298,000 herring landed in England annually during the late eleventh century—this apart from the catches at continental ports?[9]

We can be sure that only a small proportion of the total herring catch was eaten fresh. Cod, salmon, and conger eel could be transported some distance inland by cart wrapped in wet cloth or straw, but not *Clupea*. Fresh porpoise was a delicacy much prized at royal and noble tables, and by prominent abbots. The religious in houses near major fish ports like London or Southampton ate fresh fish regularly, both on feast days and on holy days, such dishes being much anticipated, especially if the cook was adept with sauces. Sturgeon was prized as a prestigious delicacy and served on special occasions. And we have seen how abbots and landowners, even kings, would honor friends and those they wished to impress. Lavish fish dishes served on holy days and for Lenten feasts were a public affirmation of religious devotion and social prestige. In medieval (just as in Roman) times, lavish fish dishes and large individual catches were a pricey way of proclaiming rank and wealth. Herring was devoid of social prestige, a food for novice monks, the poor, soldiers, and common folk. Herring joined eel as a commodity that was part of the currency of daily life.

Commodity and currency are apt terms. By the late eleventh century, tens of thousands of barrels of salted herring traveled long distances by barge, cart, and horseback. French channel ports like Dieppe shipped barrels of herring by barge as far upstream as Avignon. The marketplace for herring was towns rather than villages, which would not see much sea fish until centuries later. By the eleventh century, fishmongers and merchants plied their trade in inland towns large and small, selling salted herring and some other species in bulk. Once seafish became a commodity like eel, which had been a form of informal currency for centuries, the dynamic of fish consumption changed. Even in the early days of the North Sea fishery, the Crown purchased large amounts of herring and acquired more in taxation. In 1086 the East Anglian port of Dunwich paid 68,000 fish to the king year after year, and an additional 24,000 to the monks of Ely. While the Ely herring obviously fed the religious and helped fulfill charitable needs, the monarch used his fish for many purposes—to feed his court and large establishment, to give as gifts to impoverished religious houses, and above all to feed armies and in Tudor times the emerging navy. One peasant at a Lincolnshire manor paid twelve herrings to marry his bride.[10]

During the eleventh and twelfth centuries, *Clupea* outsold stockfish or any form of salted cod, which was still in short supply. By 975 herring shows up in considerable numbers in archaeological deposits at York in northeast England.[11] It arrived in larger numbers at Hamwic (Southampton) by 1030. A century later, *Clupea* was enjoyed in Northampton in central England. Baltic herring also traveled far. At Roskilde in Denmark, herring was 42 percent of the fish count in local middens in the late eleventh century, while 250 kilometers (155 miles) inland, no herring was eaten. A century later, herring appeared regularly on menus in Bern and Vienna.

The profits were enormous, the fish more and more abundant. Soon the wealthy were lavishing fish on the religious. During the twelfth century, Count Eustace of Boulogne could afford to endow the monastery at Cluny with 20,000 herring annually. The fishery became so important to Christian observance that in 1170 Pope Alexander III permitted Sunday fishing off the coast when the herring were running. By 1300 urban households in Paris were eating salted North Sea herring, the bones of which survive in their trash heaps and toilets. A growing number of fisherfolk provided food for a rapidly growing population, helped them follow religious doctrine, fed the poor, and brought in taxes for both lords and the church. As the chronicler Alan of Lille remarked in 1170, "Poor people can afford a little fish." As many as 4,000 people ate herring during Lent in Parisian almshouses.[12]

We probably underestimate the scale of medieval herring fisheries because the fishers operated from small working boats out of small villages. A great deal of our information comes from the arid records of medieval tax and tithe collectors, which tell us much about the seasons for different fisheries. At Dunwich in Norfolk, the fisherfolk paid doles to the town for "daysfare," fishing within a day's journey of the town, which continued year-round. Early in the year, they paid levies on inshore cod lining, then "Lentynfare," for early herring. The schedule of doles unfolds with "Northland fare" in early summer—cod fishing in northern waters—then fortylfare, the main herring drift fisheries in October and November.[13] The work of fishing, like that of farming, was never done. Thanks to the church calendar, growing armies, and new salting methods, it became extremely profitable—less for the fisherfolk but abundantly for the merchants who distributed and sold their catches. Most fishers survived by farming as well. Fortunately for them, the main herring fishery came after the harvest.

What was once a cottage industry developed into a vast enterprise, first on a regional scale and then continent-wide as properly salted *Clupea harengus* supported thousands of people during Lent and on holy days and nourished them on the battlefield. The numbers for military use alone are mind-boggling. In 1300 the garrison at Stirling Castle in Scotland received 18,500 herring. Thirty-eight years later, King Edward III obtained forty lasts of herring from Yarmouth for his Flanders army. *Clupea* even fended off an ambush. In 1429 Sir John Falstoff of Caistor near Norwich, believed to be the model for Shakespeare's Falstaff, was transporting 500 wagons of herring for the Duke of Bedford, brother of King Henry V, to a besieged Orleans when his train was ambushed. The herring barrels, in those days before firearms, formed an effective barricade for the defenders in a "Battle of Herrings," and the attackers were beaten off.[14] Herring had become part of the fabric of European society. As the Elizabethan writer Thomas Nash remarked in 1599, "The puissant red herring. . . . A red herring is wholesome on a frosty morning: it is most precious merchandise because it can be carried through all Europe. . . . The poorer sort make it three parts of their sustenance."15

# 8

# THE POWER OF
# INVENTION

> The Herring is one of those products whose use changed the
> destiny of Empires.
>
> Comte de Lacépède[1]

Many years ago, a boating friend of mine described sailing southward past Blakeney, a small eastern English village with a tidal port, where fisherfolk worked herring long before medieval times. It was a quiet, cloudy night with a light northerly wind and smooth sea. He could see the floodlights from miles away, about fifteen kilometers offshore. A great crowd of small fishing boats rose and fell on the swell, lying to their nets, hauling masses of fish into their holds. As my friend passed within half a kilometer, close enough to hear the calls of the crews as they worked the catch, the water around him frothed with the silver lightning of feeding herring.

When I called him about the subject of this chapter, he remembered the teeming fish at once. In all his years of cruising, he had never seen anything like it. "It was Victorian," he said. "They had engines, but they were just drifting with the tide as if they were under oar and sail. People must have been fishing like this for centuries." Much the same kind of scene must have played out night after night in medieval times.[2]

The decisive expansion of the herring fisheries coincided with the development of barrel brining in Baltic lands, new trade routes that brought

Biscay evaporated salt to the English Channel and North Sea, a growing demand for sea fish to feed armies and the urban poor, and an increasing shortage of freshwater fish. By the tenth century, landowners and religious houses controlled most inland fisheries through a tangle of regulation that effectively reserved such fish for the more affluent. At the same time, and with almost bewildering rapidity, herring became a staple for armies and the poor.

Barrel brining produced not only a better product than previous salting methods but one that could be shipped and marketed more efficiently. No longer a catch eaten by individual families or bundled up loosely by monastery cellarers, fish became a bulk commodity processed by the thousand, packed by the hundred, and shipped by the tens of thousands. Bulk shipping of grain, wine, and other commodities up rivers and estuaries had gone on since Charlemagne's time or earlier. Now herring and Norwegian stockfish joined the cargoes.

The growing trade centered around great fish fairs that attracted merchants from far away. The Skänia market in southwestern Sweden grew rapidly into an increasingly regulated event. Each merchant pitched camp by the shore with his own hut and booth. By the fourteenth century, when the Hanseatic League was firmly in control, each town had its own *fitte*, a precisely defined area where its merchants camped. (The Middle High German word *hanse* means "league.") The fishers camped separately. Teams of women gutted the herring and laid them in brine. A specially appointed official supervised the processing of entrails and waste into fish oil, taking care that this was done well away from the merchants. Just loading the barreled herring could be a logistical nightmare, for Skänia had no ports, only exposed beaches. First the shipper paid duty, then the barrels were hauled by horse cart to waiting barges that carried up to 100 barrels at a time out to the ships anchored offshore.[3]

The Skänia herring catch varied considerably, but between 50,000 and 300,000 barrels were shipped out each year, representing between 5,000 and 30,000 tons of fish. Philippe de Mézières tells us that thousands of small boats, each with a crew of six to ten men, caught the fish, while 500 medium- and large-size ships transported the catch. Modern estimates are considerably lower. A surviving record for 1474 speaks of 762 fishing boats at Falsterbo and Skanör, which would have provided work for about 3,500 fishers. Another 700 would have worked the 300 carts and twenty-six barges inventoried in the archive. Fish were gutted and cleaned by 174 women; in addition there were coopers and at least 200 merchants and their apprentices. In all, modern estimates have about 5,000 people involved in the fifteenth-century Skänia herring fishery; the numbers cannot have been much smaller four centuries earlier.

The North Sea fishery expanded rapidly at about the same time. An anonymous chronicler wrote, "He that will buy herring may go to the east part of England, for there is most plenty. And there as is most plenty, is best cheap, as at Scarborough [and] Yarmouth."[4] Here the herring season revolved around great fish fairs. The Scarborough Fair, in what is now Yorkshire, lasted from June 24 to the end of September and served mainly domestic buyers. Great Yarmouth, to the south, welcomed fishers and buyers from September 29 until November 10, a mere forty-five days, but appears to have been busier, with many international fish traders.

Scarborough's herring fair centered on a stone quay built in the mid-thirteenth century, where hundreds of local fishing boats landed their catches.[5] Foreign vessels came from what are now the Dutch and Belgian coasts, from Dunkirk and Calais, and even as far away as Dieppe in Normandy. Many catches were between 0.5 to 1.5 lasts, some 10,000 to 15,000 fish. The fair records tell us that owner/skippers landed catches at intervals of two or three weeks, their fish salted with foreign salt and sold to the English market. In 1304–1305, a peak year for the herring fishery, Scarborough and nearby Ravenser and Whitby handled over 820 lasts of herring from foreign boats—1,640 tons, some 8.2 million fish, valued at £1,030. All this excludes the domestic haul, which was not taxed, so we have no idea how many fish were handled altogether. Scarborough itself supported a large fishing community with a significant fleet, many of them large "fysshers" carrying crews of twenty.

The prosperity fluctuated. In 1362 the burgesses of the town noted that their income came mainly from "fish and herrings taken at sea and brought into town for sale."[6] When dues fell, they often launched investigations into the activities of those who sailed offshore and bought entire catches before they were landed to avoid taxation. By the end of the fourteenth century, the decline was so severe that the town limited drying, salting, and packaging of herring to long-term residents. Despite these limitations, Scarborough still did well. Tax records for 1414–1418 show that between thirty-five and forty-six individuals paid fish tithes annually, about a third of them part-time inshore fishers, the remainder full-time professionals with substantial investments in boats, nets, and other equipment.

Great Yarmouth, another great medieval fishing port, has a history that parallels Scarborough's. Today the town is known for its natural gas production, but its history is defined by herring. The modern borough crest bears only a few fish tails, but the medieval version displayed St. Nicholas, a patron saint of fisherfolk, on one side and a fishing boat in a sea of herring on the other. Yarmouth began as a modest fishing community at the mouth of a huge, now vanished estuary formed by several rivers.[7]

Silting in the estuary caused by fast-running tides formed an enormous sandbank several kilometers long that eventually became firm enough to support huts and temporary fish-curing stations. At first these were probably nothing more than family camps, set up during the herring season. The men did the fishing and the women and children gutted, dried, salted, or smoked the catch. Processing the fish required as much skill as catching them. Judging from well-documented nineteenth-century practice, gutting involved a single movement with a very sharp knife. An expert Victorian gutter could process up to forty fish a minute; medieval women were just as adept. It was hazardous work. A slip of the gutting knife could maim a woman for life and destroy her livelihood. Nothing was wasted. The gutted fish went into barrels filled with salty water, while the guts were sold for fertilizer.

No one knows who founded Yarmouth or when, but fishing boats from the Cinque Ports in the Dover Straits had long claimed the right to beach their vessels on the bank and may have been among the founders.

Landing and processing herring on Yarmouth beach during the nineteenth century. The scene is probably little changed from medieval times. ARTIST UNKNOWN.

By William the Conqueror's time, Yarmouth was a growing herring center. A major fish fair during herring season developed on the sandbank during medieval times. Continued silting eventually led to a town with stone quays on one side of the channel and a huge expanse of beach on the other where fishing boats dried their nets and herring were processed in enormous numbers.

At the height of the season, dozens of open fishing boats would arrive each morning and offload their catches on the filthy beach. Crude benches would have served as gutting tables where the women stood hour after hour, their knives moving with lightning speed. Children staggered with baskets of gutted herring to waiting barrels, where more women would pack them in brine. At the back of the beach would have stood row after row of brine-filled barrels, left to stew before being repacked and sealed by a team of coopers. The work continued day and night, with clouds of wood smoke from hearths and smoke houses lingering over the town. Thousands of seagulls would have wheeled and circled close overhead—fat, noisy birds that fought over fish heads and entrails, even sitting boldly on the gutting tables. The smell of decaying fish and wood smoke would have permeated the entire town, even people's clothing. Great Yarmouth was not a sweet-smelling place.*

The fair grew and grew. In 1342 and 1343, as many as 500 continental and domestic boats paid annual harbor dues.[8] At least half of them arrived during the herring season, most of the foreigners from the Low Countries. There were even a few visitors from Breton ports far to the west. English boats came from as far away as Yorkshire, Devon, and Cornwall. Each boat held at least six or seven men, bringing a huge influx of fishermen into the town. The Yarmouth catches were enormous—as many as 10 million fish in the peak year of 1336–1337. By this time the military depended heavily on salted fish. As early as 1281, King Edward I sent agents through his realm to acquire provisions for an invasion of Wales. Adam of Fuleham, an alderman of London and sheriff, was commissioned to purchase 100 barrels of sturgeon and 5,000 salt fish in Aberdeen. In 1284 Adam was asked to provide a hundred 500-pound (227-kilogram) barrels of Aberdeen salmon and deliver them to Chester. Foreign merchants exported 482 lasts—964 tons—of herring in 1310–1311, about 5 million fish.

---

*Yarmouth was famous for red herrings processed by salting and smoking. The herrings were first washed to get rid of the salt put on them aboard ship before being immersed in fresh salt for fourteen days. They were then removed, washed, rived or speared on spits or sticks through the gills and mouth, twenty-five fish to a stick, and smoked for fourteen days. The smokehouse was a lofty room about five meters square with wooden frames reaching from floor to roof with small transverse beams called loves about four feet apart. The spitted fish were laid on the loves with sixteen fires, all made of oaken billets. Fires were kept burning for two days, the smoke escaping through the uncemented tiles, which allowed a draft. The fish were then allowed to drain and drip as the fires went out before the flames were lit for a further two days. After fourteen days, the fish were "high dried" and fit for packing in barrels. A screw press was born down on the packed fish. Usually about 650 full-size fish went into a barrel.

The bloater, a later Yarmouth delicacy, was a red herring but not so smoky, although much saltier than the Yarmouth bloater of today. They were first exported from Yarmouth to Spain and Italy around 1600. The word bloater comes from the Swedish word blöta, implying soaking in brine before smoking.

# FRIED SOLE WITH ORANGE AND
# SORREL VERJUICE

Between the twelfth and fifteenth centuries, cuisine became more sophisticated and more dependent on exotic spices and other imports. The first recipe books appeared in the late thirteenth century, records of the activities of professional cooks that had been handed down over the centuries—little more than recipe collections. They provide us with the first reliable sources of information on food and cookery, especially in France.

The first true cookbook was the *Viandier de Taillevent,* which began with 133 recipes. In its later iterations, it expanded to include 220. It remained in print until the sixteenth century. Taillevent, which means "wind slicer," was the nom de plume of Guillaume Tirel (c. 1310–1395), who served in the royal kitchens with such distinction that he was ennobled. He became the king's chief cook in 1370, a post that enabled him to experiment and cook lavish dishes. His book opens with a laconic statement: "Here begins the *Viandier* of Taillevent, master chef of our Lord the King of France, by means of which can be prepared all manner of foods worthy to be served before kings, dukes, counts, lords, prelates, bourgeois, and others."

The *Viandier* was a reworking of an existing recipe collection. It was the baseline for all French cuisine that followed and remained in print until the early seventeenth century.

The recipe that follows, adapted from Chiquart's *Du fait de cuisine,* dates from somewhat later but gives an impression of the amazing things medieval cooks could do to enhance bland white fish.

## ✂ *Fried Sole with Orange and Sorrel Verjuice*

SERVES 6

*Fish*

6 fillets of sole
2 oz/60 g unsalted butter/olive oil
½ oz/15 g chopped sorrel leaves
½ oz/15 ml lemon juice
8–12 oz/250–375 ml unsweetened orange juice (about 3 oranges)
4–5 sorrel leaves, whole
4 oz/125 ml boiling water

Note: Spinach leaves can be combined with sorrel leaves to ensure a green color. Sorrel is best fresh but can sometimes be found in dried form. Farmers' markets are a good source if you don't grow your own. While not a substitute for sorrel, watercress can be used if sorrel is unavailable.

*(continues)*

*Fried Sole with Orange and Sorrel Verjuice (continued)* _____

Sauté the sole fillets in half of the butter, with a little oil added until barely cooked and opaque. Remove from pan and keep warm (caution: fillets will continue cooking).

**Sauce**

Blanche the whole sorrel leaves. Stain and reserve liquid. Chop and grind or blend in food processor. Add juice and liquid if needed. Place remaining butter in pan with the liquid, cook and reduce by one-third. Pour over fish and garnish with chopped sorrel leaves.

Big ports like Scarborough and Yarmouth were deeply engaged with the export trade. Thirty to fifty Yarmouth ships carried barreled herring to Bordeaux between October and December each year, where they traded their cargoes for wine. The largest such ships could transport 300 tons of merchandise. Smaller towns, like those on the Lincolnshire coast, focused on local needs, especially places with gently shelving beaches, where boat owners could draw up their vessels on dry land and combine fishing with farming, as they had always done.

The early centuries of the herring trade were somewhat like the Silicon Valley dot-com boom of the 1990s—uncontrolled expansion, wild gambling, and a great deal of inferior product, to say nothing of tax dodging. Inevitably herring fisheries came under tighter regulation, both by royal courts and private enterprise. During the twelfth century, the merchants of Hamburg and Lübeck, on opposite sides of the Danish peninsula, formed an alliance, the former controlling salt supplies, the latter supporting numerous herring boats in the Skänia fishery. This strategic partnership soon expanded to encompass merchant associations in Cologne, Danzig, and Rostok, evolving into the famed Hanseatic League. The Hanse suppressed piracy, imposed commercial laws, and worked hard to create monopolies

Map showing European locations in Chapters 8–10.

in grain, timber, and other bulk commodities, including salted herring and later stockfish. The profits from the bulk trade were steady and reliable for monopoly holders, always a Hanse priority. The league's commercial clout was enormous.

By 1400 the Hanse effectively controlled much of the herring trade. It raised the quality of salted herring dramatically by ending the common practice of selling poorly cured herring packed in barrels under a few

Map showing British locations in Chapters 8–10.

0    50    100 kilometers
0    50    100 miles

layers of good brine-cured fish. By importing white salt from Portugal, it eliminated wastage in the Low Countries caused by using peat salt laced with ashes. Hanse merchants searched aggressively for new markets. Imports of Skänia herring to Britain rose sharply in the late fourteenth century, partly because English merchants found it profitable to sell wool in

Baltic ports and then buy herring there. At the height of their power, Hanse merchants shipped between 10,000 and 25,000 tons of salted herring annually, an astounding volume of trade for the time. They could do this because they developed Europe's first bulk carrier, the cog.

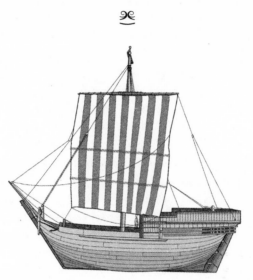

A Hanse cog, bulk carrier supreme.

In October 1962, dredging operations on the Weser River, downstream of the medieval city of Bremen in northern Germany, uncovered the wreck of a long wooden hull built in 1379–1380.[9] With this discovery, a long-forgotten but revolutionary ship reentered history. The excavator, Siegfried Fliedner of the Museum for the History of Bremen, knew nothing about cogs, which vanished during the fifteenth century. The only known depiction was on the city of Stralsund seal: it showed a high, boxlike hull of lapstrake construction with a stern-hung rudder, one mast, and a square sail. Luckily, the wreck was exceptionally well preserved, identical in every detail to the vessel on the Stralsund seal. Fliedner was even able to show from tree-ring analysis that the timber for the ship was felled in the autumn of 1378. A full-size replica based on the original hull provided useful insights into the cog's sailing qualities. Since the Bremen discovery, numerous other cog shipwrecks have been identified in Sweden, Denmark, and Germany.

The double-ended, boxlike hull had a high, straight stem and a shallow draft. This meant that the cog sailed well with the wind astern or broad on the beam but was virtually useless upwind. Like knarrs, cogs were working boats, but the thrifty Hanse built them of cheaper wood and wider sawn or split planks. Cog skippers cautiously waited for favorable winds, sometimes for weeks on end, but their ships were remarkably stable in rough weather. In earlier cogs, the deck planks ran from side to side instead of longitudinally, so that water breaking on board drained into the bilge, thereby providing additional stability and keeping the ship more upright. This meant that all perishable freight like herring, stockfish, or wool had to be transported in barrels or other waterproof containers. Sealed decks were a late innovation, combined with large scuppers that carried water through the bulwarks and back into the ocean. The crew and passengers lived on deck in all weather, sleeping in bags made of hides and pelts, the leather side facing outward. Like the Norse, the crew must have lived off stockfish or salted herring much of the time, even though live animals for slaughter were sometimes aboard.

The cog's most significant feature was its cargo capacity. The Norse built ships of great seaworthiness and ability, but even the largest knarr was a small load carrier. One of these sturdy vessels could ship out with about twenty lasts of barreled herring. The newly developed Hanse cog could carry an average of 100 lasts, sometimes as many as 200. These rugged, simple vessels were the supertankers of the medieval world, adapted above all for the shallow waters of the Baltic and Netherlands but capable of crossing the North Sea, sailing to Norway, and carrying cargoes to Iceland. During the sailing season from March to November, hundreds of cogs crowded North Sea and Baltic waters, laden with everything imaginable, from grain and timber to wine and herring barrels. Without the cog, it's questionable whether the northern fisheries could have satisfied the growing demand for salted herring and stockfish during Lent.

In the buying and selling of staple commodities like fish for holy days, the Hanse believed in close regulation and standardization, and in overwhelming the competition by ruthless and monopolistic practices. Their commercial tentacles extended as far north as Bergen, where they controlled the Norwegian stockfish trade, to the eastern Baltic and as far west as London and the English port of King's Lynn. They also shipped Baltic herring to the Low Countries, where the herring fishery thrived on lightly salted fish that did not compete with the Skänia product.

The barrel curing methods used in the Skänia fishery, vastly superior to any prior salting technology, soon became the standard wherever herring were caught for more than local consumption. Exactly when barrel curing reached a high degree of refinement is controversial, not so much over the brining but over the method used to gut the fish. Herring keep better if a cut is made at the throat and the fish is partially eviscerated, leaving part of the pancreas, the enzyme-rich pyloric caecae, in place. No one knows when this new gutting method, called *kaakharing* curing, came into use. It may have developed in the Baltic fishery, but persistent oral tradition credits a Zeeland fisherman, Wilhelm van Beukels (or Beukelzon) of Biervleit, with the invention in about 1383. Van Beukels became a national hero after his death. In 1550 none other than Emperor Charles V visited his grave and ordered a monument erected in honor of a man who had ensured that fish were plentiful on holy days and during Lent. Alas, van Beukels's innovation is almost certainly apocryphal. Biervleit was indeed an important herring curing center in the late fourteenth century, but the brining and gutting methods used there were identical to those used on Baltic shores. They existed long before van Beukels became prominent in local fishing circles. His fame is likely a product of Dutch nationalism, after the Netherlands effectively took over the North Sea herring fishery in the fifteenth century. The same curing method is still used today.[10]

*Kaakharing* curing depended on ample supplies of good-quality salt provided by the Hanse, who sent annual cog convoys south into the Bay of Biscay and beyond for evaporated salt. In this respect the Hanse were rather like the merchants of the California gold rush, who made fortunes not from gold but from the miners scrambling to find it.

North Sea herring are larger than Baltic herring, contain more nutrients, and have a higher salt content, which makes them ideal for brining in
barrels. In the fifteenth century, the Dutch developed the *vleet*, a large drift
net made up of forty to seventy smaller nets, which soon came into nearly
universal use aboard their boats. At about the same time, they started curing *kaakharing* afloat in large fishing boats known as busses, a modifica-
tion of lapstrake-planked Scandinavian cargo ships. Busses were designed
to fish for and process herring, carry heavy loads, operate in rough seas,
and stay offshore for long periods of time. The productivity of the Dutch
herring fishery soared almost immediately, as its fishing fleets entered previously inaccessible waters far to the north and followed the migrating herring southward.

Meanwhile, both the Skänia fishery and Yarmouth were in trouble. The
early 1400s saw smaller runs of Baltic herring. Yarmouth harbor was silting up. As northern supplies faltered, the Dutch lifted restrictions on the
landing of heavily salted catches by their boats and invested heavily in
busses. Soon over fifty busses were at sea, a number that climbed to some
200. English landings plummeted while their competitors across the
North Sea raked in handsome profits. The Dutch fishers were silent folk at
the best of times, and were not about to give away their secrets. Frustrated
English merchants encouraged their skippers to ply their competitors with
liquor in order to discover "their secret in gypping, salting, packing, and
curing of herringe," but to no avail.[11] French fishermen adopted Dutch
practices, with dramatic increases in productivity. Thousands of herring
barrels now traveled considerable distances. In January 1418, fish merchants in Boulogne-sur-Mer shipped 8,000 herring to the abbey of Notre
Dame du Gard in Picardy, a long journey by horse-drawn barge, possible
only with well-salted fish.[12]

By this time, herring curing was a refined art, aimed at processing a
highly standardized product. We owe this standardization both to the
Hanse, who supervised every aspect of the Baltic harvest, and to the Dutch,
who exercised increasingly rigorous official control over curing and barrel-
ing. Uniform barrel brining required precisely measured amounts of salt
and careful monitoring to ensure consistent quality. Above all, a good cure

consumed enormous quantities of salt. According to a seventeenth-century observer who witnessed highly refined brining methods identical to those of earlier centuries, a barrel of 500 to 600 herring required fifty-five pints of salt. The brine was dense enough for the fish to float.

Bulk cargoes moved slowly and anonymously in watercraft so humble that few noted their passage. We encounter salted herring in a patchwork of customs and tithe records, in kitchen accounts and occasional recipe books. Barges, cogs, and better curing brought *Clupea* to tables throughout Europe. By the start of the fourteenth century, more than 30 million salted herring arrived by barge in Paris annually. By the mid-1300s, they were commonplace on the tables of nobles and commoners as far inland as Crakow. In France, the canons of Arles regularly ate herring by 1352. Soon the trade extended to Mediterranean lands. By 1396 demand for herring in Tuscany made it profitable to ship it in barrels from Flanders.

Barreled herring became a separate line item in estate accounts. The household of the duke of Gelders at Lobith, where the Rhine enters its delta, ate local fish throughout most of 1428 and 1429. But between late November and the end of Lent the family and its servants ate herring almost exclusively. A similar pattern turns up in the accounts of the Puchaim family, who lived in a castle on a tributary of the Danube River in Austria. They consumed hundreds of brined herring between late November and the end of Lent. No other marine fish entered their kitchen, although they sometimes bought carp from local ponds.[13]

Well-off late medieval households of the Rue Fromenteau in Paris ate both carp and wild freshwater fish but relied heavily on marine fishes, fresh and preserved.[14] Unsalted cod and herring reached Paris on carts from Normandy drawn by galloping horses. Despite the inevitable ripeness of the catch, the Fromenteau households obtained as much as 55 percent of their fish from fresh sources, while salted herring and cod were not far behind. Nevertheless, the demand for preserved fish rose gradually, especially beyond the frontier of some 150 kilometers where galloping horses could transport fresh sea fish inland. Most salted herring shipments traveled up major rivers like the Elbe, Rhine, and Seine by barge. One riverboat could carry thousands of fish.[15]

During Lent, herring supported entire monasteries, poorhouses, and regiments, as well as appearing on aristocratic tables. In St. Benedict's day, the monks ate in one room, the refectory.[16] By the twelfth century, meals were served in at least two rooms, a compromise that allowed for fine distinctions as far as diet was concerned. Refectories were large rooms; the one at Westminster was forty meters long and eleven meters wide. The misericord and a third chamber used for eating, where the abbot would entertain guests and often serve more lavish dishes, were smaller. Food reached the refectory and misericord through a passage from the kitchen, which ensured that much of it was cold before it reached the table. On fast days, dinner was served only in the refectory and everyone ate fish. The food arrived at table in portions called messes, which served between one and four monks. On fast days, small messes were used to serve herring. By this time, most monks used knives, plates, and saucerlike dishes, with cups for ale or wine.

Most days, dinner at Westminster, and probably other houses too, was served at 11:00 or 11:30 A.M., as many as seventeen to eighteen hours since the previous day's supper.[17] On fast days there was only one meal.

A meal was a formal occasion. The monks washed their hands and then took their places in order of precedence. Dinner began and ended with a grace, unfolding in silence except for the voice of the reader. The intent was to lift the mind heavenward with a religious text, making the meal a form of spiritual communion. Etiquette was strict, cups often being held with two hands, fingers and knives wiped first on a piece of bread, then on the tablecloth. As far as we can tell, the monks took their time eating, since a meal was the main event of the day. Whatever the food, the choreographed ceremonial of monastic meals never altered over the centuries, whereas secular eating changed dramatically.

There were three main dishes at a refectory dinner, the first a pottage made with oatmeal and pieces of meat or fish, depending on the day. The other two consisted of fish and vegetables. Until the fifteenth century, salted herring was the staple of Lenten meals, a monotonous diet at best, each monk receiving a fixed number of sticklike fish laid out on his mess. The monastery kitchener exercised close control over individual portions, apparently four or five herring. Like everyone else, monks disliked *Clupea*, preferring white fish like cod or hake. But herring was a staple during Lent and again in the fall when Westminster, being near London's fish markets, could buy fresh herring during spawning season. Lenten herring meals, leavened with bread and vegetables, were unpalatable, even when washed down with a daily ration of ale or wine, preferred to the polluted water supply.

Monks were discerning eaters who preferred fresh or salted white fish to herring, which gradually vanished from religious menus. But the urban poor and soldiers endured herring for days on end. *Clupea* was eaten like hardtack, a formidable task in an era when people's teeth rotted early in life, but more often was cast into iron cauldrons as part of the thick stews and soups that supplemented the basically meatless diet of peasant and urban worker alike. Many people subsisted on alms, the remnants of monastery meals. At the Hundred Mens Hall at St. Cross in Winchester in 1373, 100 poor men and thirteen poverty-stricken scholars received a herring and two pilchards each daily, also coarse bread, weak beer, and pottage, perhaps to support both them and their families. Armies lived much the same way, subsisting off bread and fixed rations of herring, distributed from barrels in an unchanging diet that provided little more than basic sustenance. By the early fourteenth century, military rations were standardized, the diet being monotonous and unbalanced. By Tudor times, a sixteenth-century soldier would receive seven or eight herring a day, as well as bread, pottage, and ale for fast days.[18]

Wealthier households fared much better, especially once eating became more structured. Dinner was a formal affair, attended by all the household. In 1240 Robert Grosseteste, bishop of Lincoln, adjured the local countess to sit herself at the middle of the high table, so that "your presence as lord or lady may appear openly to all, and that you may plainly see on either side all the service and all the faults." As a result, she would be "very much feared and reverenced."[19] The food was carried first to high table and then distributed in the main body of the hall. Thus the lord and lady eating herring and other Lenten food in public with their household maintained domestic harmony and adherence to Christian teaching. High table might eat its herring soused in mustard, as was common practice at the time, but the commoners in the hall would receive a fixed allocation of bread and salted herring for dinner.

The escalating demand fueled by Christian doctrine and military commissariats stimulated the growth of offshore fisheries. The Flemish buss and the English dogger, which we will come to in Chapter 11, produced larger catches, which in turn required more people ashore handle the incoming fish and market it, build the necessary equipment, and repair the ships. Boatbuilding became a major industry on both sides of the North Sea, satisfying a constant need for replacement of fishing craft lost at sea or simply worn out. Herring ports were crowded, dirty, and increasingly polluted. Towns like Dieppe in northern France smelled of fish and roasting salt, an odor so powerful that it disgusted the members of a visiting Czech embassy in the 1460s. Here and at other fish ports, the catch was sold in bulk, "by the last and by the hundred," as English account books described the transactions. Some of the sales were enormous. In 1390 the almoner to the king of France bought 78,000 herring on the Paris market for distribution to hospices and poor households. Imported herring was charged the lowest customs duty rate, half that of fresh herring. It was the least expensive fish for Fridays and Lent—four to the penny at Coventry in 1460, as opposed to one and a half pence for an eel. A pound of herring at Frankfurt am Main cost the same as two-thirds of a pound of salt cod or a pound of beef.[20]

*Clupea* tasted like wood unless cooked with elaborate spices. It was hardly a high-class food, being sold by salt-fishmongers, or herringers, rather than fresh fish merchants. Bishop Matthias von Rammung of Speyer instructed his kitchen in 1470 that "herring shall not be considered a fish [for] one can in no way make them acceptable."[21]

By 1450 the herring fisheries were the domain of not only individual fishing communities but much larger mercantile concerns, whose loyalties lay with distant markets and whose profits depended on advance purchases. The expectation was that fish were superabundant and were there for the taking. When one fishery went into decline or the original fishing fleets were squeezed out, fishermen simply moved on in search of new stocks.

The glory years of the herring fisheries occurred in the early fourteenth century, but catches fell rapidly thereafter, recovering after 1400 but then dipping rapidly for reasons that still elude explanation—perhaps because of still unstudied changes in seawater temperatures. The annual herring runs declined; Yarmouth's trade withered. The rivalry with nearby Lowestoft intensified, the harbor silted badly, and herring demand may have fallen after the ravages of the Black Death. Competition over fishing rights quickened as Dutch, Flemish, English, and French boats vied for the same spawning grounds, leading to sporadic but unsuccessful efforts to limit catches to avoid overfishing. Sometimes rival crews came to blows. There were swordfights and drownings, as well as downright piracy, as catches ebbed and flowed from year to year.

Some of the blame for these unpredictable swings falls on a phenomenon known as the North Atlantic Oscillation (NAO). Complex interactions between the atmosphere and the ocean influence Europe's climate. A continually changing pressure gradient governs the northern Atlantic, a seesaw of atmospheric pressure between a persistent high over the Azores and a low over Iceland. Among other things, this seesaw determines the position and strength of the Atlantic storm track. Climatologists refer to high and low NAO indexes that shift constantly and unpredictably from year to year and decade to decade. A high index means low pressure over Iceland, high pressure off Portugal and the Azores. This brings persistent warm westerlies, good rainfall, and mild winters to western Europe. These are also years of warmer summers, when herring thrive in the North Sea— or did so when the area wasn't chronically overfished. A low NAO index,

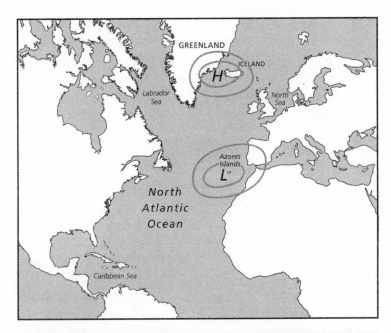

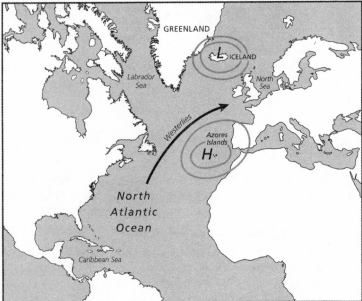

The North Atlantic Oscillation in low (top) and high (bottom) modes.

in contrast, brings shallower pressure gradients, weaker westerlies, and colder temperatures in Europe. Herring spawns in the cold water are sharply reduced. Climatologists and fisheries biologists suspect that low NAOs may have decimated herring stocks in the Baltic and North Sea at unpredictable intervals.

During the early centuries of the herring fisheries, the relatively warm conditions of the Medieval Warm Period, huge schools of *Clupea* thronged the North Sea each autumn. The Little Ice Age, a 500-year period of cooler and stormier conditions, set in around 1300. It may be no coincidence that herring schools and fish landings at Yarmouth suffered a major decline in the 1390s and that catches varied dramatically thereafter from year to year. A highly competitive marketplace, overfishing to satisfy insatiable demand, and better salting methods had an impact that varied from port to port. But in the final analysis, it may have been a climate change that tipped the northern European fish economy from sustainable to unsustainable.

What began as a food of abstinence and devotion had become a staple for the poor and the military, then a Lenten food in even the noblest homes and most devout religious houses. The herring trade was born of religious devotion, but its growth was contingent on technological innovations— better boats and better salting techniques—that allowed denizens of alms-houses and hospitals to eat fish caught hundreds of kilometers away and months before.

Until North Sea fishermen began to sail far offshore, freshwater fish was the preferred Lenten food for those who could afford it. Those who controlled the fisheries took the next logical step to secure a reliable supply.

# 2

# THE CARP BUBBLE

The mill pond. And in the seven year of the king, twenty-eighth day of January [1467/8], I brake mine greatest pond in the park, and out of that I took in great breams, sixty-five. And put them into the mill pond the which is new made; and I put the same day in to the same pond six great carps and . . . little carps, twelve score.

Anonymous monk, fifteenth century[1]

By the thirteenth century, two ways of eating in groups coexisted in European society: one set in the hall of a castle or great house, the other in the refectory of a religious community. The monastery table represented the Christian ideal, a life of moderation and abstinence. Secular consumption often gravitated to the other extreme—gluttony, sin, and purgatorial excess. These seemingly irreconcilable ways of life were epitomized by the French court of the day, where the royal table was bound by two sets of rules—those of abstinence, laid down by the Church, and those dictated by royal ceremonial.

When the court of King Louis IX assembled at Saumur in 1241, a magnificent feast unfolded, as much spectacle as meal. The king wore a tunic of dark blue satin with a scarlet surcoat. Around him sat barons and knights in velvet tunics. Twenty archbishops and bishops ate at one of the tables around the cloister. Louis's biographer, Jean of Joinville, recalled, "Many folk said that they had never seen so many surcoats or other garments of cloth of gold and silk at one feast, and that there were at least three thousand knights present."[2]

Amid all the splendor sat a monarch who lived an exemplary private life of austerity and prayer. Louis IX abstained from meat on Mondays, Wednesdays, and Fridays, ate only bread and water on many holy days, and gave up both fish and fruit on Fridays, until his health broke down and his confessor made him eat a single piece of each daily. The king's piety intensified after he led a crusade to the Holy Land. Louis now declined large fish, deliberately chose inferior food and drink, and wore only raiment of "undyed or dark-blue wool." Despite his own somewhat exhibitionistic austerity, Louis maintained all the secular ceremony of the court and a cheerful demeanor: "When any great men from abroad dined with him he was good company."[3]

Louis was one of the last monarchs to reconcile lay and religious approaches to the table at a time when the life of royal courts was becoming increasingly secular. The late medieval world saw rapid changes in court and diplomatic life. Public occasions became more formal. The grand feast became far more elaborate, the food endowed with lavish color, game displayed with gilded horns or feathers, the table a magnificent spectacle, with entirely new cuisines based on pastry, spices, sugar, and a vast range of different foods.

Logistical demands escalated accordingly. By the end of the fourteenth century, the French court employed between 700 and 800 people just to feed the enormous household. Catering such large establishments and the major feasts associated with them required a small army of men and women to provide the raw materials for food and drink. The coronation of Pope Clement VI at Avignon on May 19, 1344, is a case in point. This extravaganza, held with just six weeks' advance notice, required 15 sturgeon and 300 pike, as well as 118 cows, 1,023 sheep, and 7,428 chickens.[4] Natural ecosystems could no longer provide enough fish to satisfy such escalating demands. The only way to provide more fresh fish was to grow it, a type of farming made possible by the technology used to build water mills.

The water mill was one of those revolutionary inventions that exert a profound but quiet impact on history.[5] Not that the idea of waterpower was new. Greek artisans developed elaborate geared mechanisms as early as the fourth century B.C. but did little to develop sources of power with them. The Egyptians were among the first to experiment with hydropower; a papyrus of the second century B.C. refers to an automatic irrigation wheel along the Nile. By the late first century B.C., Vitruvius, a Roman architect and engineer whose principal claim to fame is his spreading the apocryphal story of Archimedes' bathtub, recorded instructions for building a vertical waterwheel, connected by gears to a much slower-moving horizontally mounted wheel.

Overshot wheels, with the water cups facing upward, ground grain and nothing else during Roman times, despite their potential application for other obvious and laborious tasks such as cutting stone and timber. Slaves were plentiful and there were few incentives to develop mechanical devices. As labor became scarcer and more expensive, and slavery receded in post-Roman times, water mills proliferated across Europe, especially in Frankish domains. They were commonplace by the tenth century. The Domesday Book of 1086 catalogued 5,624 water mills in 3,000 different locations in Britain alone. Toulouse in southern France had no less than sixty floating mills, replaced in the twelfth century by forty-three fixed ones.

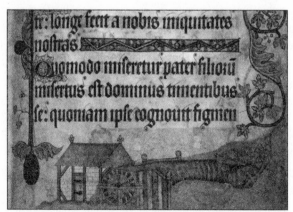

A water mill built between 1300 and 1340, from the Luttrell Psalter, begun before 1340 for Sir Geoffrey Luttrell and now a prized possession of the British Museum. HIP/ART RESOURCE, NEW YORK, N.Y.

Water mills required careful siting and engineering. Their prototypes were boat and bridge mills, which used the natural flow of rivers and streams. By building dams, the engineer could adapt the flow of water with sluices and canals to the needs of the wheel below. Medieval engineers used their dams to store water, develop a grade for the water driving the wheel, and divert stream flow. Where gradients were steep, they could site the wheel close to the dam. Wide, flat valleys might require several dams to prevent excessive flooding of valuable land and develop enough current to power the wheel using a mill race or power canal. Some of these mill races were of impressive length. The one built by the monks of Clairvaux in 1136 extended 3.5 kilometers from the Aube River to supplement the natural streams already flowing through the monastery.

Clairvaux was a Cistercian house where fish became such an important dietary supplement that Pope Clement IV in his bull *Parvus Fons* directed at the Cistercians included an ordinance forbidding any monk to take more than two helpings of fish at a sitting.[6]

The mill dam and the mill race transformed agricultural production, apart from being prodigious labor-saving devices. Historian Terry Reynolds has estimated that the earliest medieval water mills generated about two horsepower, enough to liberate between thirty and sixty people from the burdensome task of grinding grain, not to mention the food that would have been required to feed animals to operate the grinder in their place. Water technology soon extended to fulling (cleaning and beating cloth to thicken it) and tanning operations, saws, and iron foundries. Promiscuous mill construction, like monastic fish weirs, soon threatened safe river navigation, resulting in conflict between milling and shipping interests.

Hydropower dams backed up calm waters, where eels tunneled into soft mud and other fish abounded for the taking. Sluices and mill races channeled migrating eels, salmon, and other fish into narrow defiles where they were easily harvested. Mill owners were quick to cash in on this lucrative bounty. After the ninth and tenth centuries, the aristocracy and the monasteries imposed a virtual monopoly on water mills. From the monastic perspective, water mills saved labor and contributed to self-sufficiency, not only in grain but also in fresh fish for the refectory. Both secular and religious mill owners made a tidy profit from their grinding operations, but the fish in their waters also yielded substantial dividends. They trapped eels on their own account or rented out the fishing rights in exchange for a (generous) portion of the catch. Some mills made more money from fish than they did from grain. Two mills on one small Baltic stream provided Preetz convent in northern Germany with some 500 eels annually. Other religious houses received even larger payments in kind from the villagers and tenants who harvested their dams and races.[7]

The increasingly refined technology of water mills led almost inevitably to the development of fish farms. Pisciculture involved more than trapping fish in a pond and allowing them to breed. Even expert fishers, familiar with the habits of their prey, had to learn by a long process of trial and error which fish species were amenable to domestication. They had to develop feeding routines necessary to maintain a continual population of fish ready for a privileged and often fastidious clientele. Sophisticated water control methods were essential for even a small farm—methods of aerating tanks, maintaining healthy water, and creating the correct flows with sluices and runways. Here experience with water mills, where careful water control, overflows, and sluices were routine, came into play.

The first fish farming systems apparently developed between the Loire and Rhine rivers around the eleventh century, based on local species like bream or pike.[8] Elaborate dams and multipond farms soon appeared in Poitou and other parts of France, prompting complaints about illegally flooded lands. In 1160 the canons of Bourges in central France complained bitterly to the Count Étienne of Sancerré when his new fishponds inundated their property. Often such disputes ended with the parties agreeing to share rights to the fish and the land, along with the labor of cleaning the ponds. The scale of these early operations paled alongside those that developed with the introduction of the carp, an exotic fish that thrived in warm water.

Carp *(Cyprinus carpio)* are a heavy-bodied form of minnow with barbells on either side of the upper jaw. They have conspicuous fins with heavy teeth and range in color from a brassy green or yellow to golden brown or even silver. Adults spawn in very shallow, warm water each spring and usually grow to a common weight of 3.6 to 4.5 kilograms, although they can achieve enormous size. The world record for a carp caught with rod and line is thirty-four kilograms. The omnivorous carp does best in highly productive, warm, muddy water, where it eats small fish, invertebrates, and plants. Prolific, fast growing, and abundant, the carp was an ideal farm fish despite its sometimes muddy-flavored flesh.[9]

Wild *Cyprinus* flourish in the lower Danube and the rivers that drain into the Black Sea from southeast Europe, where they were a popular catch for thousands of years. These warm, often quiet waters are ideal for a fish that thrives in shallow, muddy environments. Although they would not be expected to be found in the colder, faster-moving streams to the north and west, they appeared in central and then western Europe after 1000.

Carp spread rapidly across Europe. By the late eleventh century, they thrived in the upper Danube basin, and in nearby Rhine tributaries by the mid-twelfth. In the mid-thirteenth century they appear with dramatic suddenness in French documents like those of the count of Champagne, who stocked ponds with hundreds of carp in 1258–1259. By 1260 the governor of Paris issued regulations for marketing *Cyprinus*. Despite the complexities of aquaculture, carp farming spread rapidly throughout Burgundy, through the rest of France, and then into the Low Countries by the fourteenth century. Central European landowners and monasteries also adopted carp farming. Heilsbronn monastery, a Cistercian house near Nuremberg, acquired natural and then artificial ponds starting around 1260. By the 1340s, the monks were managing a large fish-farming enterprise that extended more than thirty kilometers from the community. All the carp were for their own use. Emperor Charles IV (1347–1378) encouraged pisciculture in Czech lands on the grounds that his domains needed plenty of fish and more humid air, "so that our kingdom may abound in fish and vapours."[10] Subsequent farming operations reached an impressive size, with elaborate sluices and valve systems and ponds covering 100 hectares or more. Such was the enthusiasm for carp farming that some local landowners encountered peasant unrest when their ponds flooded cultivable land or pasture. Not that the commoners prevailed. Provincial law codes in France soon allowed a pond owner to flood neighboring lands and then compensate the owners for the damage.

The authors of contemporary encyclopedias based in Paris routinely described carp as a species whose young liked shallow, warm waters. Such fish preferred clay bottoms sown with oats and were "skilled at evading nets." Carp were nearly universal in Europe by 1300 but did not reach England until the mid-fifteenth century, perhaps because of cooler waters and different social conditions.

No one knows why carp suddenly appeared outside their natural habitat, but climatic factors may have been involved. The centuries when they spread westward coincided with the warmer summers and milder winters of the Medieval Warm Period, when higher temperatures and prolonged hot weather would have raised water temperatures in hitherto cool locations such as mill dams and fish ponds, turning them into ideal habitats for *Cyprinus*. Most likely, monks and estate fishers introduced the exotic fish into shallow waters to create prolific fishing holes. Whatever the original cause of their appearance, we know that whenever carp find warm, weed-infested waters such as ponds and dams, they colonize them rapidly.

Carp tolerate low levels of oxygen and are thus relatively easy to raise. They gather in densely vegetated shallow water, where males and females emit milt and eggs simultaneously. The parents then leave the nursery habitat. Knowing this, the farmer would introduce ripe adult carp into a warm, thickly grown pond as the water heated up in spring, allow them to breed, and then remove the adults. During the summer, the fry would grow in the shallow pond and were moved into deeper water as winter approached. After a couple of years in a growth pond, the young carp would be relocated into a fattening pool, where they would be allowed to grow to harvestable size. Feeding carp as they grew was relatively straightforward, for they consume small invertebrates found on water plants or in bottom sediment. The farmer would increase the nutrients in the water by adding manure or channeling runoff from animal or human waste into the ponds. By the fourth, fifth, or sixth year, carp would reach a table size of forty to sixty centimeters, depending on temperature and climatic conditions. The fattening pool was shallow at the sides and deep in the middle, allowing the owner to concentrate the fish as he drained the pool at harvest time. The wet ground that remained was often plowed and sown with crops.

## SALMON IN PASTRY

*Le menagier de Paris*, compiled in 1393, is one of the earliest known cookbooks, compiled by a bureaucrat of about sixty for the benefit of his fifteen-year-old bride, who had no experience in housekeeping. The book describes many aspects of running a household in an urban world with appalling sanitation, insects, and the smells of excrement and unwashed humanity. A large part of the book is concerned with ridding bedclothes and raiment of fleas and lice: placing a white sheet on the bed, then killing fleas by hand was as good a method as any. *Le menagier*'s recipes set down general instructions for dishes made for generations, using experience passed orally from one generation of cooks to the next.

Salmon in pastry was a common dish during spring and autumn runs, its relatively dry flesh easily salted and smoked. The anonymous writer gives two versions, one for Lent made with Lenten pastry, a second, only slightly more elaborate, for feast days. Either version is an attractive dish; the feast recipe is more complex in its flavorings, thanks to the ginger and bacon.

### ✄ *Salmon in Pastry*.

#### Lenten Version

Fresh salmon should be smoked. Leave in the backbone for roasting; then cut it into slices boiled in water, with wine and salt during cooking. Eat with yellow pepper or Carmelite sauce and in pastry, whatever you like, sprinkled with spices. If the salmon is salted, eat it with wine and sliced scallions.

#### A Modern Reconstruction

SERVES 6 TO 8

Lenten Pastry
For one crust:

1 lb/464 g unbleached flour (You may need more. The type of flour used, humidity, and other cooking conditions can affect pastry recipes.)
$\frac{1}{16}$ oz/5 g sea salt
1 oz/30 ml olive oil, chilled for pastry making
6–8 oz/175–250 ml very cold water

Combine all ingredients (adding water gradually as all of it may be unnecessary) and knead vigorously until a smooth, soft dough forms. Refrigerate for at least an hour wrapped in plastic wrap and/or a moist towel. Be prepared to use extra flour while kneading and rolling out the dough.

*(continues)*

*Salmon in Pastry (continued)* _____

Completing the dish:
Preheat oven to 350F/175C.

1½ to 2 lb/750–907 g (just under a kilo) fillet of skinned salmon
    (We used wild salmon.)
1 oz/30 ml red wine, preferably burgundy
⅟16 oz/5 g kosher salt
⅟16 oz/ 5 g ground cinnamon
⅟16 oz/5 g ground ginger
1 double crust pie dough (We used the one above; you may substitute
    a recipe of your choice.)
6 slices of uncooked center-cut bacon

Roll out pastry into one large rectangle piece, about 2 inches (5 cm) longer and
a little more than twice the width of the fillet. Arrange half the bacon, if used,
in the center of the pastry; place salmon on top of bacon. Sprinkle wine and
seasonings onto salmon; cover with the rest of the bacon. Bring long edges of
pastry together and pinch to close seam atop the salmon; similarly seal short
ends of pastry. Place seam side down on parchment-lined baking sheet. Bake 35
to 50 minutes until the pastry is lightly browned.

    Adapted from *Le menagier de Paris*, 1393. Available online at www.best.com/
~ddfr/Medieval/Cookbooks/Menagier/Menagier.html. Translated by Janet
Hinson. Lenten pastry: Odile Redon, Françoise Sabban, and Silvano Serventi,
*The Medieval Kitchen: Recipes from France and Italy* (Chicago: University of
Chicago Press, 1998).

The careful organization of pond works extended to their design and
construction. In most cases, the designers used specialist artisans, assisted
by local labor. Almost invariably they would build a dam, blocking a small
stream to flood an area upstream. In the early sixteenth century, a Mora-
vian prelate, Dubravius, was famously expert at calculating the level and
extent of a pond created by a dam that would stand about a meter above
water level.[11] Logs, brush, or stone facing formed the core of dams built of
compressed clay and loam. The builders would sometimes construct "stair-
cases" of ponds descending from a valley. There was an especially elaborate one at Maulbronn in the Black Forest, and another at Maubisson in

the Val d'Oise. Such ponds had bypass channels and sometimes spillways or adjustable sluices.

By the mid-fourteenth century, carp farming was big business. Operating a large farm system included coordinating dozens of pools covering a hundred or more hectares, with the carp divided into as many as six age sets, representing different stages of growth. Many farms expanded rapidly. In 1146 Châalis Abbey near Paris acquired land for a fish farm on the nearby Thève River. By 1161 the monks had constructed a single pond, then a dam that flooded eight hectares of marshland. Further west on the same river, they acquired land for another farm by 1200, whose ponds harmed those of the Count of Beaumont downstream. At its peak, the Châalis fish farm boasted forty hectares of ponds at different locations, all to feed the monks.[12]

The Châalis operations pale into insignificance alongside the huge carp-rearing operation run by the Barons Rozmberk of Trebon in southern Bohemia, on land along a tributary of the Elbe River blessed with swampy terrain underlain by loam and clay, ideal for fish tanks.[13] By 1380 the barons were operating two ponds of 190 and 305 hectares. By 1450 the Rozmberks controlled seventeen small ponds and three large ones covering more than 700 hectares, many of them on land acquired from neighbors. Trebon was a commercial operation that supplied carp down a so-called fish road to Prague and other towns, and also to people in Austria. The artisans who operated these farms acquired sterling reputations. During the 1520s and 1530s, fish master Stepanek Netolicky earned a large salary for his expertise. His work at Trebon resulted in an area called the Golden Ditch along the Luznica River, a canal that fed six new ponds, ranging in size from 150 to 415 hectares. After his retirement, he consulted for the archbishop of Salzberg and the count of Salm. Netolicky's plans remained in use long after his death. During his lifetime, he supervised the construction of nine large and thirty-seven small ponds. Today some 400 square kilometers of ponds around Trebon, including some of Netolicky's design, are still used for carp farming. An environment that was once forest and hazardous marsh is now an important wetland area of natural lakes protected by UNESCO.

Carp were a reasonably productive fish crop, but even when plentiful they were never cheap. In 1356 a hundred carp served at a wedding in Nâmur cost twice the price of a cow. For much of the fifteenth century, a pound of carp priced out at the equivalent of 1.8 kilograms of beef or twenty loaves of bread. This was a food for the wealthy and the religious, not the general populace.

Nevertheless, the demand for carp after 1400 was so great that a huge swath of Europe from the Loire and Poitou to central Poland devoted itself to a form of monoculture, especially in areas with abundant water and impermeable soils. The hectarage under fish farms was staggering. There were 25,000 ponds in Bohemia and 40,000 hectares under ponds in central France. The greatest concentration of medieval aquaculture lay inland of the 150-kilometer distance that horses, carts, or boats could carry fresh sea fish. Serried fishponds created warm, still waterways over an enormous area of medieval Europe, where there had been none before, with dire environmental and social consequences. Thousands of domesticated carp escaped from captivity and proliferated in lakes and streams. The now feral newcomers disrupted native fish populations that were already under stress from overfishing, accelerating changes in local habitats. Where once trees had shaded small streams, large lakes created humid, insect-infested environments; malaria, spread by mosquitoes that flourished in standing water, became endemic.

Large areas of France were soon notorious for a high incidence of fever and disease. The proliferating fish farms disrupted ancient farming practices and triggered disputes over flooded pastures. With the supply of fresh fish tightly controlled by wealthy landowners and monasteries, poaching by hungry and resentful peasants became rampant and labor disputes commonplace.

All of this benefited only a few. Medieval aquaculture served a well-defined constituency—the aristocracy and monastic communities. Pond masters delivered thousands of carp and other fish to barons, dukes, or abbots, the deliveries fine-tuned to the religious calendar or the whims of lords. The duke of Burgundy ate carp when residing at his castles inland and fresh seafood when he went to the coast. Large organizations like the pope's household at Avignon and demand from wealthy, larger towns like Lyon attracted suppliers from pond complexes near and far. The pope's agents traveled far up the Rhône and Saône to buy fish from Burgundy farms. Paris drew freshwater fish from the Seine and Loire basins. Apart from monastic farms, many of these enterprises became strictly commercial operations. Even a modest operation required massive investment for two to five years before yielding a return, and it demanded, as historian Richard Hoffmann reminds us, two or three times the amount of work an owner might expect from an entire farming village.[14] But the profits could be enormous. According to Jan Dubravius, Vilém of Perstejn in Moravia bragged in the fifteenth century that he made more money from selling carp than the entire wealth of ancient Roman senators. Cash returns of 15 to 25 percent were not unusual in Lower Austria.

Any humanly modified landscape is ephemeral. I remember passing through the same farming villages in southern Zambia year after year, watching the crops grow. The first year, the gardens around the village would support high stands of maize and millet. Two or three years later the crop would be more stunted, the yield smaller. By the fourth growing season, I would see the men with their axes trimming branches and undergrowth, piling it up and setting it alight so that the ash would fertilize newly cleared land. Meanwhile, the fields behind their huts lay abandoned to the native grass already invading the plots. An aerial photograph would have revealed a widening circle of active gardens ever farther from the settlement, which now lay among empty fields and confused undergrowth. The landscape changed constantly with the rhythms of sifting agriculture. Medieval carp farms were likewise never static. The fish masters labored constantly to maintain dam walls and sluices, and clean out silting ponds. They struggled with encroaching vegetation. They avoided using water from densely stocked pools close upstream, which affected the growth of their own fish. With subsistence agriculture, the soil would eventually recover, given the time to do so, providing a basic level of sustainability. But elaborate dams and pond systems suffer immediately from neglect and abandonment. They soon fill with sediment and become dry land as the natural drainage reasserts itself. Aquaculture was not self-sustaining farming.

The great flowering of carp farming took place just as salted herring and cod became readily available throughout much of Europe, even far from the English Channel and North Sea. As preservation methods improved, more and more seafood appeared on refectory tables. Increasingly, freshwater fish were luxuries, brought out at feasts, presented at royal dinner tables as symbols of wealth and power. For a while, carp farms prospered and expanded in the face of cod and herring. But by the fifteenth century, carp farming was in decline except in a few places, mainly in eastern Europe. Today virtually all of France's once bustling carp farms are dry land. Most of these enterprises dissolved in the face of political unrest, relaxed monastic diets, and changing preferences. Both aristocrat and monk came to prefer sea fish over carp's muddy flesh.

Aquaculture constructed fisheries for the benefit of a small elite living inland. The output of even large fish farms was limited. The fish masters of monasteries and noble houses created new ecosystems far from the rich ocean that surrounded so much of western Christendom. These artificial landscapes were unsustainable without constant maintenance. Changing dietary habits, the cost of labor, and competition from cheaper sea fish led to their collapse.

The forces of the piscine marketplace made themselves felt throughout western Europe after 1300, when fish consumption by the religious reached its peak and people turned from carp and herring to white fish like hake and cod.

# The Sin of Gluttony

The genius of love and the genius of hunger, those twin brothers, are the two moving forces behind all living things. All
living things are set themselves in motion to feed and to repro-
duce. Love and hunger serve the same purpose. Life must
never cease; life must be sustained and must create.

Ivan Turgenev[1]

In the summer of 1400 it would not have been uncommon to see a
string of pack horses bound from Rye on England's south coast to the
household of the archbishop of Canterbury. The animals, each carrying a
large, dripping basket slung over its back, would have trotted along
steadily under the guidance of two of the archbishop's mounted rippiers,
leaving behind a mixed scent of dead fish, live horse, and seaweed.*

The road north from Rye was well traveled. By 1400 the rippiers of that
town employed more than 300 packhorses to supply London with fresh
fish. These specialized transporters bought the catch where it was landed
and then moved it to town and monastery, covering the eighty kilometers
or so to London's Billingsgate fish markets in three or four hours. They
were part of a growing and highly regulated fish trade that linked fishers
and their catches with towns far inland.[2]

---

*Rippiers* were people who made their living transporting fish from the coast to markets inland for sale, a common occupation in late medieval times. Some wealthy
households, like the archbishop's, employed their own rippiers.

The essence of the fish trade is speed and numbers, which is why medieval fisherfolk preferred to sell their catch immediately to people who were going to eat it, fishmongers, or middlemen who sold it on. Fish are an unpredictable commodity that spoils rapidly, and processing costs time and money. Catholic dietary restrictions created a tension in the marketplace, causing enormous demand during Advent and Lent, also on holy days—a demand that did not necessarily coincide with the autumn herring spawns. Prices fluctuated wildly, especially in the hands of middlemen, so many port towns encouraged fisherfolk to sell direct from their boats. Yarmouth allowed boats to post signs at the town quay; in other places you simply walked down the beach and selected your fish from the piles on the sand. At the same time, the authorities were well aware that tolls on the fish trade were a nice source of revenue, so they turned a blind eye to abuses such as overcharging and the sale of not quite fresh catches to the unwary inland.

A traveler into a medieval town passed into a crowded world seething with people and animals. The only open space was at the center of town, where the marketplace and church stood. Narrow streets and alleyways zigzagged among wooden houses and cottages, every usable space filled with hovels and cattle byres. A steady hum of human and animal voices permeated every corner; wood smoke hovered low in the streets, where people jostled one another as they went about their daily business. Raw sewage and manure cluttered every alleyway; stall keepers shouted above the din to tout their wares.

Urban fish markets were crowded, busiest in the early morning, swarming with dealers selling from baskets or carts, even from the laden packs on the backs of horses. The crowds were largest during Lent, when people bought enough for one or two meals, sometimes slices of cod, conger eel, pike, or salmon. Officials mingled with the crowds, checking quality and price, on the lookout for scams like putting the best fish on the top of the basket. Some towns stipulated a minimum distance between sellers to allow animals and people to pass safely. The inspectors insisted that everything, including the street, be kept clean, so vendors washed their cutting and display boards constantly, sweeping entrails and other waste with the discarded washing water into the gutter. A pervasive smell of decaying fish permeated everything, including people's clothes.

The fish reached inland towns by a variety of routes. Many ports sent vessels to the Yarmouth herring fair to purchase cargoes of processed fish that were then sent inland in the hands of fishmongers. Maryanne Kowaleski has studied fish distribution from Exeter, in southwestern England, which sat at the hub of several main roads. Between 1370 and 1390, 197 fishmongers worked in the town but just 18 percent actually lived there.[3] The remainder came from small towns and villages as much as eighty kilometers away. Over a quarter of them traveled at least forty kilometers. The fish trade ebbed and flowed with the seasons, coincided with major seasonal fairs like Yarmouth and Scarborough, and reflected changing economic and social conditions. But its ultimate barometer was the Catholic Church.

By the fourteenth century, the demand for sea fish was so great that the stewards of landed gentry and religious houses flocked to buy at the source.[4] Many of them, including a group of Cistercian abbeys, invested in their own curing facilities and storehouses to ensure a reliable supply at the lowest possible price. But most fish ended up in the hands of fishmongers, who formed mercantile guilds to ensure virtual monopolies over fish purchases. The Worshipful Guild of Fishmongers was one of the most powerful in London. The guild and its equivalents in other towns claimed that their expertise ensured high quality for the purchaser, as well as stable, low prices. London's fishmongers gained the exclusive right to sell fish there; they regulated the size of fish baskets and ensured that their members were the only people allowed to buy wholesale from the boats.[5] No fisher in London could sell his catch retail on the dock. The guild owned its own ships to import processed catches from as far away as Scandinavia and the Low Countries, and supplied the royal household with enormous quantities of fresh and salted fish. The capital was a huge market. Between 1330 and 1360, 45 percent of Yarmouth's herring went there. In major ports like Yarmouth, a few merchants known as "hosts" dominated the trade. So blatant were these hosts' abuse of prices and weights that Parliament passed the Statute of Herring in 1357 to ensure a competitive marketplace. The statute was thwarted by numerous local regulations that protected the fishmonger rather than the fisher or consumer.

The abuses were just as flagrant inland. Merchants would buy fish on the road and resell it at a higher price in the market, or buy fish cheaply early in the day and then sell it at a higher price in the afternoon when supplies had run low. They were well aware that consumers were under pressure, for to break a dietary rule during Lent was a mortal sin.

The patterns of international fish trade were changing.[6] During the late fourteenth century, the Skanör herring fishery expanded dramatically under the direction of Hanse merchants. The Hanse wanted a monopoly; it prohibited English ships from buying and processing their own fish and insisted they buy filled barrels and pay for them with cash rather than the wool cloth of earlier times. Nevertheless, the trade expanded; Dutch and Hanse ships brought as many as 1,000 lasts annually to Hull and Lynn alone in the 1390s, rivaling all but the busiest years of Yarmouth in its heyday. But the Baltic herring migrations faltered at the end of the century. The Skanör trade dwindled just at the moment when herring was giving way to cod and other fish in the marketplace. The bland, oil-free flesh of *Gadus morhua* had become the fish of preference for aristocratic and monastic tables, as well as a staple for armies.

During the thirteenth and fourteenth centuries, much of the fish trade consisted of imported stockfish and salt cod in various forms from Trondheim and Bergen, most of it caught off northern Norway or in Icelandic waters. This trade peaked between June and September and stayed mainly in Norwegian hands until the Hanse took over Bergen, gaining effective control of the stockfish market. In 1390 nearly 400,000 stockfish arrived in Hanse cogs at the port of Boston in Lincolnshire, with many more arriving at Lynn, farther south. But even this trade fluctuated. As we will see, the focus of the cod trade changed when English fishing boats began to sail regularly for Icelandic waters.

The shift to cod was no coincidence; monastic diets had become more elaborate, their consumers more fastidious. So had those of secular society, which emulated the religious in fasting practices. The Benedictine diet was now more diverse, in part because the simplicity of the liturgical cycle had become complicated by a proliferation of saints' days, far more than the few allowed for in the sixth century. Saints enjoyed the privilege of a long office, when copes were worn and all the candles lit. An extra dish, an additional meal, or both commemorated the occasion. As early as the eleventh century there were few weeks without a major saint's day. By the fourteenth century, days of abstinence were in effect for well nigh half the year. Furthermore, standards of living were rising slowly outside the cloister, especially among the aristocracy. And as we have seen, religious communities had aristocratic tastes.

Still, even when cod replaced herring on the menu, Lent was an ordeal for most people. The Christian world of that era ran like a clock, its rhythms marked by fast and feast. Each fast ended in a feast—Advent before Christmas, Lent before Easter. The devout engaged in penance and then received both a lavish meal in this life and a spiritual reward in the next. Fasts were the conscious offerings of each individual, each community, society as a whole. Those of individuals could be nominal or rigorous.

Quite apart from private fasting, Catholic doctrine sanctioned official fast days to cleanse and discipline the faithful. By the tenth century there were usually three such days a week—Wednesday, the day when Judas accepted a bribe for betraying Christ; Friday, to atone for the Savior's suffering on the Cross; and Saturday, in commemoration of the Virgin Mary.

Advent was a time of personal renewal, of rebirth, when "so owe ye to begynne and renewe youre lyffe."[7] The fast was brief—four weeks or so—and relatively joyful, filled with anticipation of the celebrations to come.*

---

*Advent (from the Latin, "the coming") has been observed with varying intensity since at least the fourth century. The length has changed over the centuries, the average being about four weeks, the severity of fasting and abstinence varying considerably. Today, Advent begins on the Sunday nearest November 30, the feast of St. Andrew the Apostle, and covers four Sundays. The Canon Law of 1917 abolished obligatory fasting during Advent, but many Catholics believe that Christmas trees should not be decorated until Christmas Eve, as the season beforehand is one of penitence.

The six-week ordeal of Lent, the duration of Christ's fast in the wilderness, was another matter: a lengthy intercession for forgiveness, a time for calling on God to save humanity from its transgressions. The forty days of penance coincided with the dreary days of late winter, when food was often short. At this time people paid their tithes, up to a tenth of their harvest, to lord or parish priest.

The prolonged fast of Lent permitted one meal a day, eaten at the end of the day during the early centuries of Christianity but at noon by the ninth century. The one daily repast was no larger than one of the two or three meals normally served to working people—Lent was hard on people who labored in the fields or on other backbreaking jobs that required constant physical labor. The church encouraged the faithful by permitting a feast, a specially prepared meal of approved foods, on the fourth Sunday in Lent, sometimes called Mid-Lent Sunday. The occasion might only be marked by some small luxury like a sweet, but the introit appointed for the day came from the prophet Isaiah: "Rejoice ye with Jerusalem, and be glad with her, all ye that love her; rejoice for joy with her, all ye that mourn for her."*

The Lenten diet was difficult for everyone—fish and yet more fish, usually salted herring: "King Herring, who mounted his throne on Ash Wednesday, and stayed there, however much his subjects grumbled, until Easter Sunday," as historian Bridget Ann Henisch described it.[8] When John Gladman of Norwich arranged a procession of the months and seasons in 1448, Lent was "cladde in white with redde herrings skinnes and his hors trapped with oyster shelles after him in token that sadnesse and abstinence of mirth shulde followe and an holye time."[9]

This monotonous regime of herring ruled the households of rich and poor alike. Life was much easier for the wealthy, who moved their households to their properties near the sea or close to fishponds, so they could obtain fresh catches. Less affluent families took care to buy their salted fish after harvest in the autumn, when prices were lower, and then put it away for Lent. Prices spiked sharply as Ash Wednesday approached and

---

*An *introit* is a psalm or other chant sung by the choir as the priest approaches the altar to celebrate the Eucharist. The quote is Isaiah 66:10.

stayed high until Easter. There was money to be made off penitents, notably by religious houses and towns, which imposed tolls on barges and carts laden with salted herring during Lent.

Vigorous celebrations preceded Lent on Shrove Tuesday, when people stuffed themselves with fresh meat and other indulgences before the belt tightening of the next forty days. A fifteenth-century schoolboy lamented in his notebook: "Thou wyll not beleve how wery I am off fysshe, and how moch I desir that flesch were cum ageyn. For I have ete none other but salt fysh this Lent."[10] Imagine eating hard, kipperlike but flavorless sticks of fish week in and week out. Even the devout looked for ways around the monotony. Many found it in alcohol, taking as their text the words of St. Paul in the Scriptures: "Drink no longer water, but use a little wine for thy stomach's sake."[11] In the words of a memorable fifteenth-century sermon: "In this time of Lent, when by the law and custom of the church men fast, very few people abstain from excessive drinking: on the contrary they go to the taverns, and some imbibe and get drunk more than they do out of Lent, thinking and saying: 'Fishes *must* swim.'"[12] In fact, salted herring increased the diner's thirst, and beer and wine were safer than the unsanitary water supplies of the day.

Salted herring posed an extraordinary challenge to even the most expert cooks, who concocted ingenious sauces to disguise the dry flesh. Mustard, spooned promiscuously atop the fish, was a perennial favorite. Herring with mustard is a gourmet dish in France today; the medieval ancestor of this dish was but a crude reflection of today's refined presentation. Dried figs, raisins, currents, and almonds imported from the Mediterranean added variety to more affluent tables. Talented chefs with fresh fish to hand could bake it, grill it, simmer it, and dress it up in a myriad of sauces. They used all kinds of ingenious tricks to substitute for forbidden ingredients like butter, eggs, or meat products. Oil substituted for animal fat in the frying pan. Almonds blanched and steeped in water produced a weak "milk" that could be used in fish stews or to bind pastry. Some master cooks even devised "mock eggs," magnificent creations of white and yellow almond purée served in an empty eggshell.

None of these ingenious concoctions was an adequate substitute for the real thing. When Easter dawned, a collective sigh of gustatory relief could be felt across Europe. Church bells tolled to commemorate the Resurrection. Alleluias echoed high in cathedral naves. The artist Pieter Breughel the Elder (1525–1569) portrayed the endless tension in his *Fight Between Carnival and Lent* in 1559. We see a lively scene of celebration, with Carnival atop a barrel brandishing sausages and chickens on a spit. Lent faces him to the right, depressed and emaciated, holding forth a paddle with two herrings. Behind him the fishmongers enjoy a roaring trade and beggars solicit for alms.[13] The painting was powerfully evocative in an era when everyone, for a while, experienced at least some of the deprivation suffered by the poor year-round in urban poorhouses and slums, "bare places where every day is Lent."[14]

Behind monastery walls, the strict dietary rules of earlier centuries had been relaxed.[15] Meat had gradually crept onto the menu to the point where the question was not whether meat would be eaten but where. At the abbot's table? In a special chamber? And by how many monks at a time?

Pieter Breughel the Elder (c. 1525–1569), *Fight Between Carnival and Lent*. Lent with its miseries is at the right. KUNSTHISTORISCHES MUSEUM, VIENNA. ERICH LESSING/ ART RESOURCE, NEW YORK, N.Y.

## ROAST PIKE WITH PIQUANT HERB BUTTER

Among the affluent the number of courses and dishes at a meal varied from household to household. The sequence of different foods paid careful attention to prevailing theories about the human body, which believed that it had to be prepared, fed, then "closed" at the end of the meal. A formal repast often began with fresh fruit or salads dressed with salt or oil, also confections made with sugar or honey. Soups and other easily digestible broths followed (often the starting point for an ordinary meal). The stomach duly warmed, the guests now consumed the substantial main course of meat or, in the case of holy days and Lent, fish. Then there was a pause, perhaps enlivened by displays of spectacularly prepared foods like cooked golden peacocks or some form of entertainment. Dessert followed, sweet tarts, cheese, and light cakes, served with sweet wines—fare to "close" the stomach. We may have forgotten the rationale behind the courses, but the same general order has survived today, even if its correctness was much debated by medieval physicians.

Undue formality perhaps, but eating and drinking provided the context for not only conversation and general conviviality but also the conduct of business. Meals were an extremely important part of daily life in even a small manor house or monastery. Ray Strong quotes the example of a widow, Alice de Breyne, who presided over a manor at Acton, thirty-two kilometers north of Colchester in eastern England. Between Michaelmas 1412 and Michaelmas 1413, she served more than 16,000 meals, an average of forty-five a day, of which twenty-four were for her own people. She also threw a New Year's feast for 500 guests each year. Most of her guests were tenants and other associates "doing" lunch and conducting business at the same time.

Pike was a common dish at manorial tables. Here's a modern example from France:

### ❧ Roast Pike with Piquant Herb Butter

Pike was the food of kings, nobles, and common folk since long before medieval times. Today most pike eaten in France comes from eastern Europe, where this predatory fish still abounds. This recipe epitomizes the sophisticated dishes that can be created with pike. You can use it with almost any 4- to 5-pound (about 2 kg) whole fish.

SERVES 4 TO 6

#### The Fish

Preheat the oven to 375F/190C.

A whole pike, about 4 lb/1.8 kg, with head and fins, scaled and cleaned
2 to 3 thyme sprigs
2 to 3 marjoram or oregano sprigs
1 oz/30 g olive oil, plus more for basting

*(continues)*

*Roast Pike with Piquant Herb Butter (continued)*

Salt and pepper
2 lemons cut into wedges, for serving

Wash the pike inside and out and dry it on paper towels. Cut two or three diagonal slashes on both sides of the fish to allow the oven heat to penetrate and cook the fish more evenly. Tuck an herb sprig into each slash. Trim the tail into a neat V shape.

Set the fish in an oiled baking dish or roasting pan and sprinkle it with olive oil, salt, and pepper. (If your pan is small, try standing the fish on its belly and curve it as if swimming.)

Roast the fish, brushing occasionally with more olive oil until the skin is brown and crispy, 30 to 40 minutes. The eyes will have turned white and the flesh should no longer be transparent. Flake a small amount of flesh from the backbone to check it.

### Herb Butter

Medium bunch of watercress
Medium handful of spinach leaves
Medium bunch of parsley
Medium bunch of chervil or chives
3 anchovy fillets soaked in milk
1 medium gherkin pickle
½ oz/15 g capers, drained
1 garlic clove, peeled
3 oz/90 g butter, softened
2 oz/60 ml olive oil
⅓ oz/10 g Dijon-style mustard
Squeeze of lemon juice

Bring a large saucepan of water to the boil. Discard the stems from the watercress and spinach, and the large stalks from the parsley and chervil. Add the herbs to the boiling water and blanch them by simmering for 2 minutes. Drain, rinse with cold water, and pat dry on paper towels.

Drain the anchovies and work in a food processor with the pickle, capers, and garlic until finely chopped. Gradually add the butter and purée until smooth. Add the herbs and work until they are also finely chopped. With the blades turning, slowly pour in the oil.

The herb butter will be creamy and a lovely shade of green. Add the mustard and season the butter to taste with lemon juice, salt, and pepper.

Transfer the fish to a warm platter and decorate with lemon wedges. Serve the herb butter in a separate bowl.

Recipe by Chef Claude Vauguet, Ecôle de Cuisine La Varenne. Courtesy of Anne Willan, president of La Varenne.

Giovanni Antonio Bazzi (1477–1549), *St. Benedict and His Monks Eating in the Refectory*. SCALA/ART RESOURCE, NEW YORK, N.Y.

As is so often done in spiritual matters, the Benedictines eased the problems by making fine distinctions. Although austere orders like the Cistercians tried to banish any irregular practices, twelfth-century Benedictine monks regularly ate chickens and other birds. They consumed quadruped meat by making distinctions between muscle tissue—butcher's meat—and offal. St. Benedict had forbidden monks the flesh of quadrupeds, but the sharp minds of the religious soon picked holes in the Rule. Chickens and birds were eventually allowed. The beaver was a mammal, but because its tail was scaled and fishlike, it was considered an acceptable dish during Lent. Above all, the Benedictines distinguished between what was eaten in the refectory, where novices and junior monks ate according to the Rule, and elsewhere, in a room called the misericord.

By no means was this relaxation universal. Norman monasteries in particular gave impetus to fish eating at the expense of meat. Abbot Simeon of St. Swithun's, Winchester, seduced his monks from a meat diet with delicious fish dishes, so much so that they asked for more. He and his successors used fine sauces with such success that fish appeared at 67 percent of St. Swithun's meals by the late fifteenth century.[16] Paul of Caen,

Abbot of St. Albans between 1077 and 1093, strictly enforced St. Benedict's Rule. He adjured those who had been bled because of illness to eat herrings, which he cunningly named *karpie*, a salve, close to *kar en pie*, the meat pie to which they were accustomed. Those who ate fish received generous portions. For an everyday meal at Christ Church, Canterbury, a monk typically received a *ferculum*, or dish, of one plaice, two sole, four herring, or eight mackerel. The cellarer at Durham Abbey used sixty-five different kinds of seafood in his kitchens.

For all these attempts at reform, meat eating in the cloister had become so commonplace that in 1336 Pope Benedict XII decreed that at least half the monks in a community must eat in the refectory daily.[17] No monks were to eat irregular foods on Wednesday, Friday, or Saturday, or during Advent or Lent. Benedict's decrees were widely accepted, even if nominally obeyed. Benedict's decree, as well as a general trend toward more indulgent monastic diets, led to an explosion of fish consumption in refectory and misericord alike during Advent and Lent.

How much fish did monks actually eat, and what species did they favor? Precise statistics are hard to come by, but the amounts consumed apparently were enormous. Monastery cellarers purchased great quantities of herring, such as the twenty lasts Durham Abbey bought in 1307–1308—between 200,000 and 264,000 fish, salted in barrels, perhaps several years' supply.[18] Winchester Priory acquired its fish from Portsmouth and Southampton—42,000 red and 11,300 white herrings purchased in 1325, along with salted salmon, conger eel, hake, and mackerel. Selby Abbey in northeastern England purchased 40,000 red and white herrings from fishmongers in York. The abbot allowed himself the luxury of an occasional sturgeon, an elusive fish of high price. Selby monks also dined off eel, pike, pickerel, roach, and perch from freshwater fisheries under their ownership. Over half of the kitchen budget went to fish. Beaulieu Abbey in southern England spent more than £85 on seafood in 1269–1270, including thirteen lasts of herring, 191 salmon, 1,138 conger eel, cod, hake, 700 haddock, and 7,000 mackerel. Beaulieu not only owned quayside property at Yarmouth but also the *Salvata*, a ship that carried herring consignments from Yarmouth to home port. The same abbey also bought fish in Cornwall in the southwest and owned at least two properties where fish could be caught, dried, and shipped home without relying on outsiders. Beaulieu also maintained a fish-pond for the abbot's use.

Some monasteries near the coast employed full-time fishers or rippiers to ensure regular supplies of fresh sea fish. In 1405 Peterborough spent nearly £69 on salted herring, stockfish, and salt cod, the fish of abstinence. For the Maundy Thursday feast before Easter in that year, the house disbursed fifty-four shillings for six greenfish, two turbot, two great rays, fifteen hundred welks, twenty codling, a fresh salmon, and a large eel to satisfy a corrody.* Peterborough spent lavishly on fish, especially before 1400, after which purchases declined in favor of meat. By 1317 sea fish was common enough inland to enable Winchcombe Abbey in Gloucestershire to provide a corrody for the poor of 1,000 herring and 100 stockfish annually. The Crown bought herring specifically to donate to poor religious houses. In 1260 King Henry III purchased about 132,000 herring for £11 and ordered them distributed to "poor houses of religion."

The record of fish consumption in monasteries comes to us in snapshots from fragmentary kitchen accounts and estate records. The records of Westminster Abbey, one of the richest houses in England, from 1495 to 1525 provide us with a telling portrait of fish.[19] We learn that the monks ate fish at dinner on an average of 215 days annually. Most years, the monastery kitchen served about 570 fish meals to a community of 49 monks, plus an unknown number of visitors. The amount of fish consumed was truly enormous, at least 10,800 kilograms annually. These figures represent a minimum. Archaeological excavations under the misericord yielded the remains of at least twenty fish species.

Roughly half of the 570 fish dishes comprised dried, salted, or brine-pickled fish. Nearly all Westminster's fresh fish came from the ocean, for the abbey was close to London's bustling fish market by the Thames River. The abbey's kitchener visited the market by boat at least two or

---

*A *corrody* was a stipend granted to an individual in return for past services or a grant in kind, usually food, drink, light, sometimes clothing and laundering.

three times a week, perhaps daily, as his predecessors had done as early as the thirteenth century. The monks also owned the rights to a tithe on salmon caught along a sixty-four-kilometer stretch of the Thames between Staines and Gravesend. Feast days saw hearty dishes of salmon; dace, roach, and sometimes pike also appeared, the last an expensive luxury served with cinnamon and ginger sauce.

Various members of the cod family, also pike, plaice, and whiting, provided about three-quarters of the total weight of fish served. Eels, herring, and mackerel made up most of the fatty dishes, also salmon and conger eel. The Westminster kitchener of this era catered to the tastes of his community, who held herring in low regard. It had been much more common in the refectory in the fourteenth century, appearing on three of four fast days in January 1335. By 1495 salted herring appeared only during Lent, and fresh herring occasionally during spawning season in autumn.

Portion sizes were relatively standardized, with a sixth of a cod or a ling making up a monk's individual portion, alternatively a roach, or perhaps three or four herring. The average serving of fish appears to have been between 604 and 908 grams daily, depending on the number of dishes and the varieties available.

Outside the fast seasons of Advent and Lent, most weeks included three fish days. The dietary allowance was equivalent to about 6,210 calories per person, nearly twice the average requirements of a moderately active man today. During the severest Lenten fast the figure was still above 4,870 calories a day. Even if a monk left half of his portion to be consumed by servants and others, his intake was higher than the 3,350 calories or so required by a moderately active twenty-first-century man. Many of these men did nothing but eat and pray, and their skeletons show that obesity was commonplace. Their bones show telling signs of medical conditions associated with the overweight.

The fish-eating monks of Westminster were but the tip of an insatiable marketplace created by the demands of abstinence and fasting, of armies and lords. Nearly half the days of the year required abstinence by the laity. Between Michaelmas 1296 and 1297, the household of Joan de Valance, Countess of Pembroke, ate fish on 182 days, meat on 183. This may have been an unusually high level of fish consumption. The English soldiers in garrison at Dirleton, Scotland, in about 1300 ate fish on 122 days annually.[20] As fish consumption reached a climax in the west during the fourteenth century, the laws of supply and demand came into play, sending North Sea and western fishers far offshore in search of new fishing grounds. An insistent and ever growing demand for sea fish drove a highly competitive marketplace whose tentacles soon reached far over the western horizon.

# 11

## THE BOAT
## LOST TO HISTORY

You starvling, you elf-skin, you dried neat's tongue . . . you
stockfish, O for breath to utter what is like thee.

Falstaff[1]

Imagine a screaming winter gale off southwestern Iceland. Gray clouds
scud low over a roiling ocean, snow races horizontally across breaking
waves, flying spray cuts visibility to a few hundred meters. In the gloom
dark shapes roll and pitch in the storm, their grimly watchful steersmen
keeping the boats at an angle to the waves. Drifting slowly to leeward at
the mercy of sea and wind, the fishing boats are yet safe from the distant
rugged shore. The crews huddle in their bunks under the short decks at
the bow, waiting out the storm. Only the powerful stench of decaying
fish carried on the wind betrays their reason for being at sea.

Throughout the fourteenth century the Hanse monopolized the highly
productive Baltic and north German herring trade. Over 8,000 lasts came
from the Skänor fishery each year between 1350 and 1400, of which at
least 1,700 were exported to Flanders.* Still, herring was a minor part of
Hanse commerce with the Low Countries and was strictly regulated, with
no shipments allowed before the arbitrary date of October 9. After 1372

---

*A *last* was a widely accepted unit in the industry, between 10,000 and 15,000 herring.

cogs landed herring barrels at Damme or Sluis on the North Sea coast, where they were repacked for transshipment.

The Dutch were hardly subsistence fishers. Large fishing villages flourished along the low-lying North Sea coast, where inshore boats caught fresh herring in November and December as the shoals moved northward. These were "full" herring, best consumed fresh or smoked; the local market did not justify the salt-intensive curing methods used in the Baltic fishery. During the fourteenth century, the same villages extended their season by sailing north and west to the Scottish coast, where they intercepted the herring as they swam south for the spawn. By 1420 the Dutch were using *vleets,* large drift nets with mesh size carefully regulated to catch fish above certain dimensions, for herring were rapidly becoming a standardized commodity. The Dutch fishing boats grew accordingly to both accommodate the larger nets and hold the resulting catches.

When the Skänia fishery faltered in the early 1400s, the Dutch increasingly dominated the North Sea herring market.[2] The Scarborough and Yarmouth herring fairs declined as English landings dropped precipitously in the face of Dutch competition close offshore. By the end of the fifteenth century, most English herring came through Flanders, even if some of the catch originated in Baltic waters. The Dutch had also replaced the Hanse as the major purveyors of salted fish to the interior of northern Europe. The economic stakes grew so high that the authorities surrounded the herring industry with increasingly tight regulations, aimed at maintaining a uniform quality of herring for export. The standard was remarkably high compared with earlier centuries, when salting was at best a casual process. The taste of the herring improved markedly, as the Dutch experimented with other cures, among them a sugar and vinegar brine that produced the so-called matjes ("maiden") herring, a delicacy in the Low Countries and Scandinavia to this day.*

---

*Matjes herrings are a great delicacy. Once filleted, skinned, and soaked, they can be eaten as they are, raw, simply dressed with oil and a squeeze of lemon or smothered in sour cream or crème fraîche with a little lemon or a touch of sugar, accompanied by bread or a hot boiled potato. You can keep desalted matjes herring in a jar covered with olive oil. Cut them diagonally into five-centimeter pieces or leave them whole.

Though they were maestros of the herring cure, the Dutch achieved their near monopoly on North Sea herring not from their curing skills but from their practice of salting the catch offshore, in what became known as the "great fishery."

Norse ships—fast, maneuverable, and capable of carrying heavy loads—were well suited to the demands of trade and warfare in northern waters. But once the fishers moved to deeper waters, they required something different: a fishing boat adapted to the unique conditions of the Baltic and North Sea. Hanse cogs made poor fishing boats. Herring fishing requires a stable platform for landing enormous numbers of fish from drift nets, and the boat must lie quietly at sea in rough weather.

The Dutch fished in shallow waters, where boats would often go aground at low tide. Their flat-bottomed craft also worked well in the shoals and narrow channels of the Danish archipelago, and coped well with the short, steep seas of the Baltic and southern North Sea. Well before 1400, Dutch fishing fleets adopted *zeeschuyts*, double-ended boats about ten meters long in the Norse tradition, with lapstraked planking, the frames fitted after the hull was planked. They were broad of beam and equipped with two masts, each carrying a square sail that could be easily reduced in size during a storm. These boats could float in shallow water, lie upright on a sandbank at low tide, and navigate under oars through narrow channels. They never sailed fast. But some anonymous Dutch naval architect developed the leeboard, a streamlined board that was lowered on the leeward side of the ship when under sail to prevent it from sliding sideward when heading across or into the wind.[3] Zeeschuyts were the workhorses of the Dutch herring fleet for centuries. Clumsy to maneuver yet ideal for shallow water, they were well suited to drift net fishing, as the crew would land thousands of fish in a few hours. They were open boats with almost no decking, yet their crews would fish as far afield as the Scottish coast and the Shetland Islands, lying to their drift nets for days on end, often in gale-force winds. The casualties from storms and shipwrecks were enormous, but the profits made from the devout justified them.

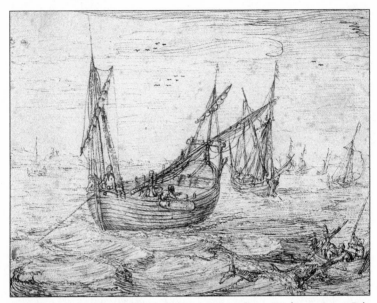

Hendrik Cornelisz Vroom (1566–1640), *A Herring Buss Catching a Large Fish.* The buss is at anchor with its mainmast lowered. © NATIONAL MARITIME MUSEUM, LONDON.

With a stroke of logical genius, the Dutch now carried their efficient salting methods offshore in a quite different vessel—the *buizen* or *buss,* which may have owed much to the Swedish cargo ship, the *kongebuss.*[4] Busses were factory ships designed to catch and process herring, pack them in barrels, and transport them to land. Like the cog, the buss is known only from drawings and paintings. They were slow, clumsy craft, with a top speed, even in a strong wind, of about three knots an hour. They shipped out with two or three masts. The crew struck two of the three spars while fishing, the sail on the third keeping pressure on the long drift net. We get a fleeting glimpse of two busses in Johannes Vermeer's famous *View of Delft,* painted in about 1660, when these craft had been in use for centuries.[5] They lie at a shipyard being prepared for the herring season, which by government regulation began on June 1. One has had its mast removed for refitting. You can see the

Jan Vermeer (1632–1675), *A View of Delft*. The busses lie at the right.

open port for hauling the catch aboard on one side. Judging from this and
the few other surviving paintings of them, busses were immensely strong,
high-sterned ships, designed for carrying loads and functioning as platforms
for fish preservation. They could lie quietly a-hull even in rough seas, their
crews hauling bulging nets and forcing gutted herrings by the thousand into
tightly packed barrels. You could smell the decaying fish guts from downwind long before the fleet came into sight.

Busses and zeeschuyts were so successful that the Dutch herring fleets
dominated the southern North Sea until 1652, when English warships destroyed hundreds of fishing vessels during the first Anglo-Dutch war. A
half century earlier, at least 5,000 Dutch fishing vessels worked in the herring fishery, 1,600 of them in English and Scottish waters. Yarmouth had,
by contrast, but 250 fishing boats in 1597, many of them "being small
and thin-sided [and easily] swallowed by rough seas."[6]

The brilliance of the Dutch enterprise lay not only in technological innovation but in a carefully choreographed sequence of investment in busses, fishing, processing, and export of the sealed barrels to the Baltic, which generated funds that paid for grain imported from the same region during the winter months and shipped home when the sea ice melted. Almost all Dutch herring passed either to the Baltic or Hamburg regions, or to the lands between the Rhine and Seine rivers.

Countries forced out of the herring trade found their opportunities elsewhere. By the early fifteenth century, cod had long surpassed *Clupea* as the preserved fish of choice for the devout. Dried stockfish, introduced to England and France by the Norse, was far more palatable than salted herring, which even the poor despised. By then the Hanse, with their control of Bergen, had effectively locked up the Norwegian stockfish market. All Lofoten stockfish passed through Bergen to East Anglian ports and into the Baltic in the holds of Hanse cogs. English ships attempted to purchase dried cod at Bergen, but their German competitors soon excluded them from the lucrative and growing trade. The demand for fish of all kinds was endless, not only for Lent and holy days but also for armies and growing navies, which consumed fish by the tens of thousands through decades of incessant war.

Cod, dried and salted, was easier to preserve and was a more reliable catch. Herring spawns could fluctuate dramatically from year to year, gyrations that are still little understood. They are thought to be connected to shifting water temperatures in the northeastern North Sea and to the abundance of the herring's favorite food, a tiny, shrimplike crustacean, *Calanus finmarchicus*. When Baltic and North Sea waters were cooler, the fish stayed away; warmer years brought them back by the millions. Stockfish supplies were more predictable. The cooler waters in the north, caused by the colder conditions of the Little Ice Age, brought *Gadus* farther south. But even with this apparent bounty, there were always potential shortages during Lent.

## BRAISED CARP IN ASPIC

"The first course oysters in gravy, pike and baked [smoked] herring, stockfish and merling [whiting] yfried. The ii course porpoises in galantine, and thereafter conger and salmon fresh endored [gilded] and roasted and flampoyntes. The iii course, rosy to pottage [coloured to resemble rose petals] and cream of almonds, therewith sturgeons and welks, great eels and lampreys, dariole [custard tarts], lech frys of fruit [tarts with spiced chopped fruits in almond milk], therewith nyrsebake [a fritter]."

Kings, nobles, wealthy merchants, and even affluent prelates rejoiced in the lavish display of freshwater and sea fish on feast days that fell during Lent. Just like Roman foodies, they cherished large fish, served whole at the table, especially the noble sturgeon—catches acquired with great effort or at a high price. When fresh fish were available, salted herring or stockfish played subordinate roles at table, which is one reason for the importance of farmed fish in medieval kitchens. The carp was a godsend, even if its sometimes muddy flavor did not appeal to the discerning.

In 1682, long after the events recounted in this chapter, the seventeenth-century author John Collins wrote *Salt and Fishery*, in which he reproduced obviously long-established recipes obtained from a Mr. Bond, who had used them for over thirty years. Here's Mr. Bond's take on carp:

> Take two living Carps, prick them in the Tail with a great Pin, rub the Scales off with a handful of Salt as clean as may be, lay them in a Deep Pan, and put to them a quart of Claret which makes them bleed, and kills them; open their Bellies and take out their Roes, then put them into a Kettle with their Roes in the middle, into which put a quart of Oysters, two Anchovies, a bunch of sweet Herbs, Stew them over a gentle Fire for about an hour, in which time they will be almost enough, and then put in a quarter of a pound of fresh Butter, take out a little of their Sauce, into which put three yolks of Eggs beat up together, then putting together in a Dish stir it about and leave it up.

*We haven't tested this recipe.*

Carp is not as common a dish as it once was, but here is a recipe from Strasbourg.

## ✂ *Braised Carp in Aspic*

This recipe originated in the Jewish community in Strasbourg, where it was prepared on Friday before sundown to be served cold on the Sabbath.

*(continues)*

*Braised Carp in Aspic (continued)*

SERVES 4

3.3 lb/1.5 kg carp
⅛ oz/10 g cooking oil
2 onions, thinly sliced
2 garlic cloves finely chopped
⅛ oz/10 g flour
15 oz/450 ml white wine
15 oz/450 ml water
Salt and pepper
Bouquet garni
¼ oz/25 ml chopped parsley

Clean the carp, discarding the fins and tail. Scale the fish. Cut into 1½-inch (4 centimeters) slices and wash thoroughly.

Heat the oil in a large pot and cook the onions until soft but not brown. Add the garlic and flour and cook over a low burner, stirring constantly, for 3 minutes or until lightly browned. Stir in the wine and water, then add the carp with salt and pepper to taste, also the bouquet garni. Bring to a boil, stirring occasionally to prevent the flour from sticking. Then simmer over a low flame for 30 minutes, or until the fish can be flaked with a fork. Transfer to a deep serving dish.

Discard the bouquet garni. Taste the sauce and, if necessary, boil to reduce until well flavored. Taste for seasoning. Remove from the heat, add parsley, and pour the sauce over the fish.

Chill overnight, which will set the liquid into a parsley-flecked aspic. Serve cold.

Recipe courtesy Anne Willan, Ecôle de Cuisine La Varenne and William Morrow and Company.

By 1100 to 1200, shortfalls in freshwater fish for Lent had helped trigger a massive expansion in herring consumption, aided by improved salting methods. Another turning point came in 1400, when tight Hanse monopolies and a potential shortage of fish in the face of growing demand and fluctuating herring migrations caused English fishers to search for new cod fisheries far from their traditional fishing grounds. They turned their eyes north and west, to the continental shelf off Iceland, where the Hanse was but a distant threat.

In medieval fishers' minds, the bounty of the ocean was inexhaustible. If one fishery declined or there were too many boats harvesting one location, the fleets would simply move elsewhere. Humans had a divine sanction to clear forest, plant the soil, and fish in lakes and oceans, and in such labor they came closer to God. "Idleness is the enemy of the soul," proclaimed the Benedictines. They pointed to St. Paul's exhortation to the Thessalonians: "If anyone will not work, let him not eat."[7] Work such as fishing was its own spiritual reward, a way of expiating sin while providing sustenance for the faithful. Whatever the risks, it was incumbent on those who fished the oceans to expand their labors into the most hazardous fishing grounds, to make a profit and serve the Lord.

Iceland was already known for its stockfish, but relatively few cargoes left local waters. The offshore passage north and west took one through bitterly cold and often stormy waters, out of sight of land for days if not weeks. Dutch busses and some smaller craft sailed as far as the Shetlands, but they chose their weather carefully for open-water passages. Venturing further offshore required deeper-draft vessels capable of weathering anything the midwinter North Atlantic could hurl at them. With quiet ingenuity, North Sea fisherfolk developed an efficient but mysterious vessel—the dogger.

The restoration of traditional sailing craft has become fashionable. Reconstructions of 200-year-old fishing smacks are common in British and French harbors.[8] It matters not that only a few fragments of the original timbers survive—the design remains for future generations. As a result, we know a great deal about the handling characteristics of open cobbles, Tudor warships, Thames barges, and deep-water tuna trawlers. But the dogger lies beneath history. Nor is there a known depiction, except for a single relief carving of a putative fishing boat on the end of a church pew in East Anglia.

Doggers were working boats, constructed on beaches and in fishing villages by shipwrights using adzes, axes, wedges, and hammers. They were built for one purpose—to fish for cod and other species far offshore. Both they and their crews were disposable in the sense that their owners expected significant losses of both boats and fishermen. A dogger's working life did not exceed ten or twenty years; its owners would repair it again and again— patching leaks, replacing planks, fashioning new spars, providing new sails practically every year. For a dogger to endure longer than a couple of generations would be a miracle. As it reached the end of its usefulness, it was abandoned on the foreshore or in a tidal estuary, to rot away without leaving a trace. Any usable timbers or spars were probably recycled into the new dogger that took its place. Lacking a chance underwater find, all we can do is reconstruct these mysterious craft based on what we know about contemporary boats, the waters they sailed in, and intelligent extrapolation.

Most nautical historians ignore the dogger even though it was a commonplace fishing vessel for centuries. Naval architect and historian John Leather is an exception. Descended from a family that owned fishing boats from the 1780s to the 1920s and once a shipbuilder himself, he has spent a lifetime studying working boats and historic craft. I'm most grateful to John for providing me with a detailed hypothetical analysis of doggers based on his unrivaled experience and his knowledge of Atlantic waters.[9]

During the Little Ice Age, the weather over northern Europe was cooler and windier than today, with a higher frequency of severe storms, such as the gale and storm surge that drowned thousands of people along the low-lying Dutch and German coasts in 1362. The Norse avoided putting to sea between November and March. An early Anglo-Saxon poem, *The Seafarer*, tells us that the prudent sailor stayed in port until the first cuckoo of summer.[10] Passage making was a seasonal activity, since gales of thirty-five knots and above are eight times more frequent in winter than in summer, with rough seas every four days or so, to say nothing of the cold. Furthermore, cloud cover is denser and endures for days on end, making navigation by sun and stars nearly impossible. Seasonal sailing was the rule for centuries until economic imperatives forced merchant ships offshore after November. By the fourteenth century, English wine merchants were sailing to Bordeaux on the stormy Bay of Biscay coast in September to buy from the harvest and sailing back in January or February. Such open-water passages were a different matter from simple coasting, which was commonplace in winter by 1440, but it meant long delays waiting for favorable weather.

An artist's generalized impression of a dogger.

Doggers had to sail from the North Sea to Iceland in February, when the North Atlantic was at its stormiest. They had the advantage of prevailing winds from the southwest, which might provide a fast passage of a week or ten days, much of it in open water, exposed to the full drift of the Atlantic swell. Even in summer, the tract of ocean between Scotland and Iceland is hardly hospitable, a bright, cold world where rain squalls and shrieking winds arrive with the rapid passage of a depression from the west. The dogger skipper knew the telltale signs of approaching bad weather—high clouds, changing swell patterns, even the behavior of seabirds. Once off-shore, in those days before weather faxes, e-mails, satellite forecasts, or even shortwave radios, they were on their own, without the luxury of being able to return to port. During the early twentieth century, decked fishing boats were not put to sea in winds above twenty-five to thirty knots. Partially decked or open boats in earlier days might have stayed ashore in anything above twenty knots. But once at sea, the dogger had to reduce sail and ride out severe storms far from land.[11]

Then there was the problem of headwinds. Replicas of Norse ships make their best progress against the wind when sailing 67.5 degrees off the wind. They make considerable leeway, with the result that they only achieve about two nautical miles an hour to windward—or even less in a heavy sea. (This contrasts dramatically with the stellar performance of modern ocean-racing yachts, which can sail as close as thirty degrees to the wind at seven to eight knots or more.) Norse skippers relied heavily on oars to make progress to windward. Most medieval ships, with their heavy, often bluff-bowed hulls, would have been even slower. The crew of a heavily laden dogger had two options—lie to the wind until it shifted to a favorable quarter or row. Rowing would have been pointless in a fishing boat measuring ten meters or more overall. The ability to lie-to was crucial.

Fishing far from home required a boat that could carry food and supplies for an entire season, including large quantities of salt for curing. The crew of four to five men and two or more boys caught cod with hook and line, sometimes landing hundreds of fish a day. They would have stood in a deep well amidships, where the boat was most stable. With individual fish coming aboard, it was easier to set up a simple production line, where some crew members brought the fish into the boat, others gutted them, and others packed the carcasses in salt. Such routines became highly refined on French and Portuguese ships working the Grand Banks off Newfoundland in later centuries. Cod fishing in the days of abundant catches was a simple task, made easier by the relative ease with which the catch could be dried or salted.[12]

John Leather believes doggers originated among working boats already familiar to North Sea fisherfolk.[13] Their ancestry clearly lay in the long tradition of lapstrake shipbuilding inherited from Norse ships and earlier prototypes. Another ancestor was the ubiquitous zeeschuyt and vessels such as cogs and hulcs. Doggers would have been built in the centuries-old tradition of northern European shipwrights—planked first with fairly large strakes, the frames then fitted to a crude but workmanlike hull, using beech, fir, oak, or whatever timber was available. The builders would have fastened the frames and planks with iron nails and wooden trenails.

Leather estimates a dogger would have displaced about thirteen tons, sufficient to carry a ton (1.02 U.S. short tons) of bait, apart from that caught at the fishing grounds. Three tons of salt, half a ton of food, and another half ton of firewood would have filled out the cargo, allowing about six tons for the catch. Boulders and coarse sand would have ballasted the hull, allowing the skipper to adjust the draft and trim of the boat. Such a displacement would require a boat about fifteen meters long, with a maximum beam of 4.5 meters and a draft of about 1.5 meters—much deeper than a Dutch inshore fishing boat. These were substantial craft, capable of carrying heavy loads and spending many weeks at sea.

Leather believes that doggers had fairly fine bows and pointed sterns, relatively high sides, and limited ability to sail against the wind. They were at their best when the wind was behind or abeam. In rough weather blowing from ahead, the skipper would have no option but to shorten sail and try and sail as close to the wind as possible. But his vessel would lose many kilometers to leeward. Despite their relatively fine bows, doggers were compact load carriers rather than swift sailors. But it was essential that they could be steered precisely in tidal waters and rough seas. For this reason they had a rudder with a long handle (tiller) attached to the stern, not a steering oar, which was far more tiring in use.

Like all North Sea vessels of the day, doggers would have had square sails, two of them set on a couple of masts, hinged at the base so they could be lowered at sea in a strong wind. Leather theorizes that the mainmast was stepped just aft of amidships, flying a single large flax or woolen sail, the material so heavy that it had to be wetted to make it set well. In lighter winds, the crew would lace two parallel cloths to the bottom of the sail to increase its area. This "bonnet" and the lower "drabbler" would be removed as the wind strengthened. The sailcloth was too weak to allow the fitting of reefing cords, which would let the sail be reduced by bundling and tying it. As on Norse ships, the sail would be edged with rope, so that it could be sheeted in tight on the windward side when trying to sail against the wind. The second, smaller mast stood in the bow and carried a much smaller square sail that could be set or furled very easily. Like Norse skippers, dogger crews knew intimately their vessels' strengths and limitations. This is where the smaller square sail came in—to act as an accelerator when the wind was abeam, to improve the handling of the ship when the mainsail tended to turn it into the wind, and to reduce uncontrolled rolling when running before an ocean swell. This combination of sails was developed on North Sea fishing boats over many centuries and made the dogger about as efficient as it could be.

The internal and deck layout is a matter of speculation. John Leather believes there was a decked area forward, a simple cuddy with shelflike berths for the crew, and possibly a stone hearth for cooking in calm water. Amidships was a hold, where the crew stood to fish and the bait and catch were stored. This may have been decked over with a small access hatch, but more likely it was open to the elements, protected by weather cloths on either side and rigged with wooden platforms where the crew fished and gutted and salted the catch. A second decked area may have covered the stern, to prevent whitewater and spray from cascading into the hold, a protected place where fishing gear and valuable equipment could be stored. Wooden partitions would have subdivided the cargo area to hold the catch.

Doggers remained stationary while fishing, so anchors were important. Each boat would have had a heavy main anchor and at least two smaller ones, sometimes weighted with stones, as well as sufficient strong rope to stay put in water up to eighteen meters deep. In the days before engines, anchors were arguably the most important survival tool for ships that had virtually no ability to sail against the wind, when a rocky shore lay close astern. Finally, each dogger would have carried a small faering-like open boat perhaps 4.5 meters long for laying out anchors and mooring lines, rearranging bait nets, or rowing ashore.

The sturdy, slow-moving dogger took North Sea fisherfolk far offshore in the depths of winter in search of cod, a food that became so fundamental to European life that it was known as the beef of the sea. To harvest it, men and boys endured great hardship. Protected only by woolen and leather garments, lashed by freezing spray and waves, subsisting day after day on cold hardtack, often the very stockfish they sought, they fished in fair weather and foul, in sun, snow, and sleet, knowing that death could come at any moment at the hands of a capricious God. They were there because doctrines based on Scriptures they could not read dictated that everyone eat fish during Lent, and because kings fought kings on the most trivial of pretexts.

# THE RISE AND FALL
# OF THE ICELANDIC FISHERY

Of Yseland to wryte is lytill need
Save of stokfische; yit for soothe in dede
Out of Bristow and costis many one
Men have practiced by needle and by stone
Thiderwardes wythine a lytel whylle,
Wythine xij yeres, and withoute parille
Gone and comen . . . unto the costes colde.[1]

Well before the twelfth century, Norway's Lofoten Islands traded dried cod south to Bergen in exchange for grain and flour. By 1200 this growing town at the head of a long, sheltered fjord in southern Norway was one of the great ports of northern Europe. Norway's kings maintained commercial treaties with England, Lübeck, and other north German ports. To England they sent furs, herring, stockfish, tallow, and timber in exchange for cloth, grain, and honey. But the staple of the trade was stockfish.

Iceland ceded its sovereignty to Norway in 1269 (a logical move given its isolation and lack of trees), which meant that all its exports traveled on Norwegian ships.[2] The Icelanders were farmers and only seasonal fishers, who cured their catches purely for domestic consumption. The union with Norway brought them into the stockfish trade, dried cod soon overtaking homespun cloth as the island's major export. Bergen became Iceland's de facto commercial capital, the conduit by which its stockfish exports reached northern Europe.

Inevitably merchants from Lübeck and other Hanseatic ports entered the lucrative trade. The Norwegians answered this threat by forbidding Hanse ships to sail north of Bergen, but to no avail. For 400 years, Norway had been the dominant maritime power in the north, a world apart from the intricate crosscurrents of European politics. Now, under the stress of climate change, this isolation broke down. The colder conditions of the Little Ice Age shortened cereal-growing seasons throughout Norway, especially in the north.[3] Occasional food shortages, made worse by the Black Death, raised the specter of famine. The opportunistic Hanse arrived in Bergen in cogs bulging with grain from their home ports. The same ships departed crammed with stockfish. The Hanse monopoly had few benefits for Norway, but it broadened the market for stockfish and provided a relatively secure return in grain.

The Norwegian knarrs, with their small cargo capacity, could never compete with the lumbering Hanse cogs. In a few generations, the newcomers had extended their monopoly over Baltic and North Sea trade to Bergen. A network of strategic Hanse ports and entrepôts extended from Novgorod in the east to Bergen, Bruges, and English ports in the west. Herring was still the dominant fish cargo, but the volume of Norwegian stockfish increased each year as demand skyrocketed.

Soon the Norwegians were catching and processing cod mostly for export. Bergen became a Hanse port, where the foreigners maintained their own docks and warehouses. As many as 3,000 merchants, clerks, and sea captains worked and lived in an independent *kontor* (merchant quarter), virtually a state within a state. Hanse clerks monitored every aspect of the fish trade, manipulated credit, and ensured that millions of processed fish flowed across their docks.

The tentacles of the Hanse monopoly extended far beyond Bergen into the North Sea, where its merchants encountered formidable competition from English traders based on east coast ports, especially at Lynn, which maintained its own guild and a small trading station in Bergen. For generations, English ships had sailed to the port to buy Lofoten and Icelandic cod. But the Hanse with its strict control of pricing and supplies, aided by aggressive pirates, gradually drove English interests out of the port.[4]

Foreign ships were expressly forbidden from trading directly with Iceland or any other Norwegian dependency. All cargoes were handled and taxed through Bergen, and by 1400 the trade through the two was exclusively Hanse.

Between 1350 and 1500, high demand meant fish prices were high relative to grain in Bergen and throughout Europe, prompting the Hanse to look for new sources of supply. Their ships visited the Shetland and Faeroe Islands, bartering fish for alcohol, cloth, meat, and eventually money. But supplies were limited by a shortage of commercial fishers. Cod fishing was still largely a part-time activity, combined with subsistence agriculture. In the Faeroes and Iceland, farmers went fishing during the winter months.[5] The Icelanders returned to the same locations for many generations, rowing offshore to long-line for cod in two- to ten-oared open boats. Hundreds of men perished every year, their heavily laden boats capsized by rogue waves and sudden storms. A few of them fished some distance offshore, but for the most part the cod came from near the coast, close to fishing camps where the boats could be beached at night on whalebone rollers above the high-tide line.

The Hanse monopoly meant little in Icelandic waters, where cod were plentiful and the local people eager to trade. As part of their sovereignty agreement, the Norwegian monarch had agreed to send six ships of provisions and other goods to Iceland each year. But the Hanse slowly strangled communications between Iceland and Bergen, leaving the islanders cut off from the outside world.

East Anglian fishing boats had long taken cod on the Dogger Bank in the central North Sea and inshore waters. Morue de Grymsby (cod of Hull) are mentioned as early as the early fourteenth century, and there was a fish market there by at least 1258.[6] In 1304 Newcastle asked the town for salt haddock and cod to feed the Scots king and his court at St. Andrews. Cod was so important that the authorities in coastal towns were regulating landings by 1357. English traders were well aware of the potential of both Norwegian and Icelandic waters, and doggers from Blakeney and Cromer are said to have fished for cod off Norway as early as 1383.[7] Barred from the Bergen marketplace and faced with faltering herring fisheries, the English now turned to the "comodius stokfysshe of Yselonde."[8]

## LENTEN FISH PIE

In 1420 the Duke of Savoy, Amadeus VIII, persuaded his personal chef to write down everything he knew about cookery and royal banquet preparation. Master Chiquart Amiczo had served a long apprenticeship in noble kitchens, where he had acquired a knowledge of the huge logistics behind formal banquets. Once he became the duke's cook, he needed all the knowledge he had, for the most important people in Europe passed through the Savoy court—Chiquart's master was elected pope in 1439.

*Du fait de cuisine* is a 235-page masterpiece, with eighty-six recipes and a summary of the logistics in preparing a feast of over fifty dishes, often for several hundred guests. After treating of the ingredients, utensils, and staff needed, Chiquart provides menus and recipes for a two-day feast. Then he confronts the classic problem facing all medieval chefs. What happens if the feast is held on a fast day? The great chef promptly starts all over again, takes all cheese, eggs, fat, grease, and milk out of the kitchen and provides an elaborate array of meatless and fish dishes. Chiquart provides extra recipes in case the feast is prolonged and recipes for the sick that conformed to the medical science of the day.

Here's a fish pie made with a double crust and plentiful spices. This version may be a trifle bland for some palates, so feel free to experiment with flavors.

### ❧ *Lenten Fish Pie*

Pastry for a 10-inch/25-cm deep-dish double-crust pie

2 lb/1 kg flaked cooked white fish fillet. (We used tuna, poached with the skin on in roasted vegetable stock, the juice of 1 lemon, 4 oz/125 ml white wine, salt and pepper, until barely cooked.)

4 oz/125 ml raisins
6–8 dried prunes
6 dried figs
6 dried dates
4 oz/125 g pinenuts
8 oz/250 ml white wine
1 oz/30 ml olive oil
⅓ oz/10 g ginger
1/16 oz/5 g cinnamon
Pinch/2 g nutmeg
Pinch/2 g cloves
8 oz/250 ml white sugar

*(continues)*

*Lenten Fish Pie (continued)* _____

Flake the cooked fillet and if there is skin, remove it. Wash fruit; cut the prunes, figs, and dates into small pieces. Place fruit, nuts, wine, and oil in a nonreactive cooking pot. Heat gently.

Combine spices and sugar and stir into the fruit. Simmer over low heat until sugar is dissolved. Gently mix in fish and place mixture into prepared pie shell.

Precook the bottom crust for about 5 minutes before putting in the filling. Cover with upper crust and make slashes for vents.

Bake at 425F/220C for 10 minutes. Then reduce heat to 375F/190C and bake until crust is golden brown, about 20 to 25 minutes.

Adapted from Chiquart's *Du fait de cuisine.*

Fifteenth-century Iceland was sparsely populated, nominally ruled by the king of Norway but in practice left largely to its own devices. The Icelanders, direct descendants of the original Norse settlers, were dairy farmers who practiced a style of animal husbandry unchanged from that of their homeland. They had only sporadic contacts with the wider world. In 1337, Icelandic annals tell us, a gale cast a crew of fifteen Scots ashore, with only five of them surviving. Sixty years later, the same annals record six foreign ships wintering over, but their nationalities are unknown. When English fishing boats came, they stayed offshore, fishing for cod on the continental shelf.

Iceland was not unknown, just a long way off the beaten track, isolated from Norway and the North Sea by perilous waters unfamiliar to sailors who were mainly inshore rock dodgers. A few English boats may have sailed there as early as 1200, but we have no record of their doings. In any case, North Sea herring boats with their bluff bows and shallow draft were hardly ideal for the open waters of the North Atlantic. North Sea fishers worked narrow channels and sandbanks, twisting creeks and tidal waters where the navigational challenges were very different from those of the great Western Ocean. Sailing the open Atlantic required a different mind-set, an ability to sail over the horizon. The Norse had done this for centuries; Hanse cogs and English hulcs* had voyaged the length of the Baltic and North Sea, but for the most part they stayed close to shore where they could anchor if necessary and wait for favorable winds. For a North Sea fisherman to venture offshore was a much greater step than is sometimes realized. These were conservative folk, surrounded by tales of great sea monsters or rapacious birds that flourished in the wastes of the Western Ocean. There were no landmarks on the horizon to steer for, just the sun, the stars, and endless heaving waters.

Every small boat sailor feels apprehension on sailing out of sight of land for the first time. I vividly remember shipping out with a retired vice admiral of the Royal Navy in his nine-meter cutter. His seamanship was formidable and his navigational ability remarkable, but I was apprehensive. We were rowing out to the mooring with a stormy passage ahead. When I asked him if he was ever afraid at sea, he rested at the oars for a moment and looked appraisingly at me. "Always, my boy," he murmured, and changed the subject. Thousands of kilometers of sailing later, I know what he means and appreciate how the first fishers to sail to Iceland must have felt. Sailing from the Faeroe Islands to Iceland on a large cruise ship, I looked out at the heaving swells roiled by a strong northeasterly wind and was glad I was not out there in a dogger or even a modern cruising yacht. But sometime around 1400, doggers began making regular fishing voyages to the north, organized by merchants who were determined to circumvent the Hanse monopoly on the immensely lucrative Lenten cod trade.

The passage between England and Iceland would have taken between a week and a month, depending on the prevailing winds. The most dangerous part of the voyage was the passage through the Pentland Firth between Caithness and the Orkney Islands, described by an anonymous

---

*Hulcs* were merchant ships similar in design to cogs, but with a curved bottom and round bilges that made for better seaworthiness. These commodious vessels carried more than cogs, had one mast and sail, and were more suitable for fighting, especially when castles were installed at bow and stern. The development of the hulc parallels that of the cog, but little is known about them. They may have appeared as early as the seventh century.

correspondent in 1542 as "the most dangerouse place of all Christendom." The *North Sea Pilot* for 1875, a sober and cautious volume, recommended that "before entering the Pentland Firth all vessels should be prepared to batten down, and the hatches of small vessels ought to be secured even in the finest weather, as it is difficult to see what may be going on in the distance, and the transition from smooth water to a broken sea is so sudden that no time is given for making arrangements." The wind blowing against the tide in that narrow channel can raise a sea "which cannot be imagined by those who have never experienced it."[9]

North of the Orkneys, the boats would have followed a well-traveled course like that steered by the warship *Marigold* accompanying the East Anglian fishing fleet in 1654.[10] They would head northwest until they made landfall on the volcanic islands of Vatnajkull of Iceland's eastern end, then set course for the Vestmann Islands to the west, and for the fishing grounds off the west coast.

By 1400 a number of North Sea skippers knew the sailing directions for Iceland, which must have come to them orally. Where one fished and how one got there was a trade secret. Lynn ships logically would have been first on the scene and may well have been, but the records are silent. The first mentions of English fishing boats in the north come not from Lynn but from other ports, and centuries after the fact. Cromer on the north Norfolk coast is famous for its crabs. "We do crabs, not herrings," an official at the local museum told me somewhat indignantly when I inquired about the local fishers' medieval forebears. His historical memory is faulty. Somewhere around 1400, a Cromer fishing boat voyaged successfully to the north. More than three centuries later, Francis Blomefield (1705–1752) reported in his *Essay Towards a Topographical History of the County of Norfolk* that "Robert Bacon, a mariner of this town of Cromer found out Iceland." The Elizabethan writer Richard Hakluyt's *Principal Navigations, Voyages, and Discoveries of the English Nation* reported in 1599 that fishermen from Blakeney in northern Norfolk fished off the coast of Iceland as early as the reign of King Edward III (1312–1377), but there is no independent confirmation of this. The Icelanders were decimated by the plague in 1402–1404, making it hard for them to supply cod to outsiders, and this may have been what prompted the English to catch the fish for themselves.[11] Icelandic annals dwell little on exotic visitors unless there was an unusual problem. In 1412 a fishing boat arrived from "England east." Five of its crew deserted the ship before it left in the autumn, complaining "they had been starved in the boat for many days."[12] The following year, an English merchantman under the command of "one Richard" cast anchor. The luxury-starved Icelanders flocked to the shore to buy her cargo. Meanwhile, less welcome English visitors fished close offshore: "30 fishing doggers or more." Some were quite large, carrying between twenty and forty men. High crew requirements, among other factors, led the Crown to consider the fisheries as the "chiefest Seminarie and Nurserie of the navy."[13]

The English fishers were a tough, unruly breed. They fished close offshore and had little to do with the Icelanders except to come ashore occasionally to steal cattle. The Icelanders in turn resented fishermen as much as they welcomed merchants. The doggermen, accustomed to the hazards of fishing in all weather in rock- and current-infested waters, adapted effortlessly to the foggy southern coast with its rip tides and offlying rocks, windy promontories and chronic magnetic disturbances that made compasses unreliable guides. I've watched a moderate southwesterly gale descend on this rugged shore. Great Atlantic rollers crash against jagged volcanic cliffs, while a low overcast and driving rain hovers over squadrons of offshore rocks. The rush of the wind drowns out everything except the harsh sound of waves breaking against gravel on the beach below us. Pity the dogger caught close inshore in even a moderate blow. Chances are it would be cast ashore in the gloom, and few crew members would survive the grounding.

The savage conditions at sea did not lead to a shortage of fishermen. The profits from the cod fisheries were so great that they never had any trouble attracting crew. Prospects were hardly better ashore: the average subsistence farmer could expect to live only into his twenties.

By 1416–1418, tithe payments at Scarborough show cod landings were second only to herring, but the investment required was substantial and the potential for losses very high. Dogger crews sailed north long before Easter into the teeth of equinoctial gales. Many were wrecked. In 1419 Icelandic annals reported a typical tragedy: "Then came on Maundy Thursday such a hard gale with snow, that far and wide around the land English ships had been wrecked, no fewer than twenty-five. All the men were lost, but the goods and splinters of the ships were cast up everywhere. The gale came on before breakfast, and lasted not quite to noon."[14]

Both fishing and trading prospered to the point that King Eirik of Denmark, who now ruled Iceland (Norway and Denmark having unified in 1397), complained to Henry V of England in 1415. He reminded him that no foreigners were allowed to trade with Iceland, the Faeroes, the Shetlands, or any other of his possessions without a license. The penalty for illegal trafficking was death or loss of cargo. Eirik also complained of depredations by the visitors. Henry V, preoccupied with a French war, appeased Denmark with a proclamation in ports from Berwick and Newcastle southward that "until the end of one year to come no subject shall repair to island parts of the realm of Denmark or Norway to fish or for other causes to the prejudice of the king thereof . . . and especially to Iceland."[15] The fishermen angrily petitioned Parliament, pointing out that "as is well known" their catch had vanished from the North Sea, whereas it abounded off Iceland. After the king rejected their pleas, the fishermen quietly continued their voyages with the tacit support of the governor of Iceland. The profits were so high that the risk was justified: English merchants paid about 50 percent more for stockfish than merchants in Bergen did. In 1415 the governor of Iceland sailed to England, accompanied by fifty lasts of cod and bags of silver coins. He and his countrymen were received as honored guests; their hosts sold them cloth and corn in defiance of the king's edict.

Iceland was so isolated that neither Norway nor Denmark could govern it effectively. The Icelanders reminded King Eirik that the promised six yearly ships of vital goods had never arrived. Therefore "we have traded with foreigners who have come peacefully on legitimate business, but we have punished those fishermen, and owners of fishing-smacks who have robbed and caused disturbance upon the sea."[16]

By the 1410s the routine of the Icelandic fisheries was well established. The fleets would leave their North Sea ports between February and April, fish for about three months, then return home in July, August, or September. Many boats fished off the north coast in the Skagafjord region, but more often they worked the shallow waters and continental shelf of the west coast. The Vestmannaeyjar, off the southwestern coast, was said to offer the best fishing off Iceland. These were fog-shrouded waters teeming with hazards, but they had the advantage of secure anchorages close to the fishing grounds. English fishers landed here, also on the Reykanes peninsula, to salt and barrel their catches. Danish authorities complained that the visitors "were building houses, putting up tents, digging ditches, working away, and making use of everything as if it was their own."17

Despite an official ban on overwintering, a few doggers stayed through the cold months. Inevitably their unruly crews caused trouble ashore, especially the "men of Hull and other English towns." They were unscrupulous, violent men who would obtain their catch by any means, legitimate or illegitimate. Hannes Palsson, a Danish governor of the island, accused English fishers of murdering royal officials, robbing and burning churches, and despoiling travelers. Many of them were little better than pirates. Some visitors effectively colonized the Vestmannaeyjar and tilled the soil without permission. They even prevented the export of stockfish to Bergen until they had filled their own holds. An Icelandic chronicler complained, "So long as the English remain in Iceland, the people cannot go to sea or carry on their fishing, for the English smash their small skiffs, and beat up, wound, and otherwise maltreat their owners."18

The islanders had no quarrel with the visitors provided they behaved well. The main conflict was between the fishermen and the royal officials responsible for collecting taxes from them. By 1425 matters had reached such a pass that the governor and another official attempted to confiscate the ships at Vestmannaeyjar by force. The fishermen beat off the attack, destroyed their foes' boats, and carried the officials off to England, an act that "few regretted."

Probably no more than fifty North Sea doggers sailed to Iceland in a good year—the distances were long, the risks high, the overheads substantial. Conditions in home ports were extremely difficult. Dunwich, Southwold, and Walberswick were in trouble from rising sea levels, the delayed result of the warm temperatures of the Medieval Warm Period. At the same time, the increased storminess of the Little Ice Age often closed their harbors. A huge gale eventually inundated Dunwich, which effectively ceased to exist as a port after 1328.

Nevertheless, the Icelandic fishery became a well-organized venture. In 1451 Walberswick alone supported "thirteen barks trading the Iceland. . . . And on their own Coast, twenty-two Fishing Boats for full and shotten Herrings."[19] Many doggers sailed in convoy, protected by warships. They sailed to Iceland purely for the fish, carrying only as much grain as "woll only suffice for ther vitallyng and expensis." But they did carry other merchandise. By the sixteenth century many doggers engaged in trading as well as cod fishing, arriving with cargoes of woolen cloth, linen, butter, and clothing. By this time too their crews had evolved into a hierarchy. In 1545 the *Jaymes* of Dunwich carried a twenty-nine-man crew that included a master and master's mate, two skiff masters, a boatswain, a carpenter and a cook, a merchant, a gunner, and a soldier.

In the late seventeenth century, John Collins described the Iceland fleet's fishing methods, which must have been centuries old.[20] The fishers used ninety-fathom (165-meter) lines with a three-kilogram lead weight at the end. A cross-stick with two baited hooks was located above the weight. The doggers also employed long lines, laid out for hundreds of meters astern, the main line buoyed at each end and fixed to the seabed with anchors. Short lines ("snoods") with baited hooks hung from the long line. Long lines were so effective during the early sixteenth century that Icelanders complained that their use prevented cod from swimming into shallow waters where they fished.

The fresh fish were prepared for curing immediately. While the Icelanders dried their catch ashore, the English laid theirs in brine-filled barrels. In later times they gutted the cod on tables, separating the livers to make oil, then salting them down in layers in the hold, with the fish piled higher in the middle so that the pickle fell to the sides. The livers were barreled and allowed to stand, yielding a "foul Oyle" that was then skimmed. Cod liver oil was an expensive commodity, selling for as much as £30 a ton.

The Hanse was aware of English doings and reluctantly began to pay closer attention to Iceland and its fisheries. Hanse cogs, designed for coastal voyaging and shallower waters, had largely confined maritime trading to the Baltic and the North Sea, as far north as Bergen. They did not undertake many deep-water voyages until a decade or more after English doggers reached Iceland. Inevitably, however, word of rich catches led the Bergen merchants to respond. By 1420 Hanse ships were sailing regularly, if fearfully, to Iceland from Bergen. So were Dutch vessels, which sometimes loaded stockfish from the Icelandic fishery, which they carried to Ireland.

Still, English fishers and merchants encountered no strenuous competition until the 1460s. By then, the Hanse and the Danish Crown were in close alliance.[21] The Danes seized English merchant ships in the Oresund by Copenhagen in retaliation for the murder of the Icelandic governor Bjorn Thorleifsson in 1467, setting off a maritime war between Denmark and England that severely disrupted English trade. The Hanse now tightened its Baltic and North Sea monopolies, greatly increasing its traffic with Iceland, especially from German ports. For more than half a century, cogs from Hamburg sailed for Iceland in March or April, usually in convoy accompanied by a warship. They departed later than the English fishers, who were more concerned with fish than trade. The Hanse brought large quantities of corn, beer, and other foodstuffs to Iceland, receiving in exchange such commodities as hides, falcons, and eiderdown—items rarely handled by English ships. The only statistics we have on this trade are the losses recorded in a September gale in 1491. Ninety Hanse vessels were wrecked; about 3,000 corpses are said to have washed ashore. Even if exaggerated, these numbers reflect a substantial trade for an island that, a century earlier, keenly felt the absence of six Norwegian ships a year.

For all its commercial acumen, the Hanse did not produce bold seafarers or expert deep-water seamen. The English and Dutch, and the Norse before them, were far more skilled. The Hanse consisted of traders and conveyors who were expert at organizing monopolies. During the fifteenth century, the league found its stranglehold on the commerce in salt and stockfish and barreled herring loosened by the growing strength of the Netherlanders, who gradually took over much of this trade and also created nearly industrial-scale herring fisheries where the catches were processed offshore, in the heart of the North Sea fishing grounds.

"Little comes from Iceland," proclaimed *The Libelle of Englyshe Polycye* in 1436, except "stokfishe." Polydore Vergil's *English History* reported in the early sixteenth century that Iceland was a place "unto which in summer season yearlie our merchaunte men doe reparie to bie their fishes."[22] The Hanse, displaced from the North Sea by the Dutch, had by this time forced English and other rivals out of the Icelandic trade. But the fisheries continued and prospered, especially after an Anglo-Danish treaty in 1490 eased restrictions on English visitors. Fishing boats applied for a seven-year license and paid a modest fee of six shillings and eightpence on departure. The Icelandic fishery had by now grown large enough to attract pirates. In 1513 Lord Howard wrote to Cardinal Thomas Worsley, King Henry VIII's chief minister, to inform him about one Hob a Barton, a privateer so notorious that "I pray God he mete not with the Island fleet."[23] In 1523 Lord Surrey warned that "the Scots entende to set forth vi or vii ships to the Ilonde to mete with the Island flete in retornying homwards, wich if they do a marvelous damage shall ensue . . . and all England shalbe destitute of fish next yere."[24]

The damage could indeed have been catastrophic, for the cod landings were now enormous, involving 150 or so ships with a mean displacement of fifty-seven tons. Some were as large as ninety tons. The Icelandic cod fleet must have represented a sizable proportion of England's offshore craft.

The Icelandic fishery was now of enormous proportions and great economic importance to the Lenten fish trade. Some documents of the day record what equipment the doggers carried with them to Iceland. It included such items as "32 hundred hooks at 6d the hundred; 1 firkin of gunpowder." There were, of course, large quantities of salt, "15 wey and a hauf . . . at 36s.8d the wey," not a cheap commodity, gutting knives, lanterns and "all kind of nayls," to say nothing of "strynges" for long lines "at 6s. 8d, the dossyn."[25]*

For unknown reasons, landings fell rapidly during the 1530s, with eighty-five ships sailing north in 1533 and only forty-three by the early 1550s. East Anglian ports suffered greatly as a result. The decline may also have been connected to a doubling of duties on English boats by the Danish authorities, who were favoring their own interests. An act of Parliament in 1534 sought to prevent flagrant overcharging in the white fish market, especially of "the fysshe that comyth from Iselande."[26] Fishers could no longer sell their catches privately to merchants on the shore, nor could crew members sell their shares to the skipper. The intent was to encourage legitimate fish brokers and prevent unscrupulous traders from cornering the market and then selling the fish for excessive prices at the great East Anglian fish fairs. But the effect was to suppress the fish trade at a time when the spread of Protestantism had reduced the number of people who ate fish during Lent. The Crown repealed the act ten years later, but the fishery did not grow again. In 1563 Parliament passed a new act, aimed at encouraging fisheries as a way of increasing the number of experienced seamen available for the growing navy. The act ordered that both Wednesdays and Saturdays be observed as fish days and made it illegal "to set price make any restraint or take or demaunde Toll or Taxe of any seafish to be brought into this realme" by Englishmen in English ships.[27]

Despite these difficulties the fishery never collapsed entirely. Some sixty to seventy ships, mostly from Hull and Norfolk, still sailed north every year. The doldrums ended in the 1590s, when the sustained growth of England's population led to increases in the price of food of all kinds. The East Anglian ports lay close to London, whose teeming urban population became the most important market for fish in the realm.

The long war between England and Spain (1585–1604) lasted beyond the events of the Armada. The Spanish continued to dominate Atlantic sea lanes, preventing the English from supplying prospective colonies in North

---

*A *wey* was a unit of measurement commonly used in the wool trade. One wey was 82.5 kgs (182 lbs) of wool, or 40 bushels of salt each weighing 25.4 kg (56 lbs).

America. James I finally negotiated an end to the war with the Treaty of London in 1604. England then began to enjoy a shipping boom in the Icelandic fishery, where it did not have to compete with aggressive herring fishers from the Low Countries. The fleets grew rapidly until King Charles I increased the toll on fish and tightened the collection of import duties on Biscay salt. The salt tax hit especially hard. In 1639 the burghers of Great Yarmouth petitioned the Crown for relief, pointing out that the number of Iceland-bound fishing boats had declined by half in five years. Their pleas were in vain. Fifty years later, the Icelandic fishery was so decayed that Britain had "not a fourth part of the trade we had twenty or thirty years since."[28] In 1702 no Yarmouth boats sailed north and what had once been a major industry was dead. Sir Francis Brewster wrote in that year, "We formerly imploy'd in the Iseland and Northern-fishing, more than 10000 men and now not 1000." Only a handful of ships now ventured to these historic waters. The great fishery vanished from memory.

The sudden collapse resulted directly from confiscatory salt taxes. The duty on English salt increased exponentially from 5 percent to 300 percent by the late eighteenth century, and foreign salt was taxed at even higher rates. Salt taxes reached a staggering 1500 percent during the Napoleonic wars before they were finally abolished in 1825. A new Icelandic fishery emerged, but by then, of course, no trace remained of the old cod trade of centuries before.

## PART THREE

# DISCOVERY

Bristol merchants towards the year 1490 . . . shared the Portuguese knowledge of the Atlantic islands already discovered. They were trading certainly with Madeira, probably with the Canaries, possibly with the Azores . . . They were already making voyages for the discovery of land west of the British Isles. . . . By their intercourse with Iceland they had, in strong probability, learned of the existence of Greenland . . . and Markland, and of the belief in Wineland the Good in a temperate western region; and they may have heard of good fishing on these western coasts. . . . The facts, as we do know them, point to a strong objective interest in Atlantic discovery, not reinforced by any of the wider knowledge that inspired Columbus and . . . John Cabot.

James A. Williamson[1]

# 13

# "SERCHE & FYNDE A CERTAIN ISLE"

It is considered certain that the cape of the said land was found and discovered in the past by the men from Bristol who found "Brasil" as your Lordship well knows. It was called the Island of Brasil, and it is assumed and believed to be the mainland that the men from Bristol found.

John Day to Christopher Columbus[1]

Even in Saxon times, the quays by the strategic crossing of the Avon River teemed with ships from afar laden with wool and wine. The Saxons called it Brigtoc, "the place by the bridge." It grew rapidly from a large village into a town, soon known as Brigstow or Bristow, with 9,500 inhabitants in the ninth century. The tides run swiftly here, between three and five knots, and up to eight knots in the narrows. The river sweeps downstream and westward through a spectacular gorge into the Severn Estuary and Bristol Channel, a waterway quite unlike the placid Avon meandering through William Shakespeare's Stratford. Bristow soon became Bristol, by 1450 a rich and thriving port, second only to London.[2]

Bristol was never a great fishing port, for it lay at the head of the long and sometimes treacherous Bristol Channel, a good distance from the rich fisheries off Cornwall and southern Ireland. The tidal streams in the estuary flow too rapidly for a sailing vessel to overcome. Arrivals and departures at Bristol depended on careful timing of the tides. In winter, gale-force winds blowing against the ebb tide pushed up monstrous waves that could shut down the port for days. Despite these obstacles, Bristol was a significant player in the Lenten fish trade, both at home and abroad.

Just like a modern shopping mall, Bristol became a trading place by virtue of its strategic location. An order from King Edward III separated it from the surrounding counties in 1373, when the town numbered around 10,000 people and was governed by a clique of leading merchants. Within Bristol's massive defense walls lay a maze of fine churches and houses, accessible by four gateways. It was a cosmopolitan town that grew wealthy from a carefully nurtured role as a transshipment port of cargos from inland, as well as from France, Ireland, and more distant places.* Bristol's merchants courted the outside world by sea and land, maintaining a flourishing trade in woolen cloth, raw wool, and wine. Cloth was manufactured and woven within or near the city itself. Barges and wagons brought thousands of wool bales from a wide area—from Devon in the south to Wales and the Midlands in the north. The town quays bustled with ships loading wool and disgorging casks of claret and Gascon wines from Bordeaux and Bayonne. There was "bastard" too, a sweet white wine from Portugal, and Spanish sherry or sack, the famous "Bristol milk" beloved by serious sherry drinkers to this day.[3] Generations of Bristol merchants grew wealthy on the Gascony wine trade until Bordeaux fell to the French at the end of the Hundred Years War in 1453, and England lost its last toehold on the Continent. The Gascon trade promptly collapsed; the town staggered but soon began exploring alternative markets in Spain, Portugal, and the Mediterranean, where there was a steady demand for dried and salted fish for holy days. Voyages to the Mediterranean and as far as the Levant sometimes ended in disaster. In 1457 the Genoese attacked three Bristol ships under Robert Sturmy, slaughtered their crews, and stole the cloth, grain, tin, and wool aboard. But the sober merchants of Bristol accepted the risks and thrived.

The end of the Gascony trade coincided with a surge in demand for salted fish of all kinds. Ecclesiastical authorities in France were cracking

---

*Bristol became a city in 1542; for convenience, I refer to it as a town here.

down on dietary practices. Though no fishing port, Bristol had surplus capital to invest in distant fishing grounds, among them Iceland and Ireland. In addition to supplying fish to the town's large hinterland, which it had done for centuries, there was money to be made farther afield in Spain and Portugal, where the Basques had traded salted fish and whale meat for centuries. Bristol's fish trade grew rapidly. In 1391 at least £305 worth of fish passed through the port; between October 1403 and March 1404, the figure rose to £1,818.[4]

Most of the fish came from Ireland, but a few Bristol merchants bought stockfish from the Icelandic fisheries as early as 1423. The town sent no fishing boats to the island, since the English vessels in the north came from North Sea ports such as Hull. Bristoleans' primary interest was in trade, so they preferred to buy dried cod at source. Had they been fishers, they would have invested more than they did in the Irish cod fisheries, which were close to home. The Icelandic trade required special licenses from the Danes, which were readily obtained until the Hanse forced English merchants out of Icelandic waters in the 1470s. In 1439, for example, the Bristol ship *Katherine* under Peter Gegge received a Danish license to trade with Iceland and the Lofoten Islands. *Katherine* returned with a full load of stockfish. John Matheue skippered the 140-ton *Mary Redcliffe* on another successful voyage the following year.[5] Perhaps one or two Bristol ships sailed out to Iceland each spring for the cod fishing, landing between £100 and £200 a year. In the memorable year of 1487, three ships returned with cargoes of various fish worth the huge sum of £540.

As the Hanse extended its stranglehold over Icelandic trade, Bristol lost interest in northern cod. Nevertheless, North Sea fisherfolk, who had dominated the Iceland fishery, continued to sail north, especially after an Anglo-Dutch treaty of 1490 eased restrictions in fishing off the island. By that time Bristol was deeply involved in the burgeoning western fisheries, especially off southwestern Ireland.

The waters of the Irish Sea and western English Channel teemed with fish species like pilchard, a relative of herring, and hake, a gadid that rarely flourished in the North Sea. The eastern fisheries worked to the rhythms of the herring spawn and the Icelandic summer season, but in the west, fishing boats were at sea most months of the year, even though many of their crews were also part-time farmers like their compatriots in the North Sea. Ocean fishing developed more slowly in the west, partly because the population was smaller but also because the region was farther from lucrative Continental markets. For centuries, most salted herring for Lent in the west came from Yarmouth and other East Anglian ports, as well as from Dieppe and other eastern English Channel harbors. By the fifteenth century, the population of western England was growing rapidly, Lenten demand was skyrocketing, and the wine and wool trade with Spain had created new shipping routes convenient to western England. Effective methods for salting the oily flesh of pilchard came into their own.

Fishing in the west antedated Roman times, but it was for local consumption until the fifteenth century. As a result, the fisheries escaped the draconian controls imposed on the heavily commercialized eastern markets. Here it was possible to search for new fishing grounds without interference or significant competition. Most fishers worked close inshore, as their North Sea counterparts had once done, catching enough to feed their families and selling the surplus at local markets. At the Stokenham mullet fishery in southern Devon and elsewhere, landowners and religious communities invested in salting houses, boats, and nets with none of the close regulation found in the east.[6]

Basic fishing methods were much the same, with seine and drift net fishing assuming great importance against shoal prey like mackerel, mullet, and herring, or for harvesting salmon. Lyme Bay, a huge bight in Dorset and Devon between Portland Bill in the east and Start Point in the west, was such a prolific fishery that boats from Cornwall, Devon, and even Brittany paid between four pence and two shillings each to fish there. It helped that Dorset produced most of England's hemp. The small town of Bridport in Lyme Bay was famous for its rope makers.

The first western fish to assume wider commercial importance was the hake. *Merluccius merluccius* is a gadid that can grow to a length of a hundred centimeters and weigh up to three kilograms. Its low-fat white flesh is easily dried and salted. Hake rapidly became a major commodity in the west, important enough that the Crown allowed the builders of Plymouth's sea defenses to levy a hake tax to pay for the construction. Fresh and salted hake also contributed significantly to church tithes. The steward of Syon Abbey on Mount St. Michael in Mount's Bay collected a £14 tithe from 1,400 dried hake in 1424–1425 alone. Hake had been a small-scale export commodity for a few centuries. As early as 1202, three merchants from Bayonne on the Bay of Biscay paid an annual fee that gave them priority over all other Gascon merchants on salted and dried hake and conger passing through Bristol. With the growth of the wine and wool trade, the hake fishery was suddenly much closer to the action, and Bristol became a major player in both the domestic and export Lenten fish markets. Salted fish were the ideal commodity. By the bundle or by weight they were a readily traded, easily carried cargo amenable to easy definition for pricing purposes. As freight, they could be readily combined with other items to fill a half-empty ship. The religious obligations of the faithful ensured a reliable profit at the other end.

Pilchard became a major commodity somewhat later; the first export references to it come from the 1460s. It was a regular export by the 1490s but not a large-scale one until the late sixteenth century.[7] New processing methods preserved it for transport. The curers salted the catch for a month, then washed it and packed it in barrels before pressing it with heavy weights to drain off the oil. More pilchard was added before the barrels were repacked for export. The result, called fumadoe pilchard, became popular in hot Mediterranean lands, because it lasted longer than North Sea herring and required less salt to cure. The oil was a lucrative by-product, useful for cooking, lighting, and other purposes such as tanning.

Most of Bristol's fish came from hake fisheries off Cornwall and the south coast of Ireland.[8] An enterprising Bristol merchant, Richard Panys, leased the entire Galway fishery in 1386, briefly cornering the market in Atlantic salmon. Herring was also plentiful here. As early as 1430, fishing boats from England and as far away as Basque country in northern Spain flocked to Irish waters each July and August spawning season. Fleets of boats from Cornwall and Devon would sail for Ireland in late May and early June, their holds laden with salt. Two or three months later, they would return home with cargos of salted herring, hake, cod, and ling.

## TART DE BRYMLENT

Medieval cooking and navigation were both imprecise arts, learned by hard experience, requiring an ability to improvise and make informed judgments. Fish cookery requires sensitive precision to avoid overcooking the catch. Boiling, grilling, poaching, and baking or roasting were the common techniques, the problem being not so much in the technique but in judging the heat source. Cooking over an open wood fire requires long experience, reflected in the instructions given in such books as Taillevent's *Viandier*. The great chef writes only of a "big fire" and a "little fire," sufficient to heat the pan. Chef Chiquart preferred to cook over coal, which provided a steadier, more constant heat, referring in his book to a "fine bright fire" or a "sprightly fire." No precise temperatures here, just the cumulative experience of thousands of dishes, some successful, some burned, others complete failures.

There was really no need for greater precision, for any cook worth his or her salt had experience of open fires, of swinging pots over them and judging when a dish was cooked sufficiently or had reached the correct temperature for the table. There were no clocks to measure the exact number of minutes a roast would turn on a spit or a fish cook in the embers. Most often the cook would revert to familiar litanies, like the time needed to recite the Lord's Prayer or Psalm 51, probably less than two minutes.

Most medieval fish cookery was simple. The elaboration came in the sauces and pies and other dishes created to showcase them and transform the often bland flavor of the flesh. Here's a wonderful Lenten fish tart.

### ✂ *Tart de Brymlent*

SERVES 6 TO 8

Dough for a 9-inch (23-cm) pie crust (use your favorite recipe)
1½ lb/680 g cod, salmon, haddock, or a mixture of white fish (we used cod)
1 oz/30 ml lemon juice for the fish
1 oz/30 g butter
2 pears, peeled, cored, and thinly sliced
2 apples, peeled, cored, and thinly sliced
8 oz/250 ml white wine
1 oz/30 ml lemon juice for the fruit
1 oz/30 g demerara organic sugar (do not use conventional brown sugar, which is just white sugar with molasses in it)
5 cubebs,* thinly crushed
Generous pinch of cloves, ground

---

*The cubeb, an aromatic pepper commonly used in medieval times, can be bought in many spice shops.

*(continues)*

*Tart de Brymlent (continued)* _____

---

Generous pinch of nutmeg, grated
Large pinch of cinnamon
4 oz/125 g raisins
10 prunes, pitted and minced
6 dates, pitted and minced
6 figs, dried and minced
3 tbs red currant jelly or damson plum preserve

Preheat the oven to 425F/218C.

Bake the pie crust for 10 minutes and let cool. When you remove the pie crust from the oven, lower the temperature to 375F/190C. (This recipe was tested in a 9x12x2½-inch (23x30x5-cm pan.)

Cut the fish into 1½-inch/4-cm chunks, salt lightly, and sprinkle with the lemon juice. Set aside. Melt the butter in a large, heavy skillet and toss the pear and apple slices in it until they are lightly coated. Combine the wine, lemon juice, brown sugar, spices, and dried fruits and add to the mixture in the skillet. Cover and simmer about 15 minutes or until the fruit is soft but still firm. Check the flavoring and drain off the excess liquid.

Paint the jelly on the bottom of the pie crust (damson plum was used for the testing). Combine the fish chunks with the fruit mixture. Drain the liquid and place the mixture in the crust. Bake at 375F/190C for 15–25 minutes or until the fish flakes easily.

Adapted from Taillevent's *Viandier*.

---

While some boats salted their catch at sea, most established shore bases for processing fish in the territories of local chieftains, who charged them for the privilege, much to the annoyance of their sworn enemies, the English authorities. Nearly all Irish catches landed at Bristol. By 1480 fish were 91 percent of all Irish imports passing through the port. Entrepreneurial merchants financed all or part of these ventures; they paid for most of the provisions and salt, and collected the profits when the boats returned.

Bristol's commercial tentacles extended to France and Spain, even into the Mediterranean. Fish were prominent among exports by 1450, and it's easy to see why. In variety and quantity, the fish passing through the port was more than enough to satisfy local needs; the surplus supplied armies and warships as well as the growing markets farther south. Given Bristol's vast experience in the wool and wine trade, adding salted fish to its cargoes equation was simplicity itself. The productivity of the western fisheries soared as fishing boats from Devon and Cornwall cast their nets as far afield as Lyme Bay, even off Winchelsea and Rye in the English Channel. On one occasion Cornish fishers sailed as far as Finmark, the far northern coast of Norway. The west gradually achieved self-sufficiency in Lenten fish. In the late fourteenth century, North Sea herring accounted for 99 percent of Exeter's fish imports. By 1460 the figure was only 29 percent, with twenty-two varieties of fish imported from elsewhere. Bristol and southwestern England were now the largest fish exporters in the country and remained so throughout the fifteenth century. The region lay near the lucrative French and Spanish markets, with cheap French baie salt a few days' sail away. At the same time, profits from cloth and tin mining combined with a successful agricultural economy provided capital for new mercantile ventures, including commercially risky fishing expeditions to Iceland and a series of speculative voyages westward into the heaving wastes of the Western Ocean in search of new lands.

Bristol was prosperous and restless, ever on the watch for fresh opportunities. Arabs from North Africa, Basques from northern Spain, Bretons, Dutchmen, Norsemen, and Spaniards drank in the town's waterside taverns, a polyglot international community of sailors with intimate knowledge of all the coasts and oceans of Europe; skippers who had navigated Pentland Firth off northern Scotland, weathered midwinter gales off Iceland, carried the tide through the Strait of Gibraltar, or sailed far south along the little-known African coast. Important navigational information passed discreetly from sea captain to sea captain—men who had been out there, often in extreme weather. For the most part they kept their counsel but in their cups would pass along stories—tales of sea monsters and mermaids; yarns of fish so large that they could sink a ship or so plentiful they could be gathered in baskets; anecdotes of exotic people of different colors, half animal, half human; and accounts of unknown lands of fabled wealth far to the west, beyond the known horizon. Above all, there were persistent stories of lands where gold and great riches would reward those who found them. It was said that a mysterious land, the Island of Brasil, lay in the vastness of the Western Sea.

In Gaelic, Hy-Brasil means "Island of the Blessed," a kind of paradise akin to St. Brendan's Land of Promise.[9] Here there was no violence, no poverty, no hard work, a place where the souls of the blessed resided on their way to heaven. Hy-Brasil was seen occasionally by lonely shepherds and fishermen, appearing suddenly out of dense mist, always floating tantalizingly on the far horizon. It was a place where no living person had landed, but it was said that if you approached close enough to throw fire ashore, you would be well received. Brasil may have been an Irish folktale, a product of the imaginations of people living on the edges of a fierce and terrifying ocean. Or the myth may have originated in Portugal and Spain, prompted by an expedition by a Frenchman to the Canary Islands in 1402, the discovery of Madeira in 1418, and the Portuguese colonization of the Azores in 1432. Or it may have come from the Basques, expert seafarers who served as captains and pilots on many Spanish and Portuguese ships.

Brasil was a fictional place—or was it? The ancient legend persisted at a time of restless exploration, improved ship design, and a greater willingness among sailors to venture far offshore. There were indeed islands in the Western Ocean such as the Azores, the Canary Islands, and Madeira that compelled further exploration, not for fishing grounds but for a sea route to the fabled gold and spices of Asia. The notion that the world was round, not flat, made it possible to sail, at least in theory, westward to China and the Indies. As always, a deep-seated curiosity about the Western Ocean was fed by the lure of untold wealth. The search for gold, spices, and new lands culminated in the classic voyages of Christopher Columbus to the Caribbean in 1492 and John Cabot to Newfoundland in 1497. With these voyages the Americas became part of popular consciousness, and large-scale European exploitation and settlement of the Americas began. But perhaps the legend of Brasil led to earlier, unrecorded voyages, a generation or more before Cabot, that did not find a route to the Indies.

Claims of discovery always raise violent passions, none more so than the European discovery of North America. No one disputes the Norse voyages that took Leif Eirikson to Newfoundland and Labrador in the late 900s. Knarrs from Greenland traveled west occasionally for 200 years before the deteriorating conditions of the Little Ice Age made such passages too hazardous. By 1450 Norse settlements there were virtually abandoned. But the lore of the western voyages lived on in Icelandic sagas that were widely read and recited for centuries. Without question, many fishing skippers and other visitors to Iceland learned of lands to the west from the sagas.

Who, then, were the next visitors to North America? Columbus and Cabot are the only names that have made it into the history books, but their voyages could just as easily have been made by others. These two men "led" Europeans into the New World in the same sense that the paint on the tip of a ship's bowsprit "leads" it into harbor. The real motivators were broader and more complex—a rapid expansion of medieval culture outward from the western European peninsula away from the frontiers of Islam, new shipbuilding technologies and innovative designs that took mariners into open water far from land, and a quest for direct routes to the gold and spices of Asia. To which one must add another often neglected economic reality—a constant search for new fishing grounds to feed armies and the devout. This expansion began as the Little Ice Age tightened its grip on Europe, bringing shorter growing seasons to a continent where most people still lived from harvest to harvest. The colder centuries also brought greater, more unpredictable storminess and more severe ice conditions in the North.

Was Cabot the first in the north or did others precede him? Whirlpools of intense academic controversy surround the early voyages, compounded by a lack of documentation. We can either dismiss claims for earlier voyages as being out of hand or grant the possibility and then examine some of the questions that result from such an admission. Did anyone actually search for Brasil before Columbus and Cabot? Could either of these voyagers have learned of lands far to the west before they left port in 1492 and 1497?

Quite apart from the findings of sober historical scholarship, the waters of discovery are muddied by wild speculation and nationalistic agendas. Who *was* first? The Basques of northern Spain are persistent candidates. They were expert sailors, consummate shipbuilders, and indefatigable hunters of northern right whales, which frequented the Bay of Biscay. By the tenth century, Basque whaling was in high gear. Their merchants sold fresh and salted red whale meat to the devout, as far inland as the Paris fish markets. They cured the fattier parts in salt like bacon and produced *craspois,* widely eaten during Lent, often with peas. But the greatest delicacy of all was the tongue, a huge organ that could account for up to 5 percent of a whale's weight, flesh so valuable that the Church demanded it as tithe payments and government officials as taxes.

According to Mark Kurlansky, author of a popular history of the Basques, contacts with Norse shipwrights and traders along the Biscay coast as early as the ninth century led to better-built ships in northern Spain, well adapted to offshore whaling and longer voyages.[10] Kurlansky also claims that the Basques learned about stockfish from their Norse contacts, *Gadus* being unknown in their home waters. He then argues that Basques, already expert at salting whale meat, now dried and salted cod, thereby enabling them to sail far north of the Bay of Biscay in search of increasingly scarce right whales: "By pursuing northern cod, and provisioning their ships with salt cod, they then were able to start chasing the whale into its summer grounds, up to Iceland, Norway, the Hebrides, and the Faeroes."[11] By 1000, he argues, the Basques were taking whales in their northern feeding grounds, more than 1,600 kilometers north of their homeland. He cites a record from a secondary source that twenty Basque whaling ships were sighted sailing westward past Iceland in 1412. In fact, the reference refers generically to twenty foreign ships *fishing* off Iceland, as the English and others were already doing in the early fifteenth century.[12] This alleged sighting and other unsubstantiated references, some of them from accounts dating to the seventeenth century and faithfully repeated by uncritical writers, have led to persistent theories that the Basques were fishing and whaling in North American waters long before John Cabot.

No one doubts that the Basques were extraordinary seamen. Basque sailors shipped out on Portuguese caravels down the coast of Africa and accompanied Columbus to the Indies. They skippered merchant ships sailing from Spain to Bristol and other English ports to North Sea coasts and as far as the Baltic. Their reputation as expert whalers is unchallenged. But when did large-scale Basque whaling actually begin outside the Bay of Biscay? It's tempting to write, as Kurlansky and other nonscholars have done, of the Basques sailing, Ahab-like, in pursuit of whales as far north as Spitzbergen soon after the possible (and controversial) discovery of these Arctic islands by the Norse in the twelfth century. In fact this is a myth. There is no archival evidence—and people have looked carefully. Records of Basque inshore whaling in the Bay of Biscay abound, dating to the eleventh or twelfth centuries. However, despite exhaustive search, no one has yet found archaeological or historical data for anything more until the early sixteenth century, when the Basques entered the North American fishery.[13] There's no reason to believe that serious whaling began in Spitzbergen until Dutch explorer Willem Barentsz made his well-documented visit on June 17, 1596.[14]

Unfortunately Basque Atlantic voyaging is cloaked in the passions of nationalist mythmaking. Writes the Canadian historian Selma Barkham, "Those cheerful fellows who chased whales further and further out into the Atlantic (having first eliminated, in theory, all whales along their own Cantabrian coast), those pioneer Basques who sailed up to Iceland and then on to Greenland in medieval times, accompanied by some obliging pilot . . . those men who miraculously bumped into Terranova (and kept it secret) more than a hundred years before Cabot, those men are rather different from . . . more mundane Basques who installed a flourishing and efficient whaling industry during the . . . sixteenth century."[15] Barkham knows of what she writes, for she has combed Basque archives for information on Terre Neuve (new land) whaling.

The English, not the Basques, had knowledge of northern waters during the fifteenth century. They had frequented Icelandic waters for generations, sailing there from the North Sea and the west coast of Ireland. Bristol's merchants had their money from the mundane but profitable cloth and wool trade. Their skippers, having sailed to Iceland to buy cod, were well aware of the existence of Greenland. They knew the wind patterns, the wisdom of sailing north from Ireland, then west, when making passage in waters explored by the Norse centuries earlier. It would be surprising if the same mariners had not heard the ancient tales of Viking journeys to lands far to the west, which must have circulated freely in the close-knit, private world of fisherfolk and mariners. And we know for certain that a few Bristol entrepreneurs financed ships to sail westward long before John Cabot sought the backing of the English court for a northern expedition to Asia.[16]

On July 15, 1480, somewhat late in the season to sail west, an eighty-tun ship owned by customs officer Thomas Croft and merchant John Jay Jr. weighed anchor and sailed on a voyage, customs records tell us, "ad insulam de Brasylle in occidentali parte Hibernie" [to the island of Brasylle in the western part of the Hibernian Sea].* Jay was well-known in the town, having served as sheriff in 1472–1473.[17] With the resources to hire the best and most experienced skipper around, he hired one Thloyde, or Lloyd, "the most scientific mariner in all England." But nine weeks after setting off, Lloyd took refuge in an Irish port, forced by fierce storms to turn back without sighting land.

Croft and Jay lost money on Lloyd's voyage, but the potential returns from Brasil were thought to be so enormous that exploration continued. The following year two small ships, *George* and *Trinity,* set out on a similar voyage with instructions to "serch & fynde a certain Isle called the Isle of Brazil."[18] The ships carried large quantities of salt for "the reparacion and sustentacion of the said shippes." This "sustentacion" must have been a form of insurance, for the crew could always buy Icelandic cod for salt or even catch and salt their own. The ships returned intact, but there's no record of the outcome of the expedition. The returning crew and their sponsors both kept their own counsel.

---

*A *tun* was a large barrel capable of carrying two butts or 1,146 liters (252 English gallons) of wine. Tuns were often used to record the capacity of a merchant ship.

But there are grounds for thinking the journey was profitable in terms of lucrative stockfish cargoes from Iceland or further west, for there were more forays westward in search of Brasil. We know this because in 1498, a year after John Cabot's voyage to Newfoundland, the Spanish ambassador to London, Pedro de Ayala, reported to Ferdinand and Isabella that "the people of Bristol have, for the past seven years, sent out every year two, three, or four light ships *(caraveles)* in search of the island of Brasil and the Seven Cities."[19] His report received startling confirmation in 1956 from the discovery of a letter written by London textile merchant John Day. In the winter of 1497–1498, having recently arrived in Andalusia from England, Day wrote to an important personage styled the "Grand Admiral" (commonly assumed to be Christopher Columbus) making reference to a landfall far to the west made by an unknown vessel from Bristol "in the past." "It is considered certain," wrote Day, "that the cape of the said land [Cabot's New Found Land] was found and discovered in the past by the men from Bristol who found 'Brasil' as your lordship well knows. It was called the Island of Brasil, and it is assumed and believed to be the mainland that the men from Bristol found."[20]

If Ayala and Day are to be believed, there were at least irregular voyages from Bristol that discovered Newfoundland and even fished there well before Cabot's well-publicized venture. Why, then, did the Bristoleans cloak their discoveries in secrecy?

Bristol was not concerned with imperial conquest but sought gold, spices, and new markets. When her ships made landfall on fog-shrouded Newfoundland and the mainland beyond it, they stumbled on an unknown fishing ground teeming with cod of vast size. The merchants behind the voyages were shrewd enough to recognize their potentially huge commercial advantage and kept their mouths shut. But the fishery, if it existed, never reached a large size, perhaps because of the need for secrecy and because of the enormous financial risks involved. From the backers' point of view, cod cargoes were sound insurance, for they paid the expenses of voyages searching for something more glamorous: a direct route to Asia and its spices.

∝

Ayala refers specifically to caravels, not the familiar dogger used by English fishers to take cod in the north for more than a century. The *Trinity* and its ilk were very different vessels from their cod-fishing predecessors and contemporaries.

Caravels probably originated among fishing boats with lateen rigs used by Islamic fishers off the coast of western North Africa and Spain. Soon they came into use in the Bay of Biscay inshore fisheries.[21] By 1440 caravels had become large enough to serve as oceangoing vessels, used by Portugal's captains to sail south into the Atlantic. These were two- or three-masted vessels with lateen sails, designed to be fast, maneuverable, and capable of operating in shallow waters. They could point as high as forty-five to fifty degrees to the wind, which made them ideal for passages against contrary winds and currents. Because the lateen rig was difficult to handle on long downwind passages, many skippers hoisted square sails on the fore and mainmasts, with only a lateen at the stern. Thus was born the full-rigged ship, the most important maritime innovation of medieval times, capable of making long passages far from land and surviving severe weather in the open Atlantic.

A lateen-rigged caravel.

Oceangoing full-rigged caravel used widely for exploration.

Caravels may have carried Columbus to the Indies and Vasco da Gama to India, but they were first and foremost workhorses—warships, trading vessels, and fishing boats. By 1448 Portuguese fishers were already working far from home off the Saharan coast of Morocco and West Africa. Portuguese caravels not only caught fish but transported them to ports large and small. They carried salt to Ireland and southwestern England in exchange for cloth and regularly traded in Icelandic waters. Such versatile craft soon caught on in northern Europe, acquired by purchase or capture. One was built in Brussels in 1438–1440. A Breton owner in Dieppe, France, took delivery of another in 1451. In about 1449 caravels were under construction in Flanders, following the example of a Breton named Julian. A three-master was built at Dunwich in East Anglia between 1463 and 1466.[22] It would have been easy for Bristol shipowners to acquire a caravel.

The caravel's seagoing qualities, speed, and maneuverability convinced northern European builders to adopt it. The shipwrights now used new techniques that erected a skeleton framework of the hull first, then completed it with planks laid one against the other. This method, known as carvel construction, produces a tough, rigid hull, quite different from flexible Norse designs and a better load carrier. But there were formidable challenges. Building the frame first may have required less-skilled workers,

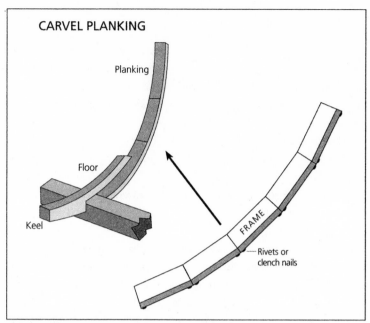

CARVEL PLANKING

Planking

Floor

Keel

FRAME

Rivets or clench nails

Carvel hull construction, the frame being built first.

but the master builder had to define the three-dimensional form of the hull before a single frame rose on the keel. As a fifteenth-century Venetian treatise tells us, the main dimensions of the hull were expressed as proportions of a convenient modular unit such as the keel. As a result, the same basic shipbuilding methods came into use over a wide area of the Mediterranean and western Europe.

The *Trinity* and her contemporaries survive as crabbed depictions on early maps and in a half a dozen or so fragmentary shipwrecks, among them the remarkably complete hull of the Basque whaler *San Juan*, which sank during a storm in Red Bay, Labrador, in 1565.[23] All of these ships shared common features—full-bodied hulls constructed with closely spaced, heavy frames assembled before they were erected and fastened to a heavy keel. Each had a gently curved stem and a sloping transom, with smooth (carvel) planking. Caravels and naos, larger load-carrying ships of similar design, had massive wooden steps for their masts—a sign of the harsh realities of Atlantic sailing.

While they served various purposes, caravels, naos, and their relatives shared a common shipbuilding tradition of plank-and-frame construction— ship designs that evolved along the rockbound western coasts of Spain and Portugal and in Biscayan waters. The shipbuilders and sailors of these waters saw vessels of every kind—lapstrake Norse ships, cogs, flat-bottomed Dutch ships, slender galleys, and carracks. Their eclectic knowledge led to a melding of northern and Mediterranean shipbuilding traditions in thousands of oceangoing vessels large and small, all constructed with more or less standardized building methods and proven designs, relatively simple to construct and, above all, capable of carrying people and their cargo safely across a stormy, cold ocean.[24]

The Western Ocean was still a dangerous place; shipwrecks were common, casualty rates high. But most wrecks came when sailors were caught close to land in thick weather or in sudden gales, not in the open ocean, where a well-handled vessel such as a caravel or nao had an excellent chance of surviving. Eloquent testimony comes from the Spanish Armada of 1588, whose ships scattered in front of a vicious southwesterly gale in the southern North Sea, then rounded northern Scotland and sailed home under appalling conditions. Most ships of the armada were carrack-like warships or cargo vessels, clumsy sailors for the most part. In the end, only 16 percent of the Iberian-built naos in the fleet perished, as opposed to 41 percent of the heavy North Sea vessels hired by the king of Spain and 62 percent of the largest ships, the carracks.[25]

By the fifteenth and sixteenth centuries, the Basques of northern Spain had acquired a sterling reputation for their boatbuilding skills. Shipyards from Bayonne to Bilbao produced hundreds of vessels of every size, notably cargo ships and fishing boats for inshore and offshore use.[26] Planking oak was abundant, iron ore plentiful. Basque shipbuilders worked in small village yards to produce essentially disposable oceangoing ships and fishing craft that would have hard lives. The tools of boatbuilding had changed little from earlier times; what was different was a broad standardization of designs. Ships were constructed on lines that had proved themselves over thousands of miles of open-water sailing: sloping prows, beamy hulls capable of carrying heavy loads, transoms with stout rudder posts, and heavy mast steps that supported the spars in all conditions.

We should not be surprised that some form of caravel or nao was the vessel of choice for mariner Lloyd and the Bristol skippers who followed in his wake.

By the 1480s, long trading voyages were routine along the Atlantic coast and out to the Canaries, Madeira, and the Azores. By fortunate historical coincidence, we know something of the earlier voyages of the ship *Trinity* that sailed west in 1481.[27] A large ship by contemporary standards, displacing more than 300 tons, she had carried wine from Gascony and Lisbon since the mid-1460s, then voyaged to the Mediterranean in 1480–1481. Her purser on this trip, John Balsall, records how the ship left Bristol in October 1480 with a crew of thirty-four, including eight soldiers and a gunner. *Trinity* sailed nonstop to Huelva in southern Spain, stayed there four or five weeks, then coasted to the Strait of Gibraltar, where a pilot came aboard to guide her to Oran in North Africa, a lucrative but pirate-infested port. On her return to Huelva, the ship was beached and her hull caulked by two Spaniards who took four days to complete the job. Then she returned home, carrying a cargo of fruit and wine, with only one stop to revictual.

At Huelva, Balsall arranged for the Franciscan friars of Santa Maria de la Rabida to say prayers for the ship. A few years later, the community gave Columbus important backing as he sought sponsors for his westward voyage. Only two months after its return, John Jay and his partners sent the refitted *Trinity* west on a search for the islands of Brasil. Could the Franciscans of Santa Maria have learned of western lands from Balsall, information that they then passed on to Columbus? We shall never know, but the possibility is intriguing.

The purser recorded no details of *Trinity*'s rig, but his purchase in Spain of a new mizzen mast and two topmasts suggests she was a three-master. Almost certainly she was some form of caravel, perhaps a nao, one of a new generation of oceangoing ships that were to carry Europeans to North America and distant fishing grounds.

∂℃

Ambassador Ayala, John Day, and some sparse customs records are the only records of the Bristol journeys. No skippers' logbooks or passengers' accounts survive to tell us where these voyages went and how they traveled west. This could arguably mean that such passages never took place, since there is no record of them. But we should not be surprised at the lack of records. More likely, most skippers were illiterate, even "the most scientific mariner in England," and not given to loose talk. Fishing boat captains are notoriously closemouthed about their fishing grounds, and the masters of the westbound vessels would almost certainly have been either expert cod fishers or merchant seamen used to operating in waters infested with pirates and unscrupulous competitors. The knowledge acquired on the voyages was secreted in the skippers' heads and passed from generation to generation, acquired not from book learning but hard-won experience.

In the absence of written records, we can only approach the voyages from their likely routings. Atlantic wind patterns have changed little since medieval times, so we can safely assume that the strategies for sailing west in vessels with limited ability to sail against the wind were in use centuries earlier. The knowledge came from generations of voyages from Bristol to Iceland, where the best sailing routes in the face of the prevailing westerlies would have gone west to Galway and western Ireland, then northward toward Iceland, scudding before the now favorable wind. North of latitude sixty degrees, perhaps even in sight of the island, the mariner could turn west, taking advantage of the easterlies that blow persistently in this region, especially in spring and early summer.

By the time the *George* and *Trinity* sailed, Bristol skippers would have had an intimate knowledge of Icelandic waters and the fretted western coast where most fishing and trading took place. These are stormy seas. Many fishing boats would have been blown far offshore by easterly gales. When the weather passed and the wind blew strong out of a clear, blue sky, they would have sighted the mountain peaks of Greenland to the west, which are visible only a day's sail from Iceland on a luminous northern day. In any case, they would have heard of this mountainous land from the Icelanders, who were raised on the Norse sagas.

The existence of Greenland was common knowledge in the fifteenth century, but did English skippers sail that far? In 1996 the historian

Kirsten Seaver wrote of an "information chain" that linked the English fishers in the north with the Icelanders' firsthand experience of Greenland.[28] She developed her scenario from an intricate skein of historical and archaeological clues. As competition for cod intensified off Iceland, she argued, English ships may have sailed westward in search of fish off the western lands. There they anchored off the old Norse settlements, perhaps using local pilots to guide them through ice-free passages near land. The Greenlanders, by this time effectively isolated from Norwegian goods, traded dried cod for clothing and other imports, knowing that the English paid far more for stockfish than the Norwegians did.

Seaver believes that English ships traded with Herjolfsnes on the east coast and other Norse settlements for stockfish, train oil, and other profitable commodities through much of the fifteenth century, long before John Jay sent the *Trinity* westward. The primary attraction was dried cod, processed ashore by the Greenlanders, not the English, who did not stay around long enough to conduct proper drying. If this trade did take place, it must have been on the quiet in goods that were easily and inconspicuously absorbed into the stream of commodities passing through Bristol and other ports without drawing the attention of tax collectors. Seaver points to archaeological finds at Herjolfsnes that provide evidence of at least sporadic European contact after Norwegian ships no longer sailed to Greenland—a local copy of a Burgundian style of tall hat and Norse replicas of women's clothing fashionable in Europe during the late fifteenth century.

By the mid- to late fifteenth century, Seaver argues, conditions in the Icelandic fishery were viciously competitive, compounded by political instability and violence on the island itself. She thinks there were plenty of incentives to sail to Greenland waters.

Seaver's arguments rest on shaky foundations. Several archaeologists have pointed out that the imports found in Greenland Norse settlements could have been carried there by Norwegian ships, Hanse vessels, or almost any seafarers in Europe, including the English. Furthermore, new, very accurate radiocarbon dates tell us that the Norse settlements in Greenland were almost certainly abandoned by 1450, when the intensifying cold of the Little Ice Age was making life in general, as well as navigation between Iceland and Greenland, very difficult. Any English visits to Greenland would probably have been little more than blind gropings in unfamiliar, ice-strewn waters.

A new generation of archaeological research has hammered a final nail into the English-in-Greenland coffin.[29] Inquiries by Sophia Perdikaris and Tom McGovern, among others, show that the Norse who settled Iceland and Greenland began their colonization with similar dairying economies imported from Europe. But soon after settlement their economies diverged sharply. The Icelanders combined farming with seasonal inshore fishing and then were drawn inexorably into the widening orbit of the international stockfish trade of later medieval Europe. Fish bones abound in early Icelandic middens. In stark contrast, Greenland sites yield abundant remains of walrus and other sea mammals but almost no fish bones—and not because of imperfect preservation in the soil. The original settlers imported the farming culture of their homeland, with its cattle, pigs, goats, and sheep. Here harp seals, not fish, became all-important, especially by the colder decades of the fifteenth century. Many were killed with clubs during their annual northward migration from their pupping grounds off Newfoundland. But the Norse rarely took ring seal, hunted by Inuit at the edge of the ice and through floes with harpoons.

Years of meticulous research conducted on sites so carefully excavated that even insects and seeds are recovered have yielded almost no cod remains. Nor do analyses of domestic animal bones from these sites display the telltale carbon isotope ratios that would indicate that these animals were fed fish products, as they were in Iceland. Fish were simply unimportant in Norse Greenland society. Potential causes include a shortage of boats in a timberless land, few materials for making nets or fishing lines, even a dietary preference for fattier sea mammal flesh. Cod fishing is a winter activity in Iceland, as is the production of stockfish. In Greenland, where temperatures are much lower and ice conditions more severe, both fishing and stockfish drying are virtually impossible in winter. In summer, fishing would have competed directly with the demands of farming and of the walrus hunt and other activities that produced prestigious commodities such as falcons and sea mammal oil for traders from Europe.

The severe cold of the Little Ice Age brought Norse settlement in Greenland to a standstill. As early as 1250, the number of ships traveling between Iceland and Greenland shrank rapidly. Those that did attempt the journey sailed far south and west to avoid the ice pack, which was farther south than today, even in summer. Once well clear of the ice front, they would steer northwest toward Cape Farewell at the southern tip and into the David Strait. There were no incentives for English ships, or anyone, to visit Greenland. Unless there was a specific reason to go there, no caravel would have traveled to a place that lacked gold and cod. Greenland was a known quantity and off any direct route to the fabled Brasil.

A Bristol ship sailing westward from Iceland would have used latitude sailing. Like all mariners of the day, the skipper would have traversed the ocean by sailing along a latitude line, checking his position with the sun and stars, a time-tested way of crossing open water used by the Norse. His strategy would have drawn on knowledge acquired from years of Bristol passages to the Icelandic fishery. Once at about sixty degrees north, he would have turned west, in an area where polar easterlies blow strongly in the early months of the year. Both the Irminger and East Greenland currents would also have helped propel the ship westward. Keeping well south of the pack and clear of Cape Farewell, the ship could have sailed a further 1,100 kilometers or so to make landfall on Labrador. The explorers might encounter the occasional severe gale and would have been at the mercy of icebergs, but the extra distance would not have been significant to experienced deep-water sailors using a favorable wind and with every incentive to find their way to Asia. Unlike doggers, caravels and naos had the sailing ability and the range to sail thousands of kilometers independent of the shore.

In the end, the *Trinity* and other Bristol ships may indeed have found their Brasil, not an island of fabled wealth but a place where cod swarms beggared the imagination. Beyond may have been a route to Asia, but a hold full of cod guaranteed a profit even if it lacked the glamour of spices and precious metals. So the early Bristol voyages, if they took place, stopped at what later became known as Newfoundland or Terre Neuve and on the adjacent coasts. With luck, the return journey in late summer or early autumn would have been a fast passage, taking advantage of the prevailing westerly winds that carried a laden ship back to England in a few weeks. The same general passage strategy remained commonplace long after John Cabot followed it in 1497, until larger ships began sailing directly against the westerlies.

If the *Trinity* and other ships did reach Newfoundland, they had little company. The risks were enormous—fog, icebergs, severe gales far offshore, and all the dangers of shipwreck on rugged shores at home and in North America. But the profits would have been substantial, and we can be sure that the few Bristol merchants who risked investing in such voyages would have been smart enough to take their money and keep quiet about where their catches came from. Fishers don't talk. Nor do merchants who find a highly profitable if unspectacular island of Brasil of their own. As for the legendary Brasil, it remained a fabled isle floating around on charts of the North Atlantic, sometimes near Newfoundland, sometimes west of southern Ireland. The British admiralty finally removed Brasil from its charts in 1873.

Ambassador Ayala and John Day wrote of the earlier voyages when reports of Cabot's voyage became common knowledge. By then there was no incentive for secrecy, for the Spanish Crown boldly announced Columbus's discoveries and laid claim to the Indies and a new continent. If Bristol shipowners already knew of the Newfoundland cod fisheries, they kept quiet about them for sound commercial reasons. As always, Bristol's leaders were merchants who put profit first, not empire building. John Cabot was an outsider who came to Bristol seeking sponsorship to find a route to the wealth of Asia. He was an expert on spices who knew from Columbus's voyage and perhaps from discreet Bristol sources that there was land to the west. Cabot surmised correctly that King Henry VII regretted not sponsoring Columbus's voyage and the wealth it produced. So he dangled spices, not fish, before the Crown and Henry invested.

The putative Bristol voyages could never have taken place without generations of fishing in the open Atlantic, in the western approaches of the

English Channel, off the stormy western coast of Ireland, and on Iceland's continental shelf. It was cod that took doggers and then caravels offshore, and the local knowledge acquired by these fishers that put substance behind the legends of Brasil.

In 1477 Christopher Columbus sailed north from Lisbon, perhaps in a Bristol ship to its home port, then to Galway in Ireland and perhaps on to Iceland and as much as 100 leagues north of it during a mild, relatively ice-free year. But his visit there is questionable. In Galway, a common stopping place for Iceland-bound ships as well as sailors and pilgrims, he saw "many remarkable things," including "a man and woman of extraordinary appearance in two boats adrift," whom David Quinn convincingly identifies as Inuit—like the man in his kayak who appeared in the Orkney Islands in 1690 during the height of the Little Ice Age.[30] Being a mariner himself, the young sailor would have heard the bar talk of mysterious islands and lands to the west from people who knew more about the Western Ocean than anyone else. Columbus may have gained considerable assurance from his conversations with sailors in the north. Perhaps it was no coincidence that his brother Bartholomew unsuccessfully approached King Henry VII of England for sponsorship in 1489. All we know is that twelve years after mariner Lloyd set forth from Bristol in search of Brasil, Christopher Columbus sailed confidently across the Atlantic with the northeast trade winds under the Spanish flag and became a legend of discovery.

## 14

# A NEW FOUND LANDE

Newfoundland—the fish of the Banks, the inshore cod fishery,
the whale fishery on its northern flank—may in the end prove
to have been for Europe during the sixteenth and early seventeenth centuries as valuable a discovery as the gold and silver
of the Spanish empire.

David B. Quinn[1]

The tides at Avonmouth rise and fall 12 meters in the spring, when the
moon is new or full, 6.4 meters at neaps, the time of the half-moon. Despite the scouring currents, Bristol (or rather Bristowe) was the second
port in England in 1450. Its quays lay close to a strategic river crossing
and the harbor was well protected from pirates and other enemies. The
town was the natural transshipment point for wool from the lush
Cotswold country nearby. Bristol lay at the center of long medieval trade
routes, halfway between Iceland and the Iberian Peninsula, close to Ireland's rich fisheries and English Channel ports like Plymouth. Merchants,
men like William Canynges and John Jay, built and owned ships in Bristol, made fortunes from wine and wool, Lenten herring and cod.[2] Jay and
his contemporaries probed unknown seas to the west, perhaps finding
rich cod fisheries off Newfoundland and Labrador in the early 1480s. We
may never know what their skippers found, but the voyages must have
been profitable, for prudent merchants do not throw money away on
fruitless ventures. They operated discreetly, keeping their mouths firmly
closed. Inevitably, however, tales of earlier voyages circulated after Cabot

made Newfoundland common knowledge. The first crossing known from contemporary records is that of John Cabot, a famous but shadowy immortal of Atlantic exploration.

Although Jay and his ilk sent their ships west in the 1580s, they also had in mind a route to spice-rich Asia. Spices were the most lucrative commodity of all—exotic, expensive, and obtainable only from merchants in Alexandria and the Levant. England lay at the end of a long trading route that passed from the eastern Mediterranean to Italy, France, Spain, and Portugal, then north, so the English paid the highest prices for cloves, nutmeg, and pepper. Spices became more plentiful when Vasco da Gama and his successors sailed to India and southeast Asia after 1497 and made Portugal a spice exporter. Bristol had long tried to become a player in the trade; witness the ill-fated voyage of Robert Sturmy, whose ships were destroyed by Genoese competitors in 1457. The town was strategically placed for a western route to Asia, lying farther west than Portugal and Spain, with mariners expert at sailing in northern waters. In 1492 Bristol's skippers probably knew more about the Western Ocean than anyone in Europe, except perhaps the Portuguese. A handful of them may have known that there was land a month's sailing or more over the horizon. Had Henry VII responded favorably to the Columbus brothers' petition for sponsorship in about 1489, the course of history might have been different.[3]

Bristol lay closer to the newly discovered Indies, offering the prospect of a shorter, more direct route to Asia north of the lands described by Columbus. The Bristoleans must have contemplated searching for a strait to the west, but they apparently did nothing about it. Perhaps they already knew there was no such route or perhaps the venture was too speculative for their conservative tastes; we will probably never know. But when a Venetian, John Cabot, arrived in Bristol with a proposal for a voyage westward across the North Atlantic in 1495, his plans attracted immediate attention from the Crown. Henry VII had begun to regret turning down the Columbus brothers. He was not about to make the same mistake again.

We don't know what John Cabot (Zuan Cabotto, c. 1453–1498) looked like, and he left no writings. The log of his voyage, if it ever existed, has not survived, nor did any crew member record his adventures. We know Cabot was an Italian, probably from Genoa, but he became a citizen of Venice in 1476. According to Raimondo Soncino, the Milanese envoy in London who knew him well, Cabot was an expert seaman and navigator.[4] Earlier in his career, he had traded spices and was aware that the best came from China and the northern regions of Asia. Between 1490 and 1493, he lived in Valencia, Spain, and sold real estate. Encouraged by Columbus's triumphant return from the Indies, Cabot approached the Portuguese and Spanish courts about a northern voyage but was turned down. He then settled in Bristol with his wife and three sons, offering to sail in search of a spice route and pay the expenses himself. This time he was successful. On March 5, 1496, Henry VII granted letters-patent to Cabot for an expedition of five ships to explore "iles, countries, regions or provinces of the heathen and infidelles, whatever they bee, and in what part of the world soever they be, which before have beene unknowne to all Christians."[5] Following the usual practice, one-fifth of the profits would go to the Crown.

Cabot's move to Bristol was astute, for the town's merchants were well aware of the potential profits in the spice route. But he was an outsider and perhaps distrusted. According to John Day's famous 1497–1498 letter to Columbus, Cabot attempted to sail west in 1496 but turned back in the face of strong winds and a crew that "confused" him. We know nothing more of the abortive venture. In 1497 he obtained a single ship, the *Mathew* or *Matthew*, a small caravel capable of transporting fifty tons of wine. Its rig and hull are a matter of conjecture. A modern replica built from the best available sources is a three-masted ship 23.7 meters long overall, with a beam of 6 meters, a draft of 2.1 meters, and a displacement of 85 tons.[6] A lateen sail on the mizzen (or aftermost) spar enhances her maneuverability. Cabot shipped out on May 20, 1497, with a crew of eighteen and a surgeon who doubled as the ship's barber.

The *Matthew* set a course "north and then west," clearing Dursey Head in western Ireland two days later. Like all mariners of the day, Cabot used latitude sailing, checking his position with the sun and stars, a time-tested way

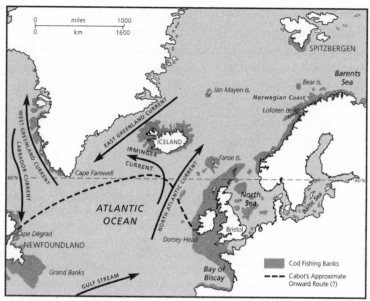

A map of John Cabot's possible route, with Atlantic cod fisheries and New-foundland, showing locations mentioned in Chapters 14 and 15. Cabot's landfall is controversial, but this is my take on it.

of crossing open water used by the Norse but worthless for days on end in the North Atlantic with its frequently cloudy skies. But unlike them, he carried a compass, a quadrant, and a traverse table, all of which enabled him to correct his latitude course if need be. His strategy must have drawn on knowledge acquired from years of Bristol passages to the Icelandic fishery and perhaps farther west.[7] Like fisherfolk from western England and Bristol's putative western voyagers, he sailed north from Ireland to about sixty degrees north and then turned west with the polar easterlies and favorable currents behind him, keeping far south of the pack and well clear of Cape Farewell and Greenland. The *Matthew* was fortunate. Apart from a single gale near the end of the voyage, the weather was good, with persistent east and northeast winds and smooth seas.

On June 24, after a crossing of thirty-five days, Cabot made landfall on Newfoundland's northern peninsula, probably on Cape Dégrad, about eight kilometers from L'Anse aux Meadows, where Leif Eirikson overwintered 500 years earlier.[8] Instead of entering the Strait of Belle Isle, which may have been congested with ice, he turned south and probably landed at Griquet Bay, where he claimed the land for Henry VII. Cabot then sailed southward, probably keeping relatively close to land, both to explore the shoreline and keep track of soundings. Dense fog is common in that part of the world, especially in the morning hours, and he would have navigated by lead and line, following the shore by keeping to a constant depth.

The crew saw timber suitable for masts as well as possible evidence of cultivation and other human activities. They fished for cod, or more accurately gathered them in baskets as they teemed near the surface of the water. The *Matthew* coasted about 1,400 kilometers around Cape Race at Newfoundland's southern end and then into Placentia Bay. There was clear water to the west with no land in sight. Cabot turned back at Placentia and retraced course to his landfall, apparently satisfied that he had found a strait that led to Asia. After a quick return passage of fifteen days before strong westerlies, he landed in Bristol on August 6.

By any standards, Cabot's was a remarkable achievement, attained at minimal cost with respectable and even fast passage times. What is even more remarkable is his uncanny landfall on the northern tip of Newfoundland, achieved after some stormy weather and by latitude sailing along sixty degrees north. Did he know that this particular westerly course would bring him to land? Could it be that he was following in the footsteps of earlier ships to fisheries far richer than those of Iceland and southern Ireland? Given that he set out from Bristol, it's not beyond the realm of possibility that he had verbal sailing directions to take him north and west. We will probably never know for certain.

A delighted Henry VII rewarded Cabot with £10 and an annuity of £20 to be paid from Bristol customs dues. The Milanese envoy, Raimondo de Soncino, conveyed impressions of Cabot and his men to his patron, the Duke of Milan: "They say that the land is excellent and temperate. . . . They assert that the sea there is swarming with fish, which can be taken not only with the net, but in baskets let down with a stone, so that it sinks in the water." He added, "These same English, his companions, say that they could bring so many fish that this kingdom would have no further need of

Iceland, from which place there comes a very great quantity of the fish called stockfish."[9] This may not have been news to a few Bristol merchants.

The Admiral, as people now called him, strutted around as if he were a prince. He promised friars rapid preferment if they sailed with him, gave his companions small islands, and even offered Soncino an archbishopric. But Soncino declined: "The benefices which your Excellency reserves for me are safer. . . . I stay on in this country, eating ten or twelve courses at every meal, and spending three hours at table twice each day, for the love of your Excellency." He was wise to stay home. In early May 1498, Cabot set out on a second voyage, this time with five ships, one outfitted by the king and London merchants, the others by Bristol traders with "coarse cloth, Caps, Laces, points, and other trifles" as gifts for peoples encountered on the way. According to Soncino, Cabot planned to coast westward from Newfoundland until he reached "an island which he calls *Cipango*, situated in the equinoctial region, where he thinks all the spices of the world have their origin." There he would found a trading station that would turn London into a major center of the spice trade. But the expedition ended in disaster. One ship turned back with storm damage; Cabot and the other four disappeared without a trace. According to the historian Polydore Vergil, Cabot "is believed to have found the new lands nowhere but on the very bottom of the ocean."[10]

The momentary flurry of interest in Cabot's voyage was overshadowed by the sensational tidings of fabulous wealth and new lands emanating from Spain and Portugal. Gold from the Indies soon flowed into Spanish coffers. In 1499 one of Portuguese captain Vasco da Gama's ships returned to Lisbon with news of a sea route to India. By 1500 Portuguese and Spanish ships were exploring the riches of South America.

The search for a northern route to Cathay was abandoned, except for an expedition led by an Azorean, João Fernandes. He sailed north and sighted Cape Farewell at the southern tip of Greenland in 1500. He failed to recognize it and gave it the name Tierra del Labrador. A century would pass before the old Norse name was rediscovered and revived. The name

## Salt Cod *(Bacalhau)*

Religious doctrine may have driven the expansion of the international fish trade, but a need to provide hardtack for armies and sailors became a critical foundation of the industry after 1200. Preserved cod was an integral part of naval rations until the eighteenth century. As the Norse discovered centuries earlier, stockfish was light and easily compacted into tight spaces, and it kept well even in humid tropical climates. Sailors may have disliked it, but it was cheap, easy to store, and relatively palatable. When the Newfoundland fisheries came into their own, purchasing agents would await the arrival of laden fishing boats at major ports in the west of England.

King Henry VIII's warship *Mary Rose* sank with all hands off Portsmouth Harbor in July 1545, at a time when the navy was expanding from five ships to over eighty. Only 30 sailors and soldiers out of 700 survived the catastrophe. Over 30,000 fish bones came from the orlop deck and the hold of the ship. Over 90 percent of them were from *Gadus morhua,* fish that had been prepared by beheading before preservation, fish that were about sixty centimeters long after processing. Few of the more than 100 fish in this sample were caught locally. They were imported tax free from Iceland, Ireland, the Scottish Isles, and Newfoundland. How many fish were required for a crew of 700 people is unknown, but one documentary source in the British Museum quotes a requirement of 18,000 salted fish a week for 3,000 men for eight weeks—one piece of unspecified size a day to every four men on the three fish days during the week. Interestingly, the *Mary Rose* wreck contained few eel or herring bones, presumably because cod kept better than saltier fish.

Here's a recipe for salt cod from Newfoundland, which makes *bacalhau* quite palatable.

### *Salt Cod (Bacalhau)*

SERVES 6–8

1½ lb/680 g salt cod
4–5 boiled potatoes, sliced
3 onions, sliced
4 oz/125 ml olive oil
4 hard-boiled eggs
3 garlic cloves
Parsley and black olives for garnish
Black pepper to taste

Preheat oven to 350F/180C.

Soak salt cod overnight. Change the water and boil for 20 to 25 minutes. Flake fish and remove all bones. Heat oil in skillet. Add onion and garlic and sauté for 2 to 3 minutes.

In a greased casserole, layer potatoes, fish, onions, and garlic with the olive oil. Repeat layers if necessary. Arrange sliced egg on top and dot with black olives and parsley. Bake for 10 to 15 minutes, until everything is thoroughly warmed through.

Recipe by Newfoundland Department of Agriculture and Fisheries.

Labrador then passed to eastern Canada. Another Azorean, Gaspar Corte Real, also sailed north in 1500 and sighted a land "that was very cool and with big trees" at about fifty degrees north, almost certainly Newfoundland.[11] On a subsequent voyage in the next year, Real's ship vanished, as did two ships sent out under his brother Miguel in 1502.

Bristol merchants continued to finance discreet westerly voyages—so discreet, unfortunately, that we have no direct record of them. João Fernandes moved to Bristol, where he had trading connections, and formed a syndicate with local traders that made at least one voyage after 1501. According to the chronicler Robert Fabyan, they brought back three "men taken in the Newe-Found Island," who appeared at court despite having the manners of "bruyt bestis," and unintelligible speech.[12] The syndicate's voyage or voyages brought no new discoveries, nor did an alleged voyage by John Cabot's son Sebastian in 1508.[13] Clearly the rocky coasts to the west were part of a hitherto unknown land that lay between Europe and Japan.

Cabot's voyage was a pebble cast in the pond of Bristol's merchant class. In 1502 Hugh Elyot's ship *Gabriel* returned to Bristol with the first recorded cargo of Newfoundland cod. After years of fruitless transatlantic ventures, the patient Elyot earned the huge sum of £180 from the voyage.[14] The ripples from Cabot's discoveries extended far from Britain. News of the incredible riches of the Newfoundland cod fishery spread rapidly through European fishing communities. Word of the new fishing grounds came at a time of population growth and mounting demand for fish for armies, urban customers, and the religious. With cod prices rising steadily, continental merchants were quick to seize on a new opportunity offshore. By 1510 fishing boats manned by Bretons and Normans were fishing the coasts of Terre Neuve—the "new land"—every summer. Over the next four and a half centuries, the brutally tough Newfoundland cod fisheries would generate more wealth in Europe than all the gold of the Indies.

*Gadus morhua* spawns in water less than fifty-five meters deep. Such conditions occur off New England, Maine, Nova Scotia, and Newfoundland.[15]

A vast continental shelf of shallow banks, separated by deeper troughs, extends along the coast of the northeastern United States and Atlantic Canada. Newfoundland's Grand Banks are the shelf's northern and eastern extremity. They consist of a series of submerged plateaus between 36.5 and 185 meters deep that extend for some 730 kilometers along Newfoundland's south coast. Troughs more than 200 meters deep dissect the banks, as do coastal fjords, some bottoming at more than 700 meters. The Labrador Current flows south onto the banks at a rate of about thirty-five kilometers a day, keeping the ocean water cold throughout the year. The much warmer Gulf Stream floods north and east, mingling with colder water from the Labrador coast around the Flemish Cap, a shallow that rises within fifty-one meters of the surface at the far eastern edge of the banks. Beyond this edge, the Atlantic is over 2,000 meters deep.

Nutrients upwelling from the depths supply plentiful food for a variety of fish and shellfish. Light reaches the seabed in shallow areas of the banks, allowing phytoplankton to grow. Lobster and scallops abound; so do capelin, herring, and numerous flatfish, but above all cod and haddock.

The annual cod spawn runs from south to north. Atlantic cod breed in winter in the restricted waters of the Gulf of Maine and somewhat later along the Newfoundland coast, then on the Grand Banks and in the Gulf of St. Lawrence in summer. The eggs float in the upper levels of the ocean, yielding hatchlings that feed on surface-level plankton. Then the young migrate to the bottom, where they reach maturity. Mature fish feed on shellfish, squid, smaller fish, oil cans, jewelry, rope, even boots and clothing.

By the time they become adults, the cod off Newfoundland have three dorsal and two anal fins, a heavy body, and a head that is about a quarter the length of the entire fish. The ones caught today are puny next to those taken from Newfoundland and New England waters in the early days of the fishery, when fish more than a meter long were commonplace, the cod "so thicke by the shoare that we nearlie have been able to row through them. I have killed of them with a pike."[16] The fish caught close inshore off Newfoundland could average between 4.5 and 5.5 kilograms, but adults from the banks were considerably larger, often weighing more than eleven to fifteen kilograms. Fish from the Gulf of Maine were even bigger, in the sixteen-kilogram range. But by the time the known record was set—a ninety-six-kilogram fish over 1.8 meters long caught off Massachu-setts in May 1895—large cod were rare. Adolphe Bellet, describing the Newfoundland cod fisheries, remarked in 1902 that the average weight of the fish taken was "only half the weight of cod caught a century ago. 'Tho their number is still immense, they are evidently diminished. . . . Much fewer are now caught in the same space of time, than there were twenty-five or thirty years ago."[17] The average weight of a Newfoundland cod caught today is under nine kilograms.

Capelin, *Millotus vollosus.*

Cod withdraw to deep water during winter; as the ice retreats, they fol-low the capelin inshore and onto the banks, where they spawn.* Although they prefer waters between zero and thirteen degrees Celsius, they have an-tifreeze nitroglycerins in their blood that permit them to withstand tem-peratures below freezing when inshore in winter. Little is known about their migrations. Many stay in one general location for life, especially south of the Grand Banks. The record for long-distance travel belongs to a cod tagged in the North Sea in June 1957 and caught on the Grand Banks in January 1962 after a journey of about 3,200 kilometers. Recent DNA studies, however, make it clear that the banks cod are largely a different stock even from those living nearer to Newfoundland and Maine.[18]

---

*Capelin *(Mallotus villosus)* are slender fish that prefer cold, deep water but come in-shore to spawn. They are a favored prey for many larger fish, including cod and At-lantic salmon. Highly nutritious, they are caught today for fish meal but are still prized as food in many non-Western cultures.

This, then, was the fishing ground—an offshore bank covering thousands of square kilometers and inshore fisheries around the coast of Newfoundland and the Gulf of St. Lawrence. There were good and bad years, for the movements of *Gadus* can be unpredictable. But the cod were always there, usually in immense numbers—fat, voracious, and easy to catch.

Two fisheries took hold in these waters. The earlier was along the coast of Newfoundland, Cape Breton Island, and the Gulf of St. Lawrence, where the fish were smaller. Here fishers worked during the summer months, from late May or June to early November. The other fishery was farther offshore, on what is now known as the Grand Banks, where Breton and Norman boats almost certainly stopped during the early sixteenth century. Fishing on the banks began before April and moved gradually northward until October, when the season ended. The timing of both Newfoundland fisheries was perfect for the Advent and Lenten fish trade, the catches being landed in Europe by September-October, then shipped out to their final destinations soon afterward.

These migrant fisheries danced to the tune of neither cod nor climate but to the moods and swings of the marketplace back in Europe. Unlike the fur trade far up the St. Lawrence River, which depended on close collaboration with native Americans, the North Atlantic cod trade was entirely in the hands of Europeans, who generally had little contact with Indians. For centuries the fishers were not permanent residents but seasonal visitors. To both the fisherfolk and the merchants who financed them, the Newfoundland fishery was just another element in a complex mosaic of fisheries that fed the devout, the poor, and the military. The journey out and back was longer, stormier, sometimes more dangerous, but the Newe Found Land was still part of the economic, political, and social forces that shaped the European fish trade. It was not a new land at all, but an extension of the old.

The Bretons and Normans who came to Newfoundland waters in the early sixteenth century were long accustomed to fishing off southern Ireland and

Iceland. English fisherfolk had invented the light salting and drying cure while fishing in Icelandic waters. They gutted and split the fish, then salted them for several days before drying them on shore in the sun and wind. These "dry" fish were tastier than the simple dried stockfish of earlier times and fetched a higher price. This type of salting was especially good for moderate- and smaller-size cod, which were not too fat when gutted and thus easier to salt and dry. Lightly salted and dried cod appealed to the English palate and also found a ready market in Spain. In warmer climates, it had the priceless advantage of a longer shelf life than Icelandic stockfish. From the merchants' and fishers' perspective, this type of "dry cod," known to the English as "Poor John" or "Newland fish," required less salt and was cheaper to process. Nor did it need another cure after it crossed the Atlantic. Consequently, dry cod was the first product to emerge from the Newfoundland fisheries.

Newfoundland attracted Bretons and Normans and later Basques and a few Spanish and Portuguese—a polyglot fleet of caravels and naos, North Sea fishing boats, even a few doggers. The fishery was a haphazard affair; all kinds of ports sent one or two ships, or, in the case of Dieppe, considerably more. These waters became part of the enormous migratory fishery that supplied Lenten fare to all of Europe.

At the time of Cabot's voyage, Brittany and Normandy were still recovering from the Hundred Years War, which had ended in 1453 with England losing her last foothold in France. Dieppe and other Norman ports, long major players in the herring trade, were devastated by the war. Recovery was slow and the fish business sluggish, since the English and the Dutch effectively controlled both the North Sea herring trade and the Icelandic cod fisheries. Dieppe herring traveled to Rouen and France, even as far as the pope's table at Avignon. Many boats from ports large and small fished for herring and hake off southern Ireland, where they built salting and drying bases ashore. Despite the Icelandic and Irish landings, the demand for cod continued to expand. Cod also fed the growing navies, which protected the convoys of fishing boats as they returned home with full holds.

Dieppe's financiers and merchants were hungry for new opportunities, and, for all its hazards, the Newfoundland fishery's potential profits were enormous. But not many boats sailed west at first. In 1504 Jean Denys of Honfleur fished the eastern coast of Newfoundland. In 1508–1510, the *La Pensée* of Dieppe and the *La Jacquette* of Plénef under Thomas Aubert fished off the island.[19] Dieppe and Rouen became famous for their influential trading families, who financed and built ships and supported their crews, accepting staggering losses at sea as part of what soon became a highly profitable business. Their greatest asset was their tough seamen bred in some of the most demanding waters in the world.

Anyone who sails the northern French coast must acquire an intimate knowledge of tides and tidal overfalls, sandbanks and narrow channels between rocky outcrops. Before electronic depth sounders and satellites eliminated the guesswork, sailors had to contend with fog, poor visibility, and moonless, calm nights feeling their way with lead and line, a lookout peering into the gloom, straining for a sound of breakers close ahead. I remember once anchoring off the entrance to Brittany's Morlaix River in a thick fog with nine meters of water under our keel at low tide, waiting for the visibility to improve. We had only a general idea of where we were; the tide sluiced under our keel, the anchor chain taut like a piano string. We sat there for two days, unable to move, until welcome rays of sunlight showed the mouth of the river a kilometer away. Like the Labrador and Newfoundland coasts, Brittany and Normandy are not for the timid, which is probably why French mariners flourished in the North Atlantic fishery.

The Bretons had another important advantage in that the climate on the Biscay coast was sunny enough to allow evaporation pans. These produced a grayish salt that was of lesser quality than the white salt from Aveiro, Setubal, or Cadiz Bay, but was ideal for salting fish.

When King Charles VIII (1470–1498) married Anne of Brittany in 1491, her duchy became part of France. As part of the marriage settlement, Charles exempted all Bretons from the *gabelle*, or salt tax. Overnight, Breton fishers gained a significant advantage over their competitors. With tax-free salt at hand, the Newfoundland fisheries became economically viable in a way they would never be for English merchants, who had to import expensive salt from the Continent. Breton ships could load cargoes of top-quality salt from the Guienne area or from the salt pans of the Île de Oléron, then sail directly offshore to the fishing grounds.[20]

As always, the records tell only part of the story, but we know the catch for the French market rose rapidly from virtually nothing. For instance, in 1515 Breton merchant Michel Le Bail sold 17,500 salt codfish in Rouen. Each year, several ships from Terre Neuve discharged Newfoundland stockfish at Norman ports. The French commonly made landfall on Cape Bonavista and often fished the northern parts of the island. Portuguese boats were active along the east coast, but the fishery expanded into the Gulf of St. Lawrence as Jacques Cartier and others explored the mouth of the great river. By the 1530s, fishers from Normandy, Brittany, and western England, as well as Basques, fished both shores of the Strait of Belle Isle, the Gaspé Peninsula in the Gulf of St. Lawrence, Cape Breton Island, and the Madeleine Islands. St. John's Harbor became an important rendezvous point. In August 1527, John Rut of the *Mary of Guildford* reported seeing at various times "eleven sails of the Normans, and one Brittaine, and two Portugall Barkes and all a-fishing."[21]

Only a handful of English ships fished in Newfoundland. The canny Bristol merchants looked closely at the risks involved and turned away. The passage was long and potentially stormy, the rocky coast at the other end beset by fog and ice. Bristol was wealthy on wool and wine, and the Icelandic fisheries through Hull were providing large supplies of cod. As a trading city interested in commodities rather than fishing, Bristol had little incentive to expand into high-risk ventures. Without the potential profits of the spice trade, Bristoleans saw no profit in the business. Nor did they need the insurance of cod cargoes to cover the cost of exploration in the North Atlantic. Closer to home, the fisheries of the western Channel and Ireland boomed in the hands of fishers from the Continent and English Channel ports like Dartmouth, Fowey, and Plymouth.

By midcentury, Cornish and Devonshire fishing boats operated as far away as the North Sea and Dogger Bank. Western fisherfolk had become part of the international fishing industry, a huge network of large and small fishing communities that transcended nationality and religious belief.[22] But the English largely ignored Newfoundland until the 1570s. In 1578 the Bristol merchant Anthony Parkhurst remarked, "The trade that our nation hath to island [Iceland] maketh that the English are not there [in Newfoundland] in such numbers as other nations."[23]

As the population of western England grew and prospered, the demand for fish of all kinds increased. By 1529 Rouen was selling Newfoundland fish to England, and French catches were landed at Exeter and Plymouth, undoubtedly in response to growing demand. Rouen was now the major distribution center for North American fish for towns throughout France. The far tastier Newfoundland cod was giving salted herring a run for its money. The dry fish did not have to be transported in sealed barrels and could be stacked in odd corners, was light enough to be carried easily, and could be used to fill out a cargo of other goods.

The numbers of Breton, Norman, and Basque fishing boats rose dramatically after 1540. By 1542 at least sixty French boats departed for the Grand Banks from Rouen alone. Basque merchants out of San Sebastián and other towns financed whale hunts in the Strait of Belle Isle, leaving artifacts for the twentieth century's remarkable archaeological excavations on shore and underwater at Red Bay, Labrador. Here Basque whale hunters processed their catch on wooden stages at the side of the bay, rendering the blubber in iron cauldrons and then shipping it out in wooden barrels. The Basques also took cod, but they faded from the scene toward the end of the century when whales apparently became scarce.

Most of the ships in the early trade were relatively small, 80 tons or under, but a few were as large as 100, the crew averaging between eighteen and twenty-five men and boys, including a first mate, second mate, surgeon, and carpenter. A flourishing shipbuilding industry developed in Normandy, Bordeaux, and northern Spain in response to a huge increase in transatlantic voyaging. Even in summer, the North Atlantic was a harsh place, with huge seas, icebergs, fog, and ironbound coasts. There were no diesel engines to rescue a fishing boat driven against a lee shore; cloudy skies prevented celestial navigation much of the time; compasses were primitive and unreliable. Even in the best of times, fishing boats did not last long and shipyards were kept busy just replacing existing vessels, quite apart from expansion. Samuel Eliot Morison remarked that shipping losses in the North Atlantic and off Newfoundland between 1530 and 1600 were probably greater than those in World War II.[24] The greatest danger of shipwreck lay close to home, among the rocks and fast-moving tides of the English Channel.

No one knows how many French fishing vessels fished Newfoundland in the years before the English arrived in the 1570s. Anthony Parkhurst, who fished from 1575 to 1578, counted at least 350 boats along the eastern shore of the island in 1577. The archives of Bordeaux, La Rochelle, and Rouen show that by midcentury as many as 150 ships a year set off for the fishery from each town.[25] The rapid expansion of the French presence may have been a consequence of the Council of Trent, which tightened church discipline in the face of a rising tide of Protestantism.[26] A half century after it became widely known, the Newfoundland fishery was an enormous European industry, equal to the entire Spanish trade with the Americas.

## PART FOUR

# HARVEST AND SETTLEMENT

I believe . . . that the cod fishery, the herring fishery, the pilchard fishery, the mackerel fishery and probably all the great sea fisheries are inexhaustible; that is to say, that nothing we do seriously affects the numbers of the fish. And any attempt to regulate the fisheries seems consequently, from the nature of the case to be useless.

Thomas Henry Huxley[1]

## 15

# THE MIGRANT FISHERY

> In Newfoundland as nowhere else can one be made to feel the
> contrast between a land that is infinitely silent, motionless,
> poor in vegetation, above all poor in its variety of living crea-
> tures, and a sea which harbors every form of life.
>
> Robert Perret[1]

To sixteenth-century Europeans, Newfoundland was the place cod came
from. Information about the island and the fisheries was hard to come by.
Those who fished or whaled these waters learned the sailing directions,
the best bays, and the key fishing spots by word of mouth, passed from
one skipper to the next.

Fishing boats swarmed around the mouth of a wide river leading into the
heart of an enormous continent. When French historian Marc Lescarbot
wrote his *Histoire de la Nouvelle France* in 1609, he said little about Newfoundland. But popular sentiment was changing. His third edition, dedi-
cated to King Louis XIII in 1619, devoted more attention to the island,
which "hath long time supported by her fish the whole of Europe alike on
sea and on land." Lescarbot added that sailors from throughout Europe "find
excellent mines in the depths of the waters. . . . Let this much be said in passing with regard to Newfoundland, which though thinly inhabited and in a
cold climate, is yet visited by a great number of people who yearly pay their
homage from further afield than is done to the greatest Kings of the earth."[2]

Fishing might be big business, but it was not a prestigious industry. Fishers were lowly men who enjoyed none of the glamour of the gold and fur

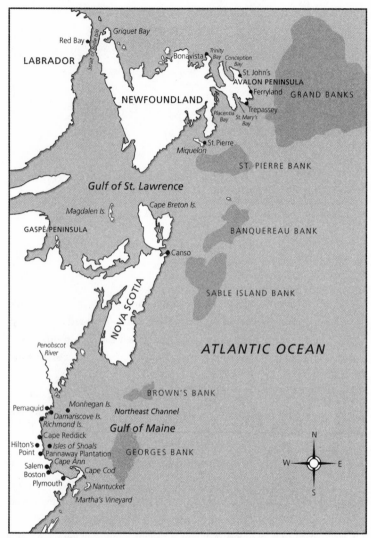

Fishing banks off Newfoundland, Nova Scotia, and New England.

trades. Those who ate cod and used train oil for leather work and other purposes cared nothing about Newfoundland; nor did the thousands of bankers, fishers, merchants, shipbuilders, and victuallers who were engaged in the cod trade. Few people appreciated the growing economic power of an industry that was worth as much as all the gold transported laboriously from the Indies.

By the time the English joined the action, the cycle of the fisheries was well established. The fleets departed between February and April, with many English boats heading to Portugal to load salt before sailing across the Atlantic. The passage took about five weeks, bringing most ships to Newfoundland by April or May. Everyone returned home in August or September. So-called sack ships, the Dutch-, French-, or Spanish-owned trading vessels sent to Newfoundland to pick up cargoes of salted fish, departed later, for there was no cod to load until July or August.

In every sense, Newfoundland was a natural extension of the Irish and Icelandic fisheries. Nowhere do you see this more clearly than in the lives of the fishermen. They were true migrant workers, part-time farmers or shepherds, carpenters or cobblers who left their families for months at a time to fish. They moved from fishery to fishery as readily as a modern-day Mexican farm laborer travels north for the California vegetable and grape harvests. One year they might go to Iceland, then to Ireland, then perhaps three years running to Newfoundland before returning to Iceland. Many of them owned farms, herds of animals, and real estate. Their fishing generated maybe £20 to £30 a year in extra income. The economist Lewes Roberts aptly remarked in 1638, "Their lives may be compared to the Otter, which [is] spent halfe on lande and halfe in Sea."[3]

All of this activity had no economic impact on Newfoundland, which had no permanent European settlement, or on its sparse Native American population.

The big growth in the cod industry came in the 1540s, when increasing numbers of French boats crossed the Atlantic each year.[4] The Spanish Basques were a significant presence, but the Portuguese were minor players, preoccupied instead with their southern ventures and other fishing grounds such as the Cape Verde Islands. Few English ships engaged in the fishery until the Reformation and the signing of a treaty of reconciliation between the major Catholic powers, France and Spain, in 1559. A new balance of power emerged in Europe, with the main conflict now existing between the Protestant north and the Catholic south. Over the next half century, Philip II of Spain placed onerous demands on Portuguese and Spanish Basque fisherfolk by requisitioning their ships for cargo work and also for his great Armada against England in 1588. At the same time, the number of whales in the Strait of Belle Isle declined, perhaps from overhunting and perhaps as a result of climatic change during one of the climaxes of the Little Ice Age; we do not know. Even inshore cod catches fell, prompting a greater emphasis on the wet fishery of the Grand Banks. By the early 1600s, the number of Spanish Basque ships in the Terre Neuve cod and whale fisheries had fallen to about half a dozen on account of royal demands for seamen and shipping.

The English soon displaced everyone except the French. England's maritime star was on the rise, while Spain's was in decline. English involvement in the fisheries rose dramatically to 100 boats in 1592 and 250 in 1615—a year, a government return tells us, that yielded 300,000 quintals of cod.* The number of boats was not the whole story; the business now involved at least 6,000 people, most of them ashore in England—rope makers and shipwrights, merchants and fish processors, the extended support network needed to maintain a long-distance fishery.[5] Western ports such as Dartmouth and Plymouth were now major players in the trade; Newfoundland dominated Dartmouth's economic life for two and a half centuries. Great-power politics began to cross the ocean as well. In 1585 Bernard Drake, one of Elizabeth I's privateers, was diverted from a trip to

---

*Fish yields were often quoted in quintals, a unit of fifty-one kilograms, about 120 dry fish.

the Roanoke colony in what is now Virginia and ordered to sail to New-foundland to warn the ships there not to sail directly to Spain, following Philip's sudden embargo on all English ships within his domains.[6] Drake attacked a convoy of twenty Portuguese fishing and treasure ships and brought more than half of them back to England as prizes.

The Protestant Reformation took hold in 1517 at Wittenburg, Germany, after Martin Luther's famous protest. The tidal streams of theological dissent permanently reshaped England when King Henry VIII challenged the authority of the Catholic Church with an eye to acquiring the vast wealth of the Church and its religious foundations. Elizabeth I steered a more cautious path but prevailed over the Spanish Armada in 1588. With the Reformation, Europe became home to both Protestants and Catholics. Britain, the Low Countries, Scandinavia, and large parts of Germany and Switzerland formed a Protestant enclave where Catholic doctrines, including dietary teachings, were no longer strictly followed.

The Reformation was affected by the unpredictable climatic fluctuations that defined the height of the Little Ice Age. The Armada succumbed in large part to hurricane-force winds in the North Sea. A series of exceptionally cold winters descended on Britain and the Continent, causing widespread suffering. Elizabeth I found herself struggling to feed her people, especially the burgeoning urban poor. A Tudor monarch's greatest fear was food shortages, for political stability depended on there being enough to eat. Fish provided one answer to a poor harvest, but with people increasingly disregarding the ancient rules of the Church, salted herring and cod were hardly favored foods. But religious wars on land and sea and exploding international commerce meant that salted herring and stockfish were vital staples for soldiers, sailors, and cargo ships. A shortfall in preserved fish of any kind would have had serious economic, political, and social consequences. The Tudors cast around for ways to encourage fishing.

Though they eliminated many popish trappings, Martin Luther and his fellow Protestants did not dispense with fish on Fridays and during Lent.

Meat was in short supply during the late sixteenth century, so "Fysshe Days" and the observance of Lent were strictly enforced as a stimulus for the fishing industry. In 1548 Parliament made Saturday another meatless day, "considering that due and godly abstinence is a means to virtue and to subdue men's bodies to their soul and spirit, and considering, also specially that fishers . . . may thereby be rather set to work, and that by eating of fish much flesh shall be saved."[7] King Edward VI issued a stern proclamation on February 13, 1552, recalling the 1548 act: "No person, or persones should after a certaine time willingly, or unwittingly eate any kinds of fleshe upon any Fridaie, Saterdaie, any day within the time of Lent, nor at any such other day, as was at that time, or should be at any time afterwards, comonly accepted . . . under divers penalties." The act had been flouted "by divers and many fearelesse subjectes, most disobediently and stubbernely, infringed, broken, and neglected . . . His maiestie hauvng due consideration of the great scarcetie of victual, especially of fleshe, that is grown within this realme." Edward ordered tavern- and innkeepers not to sell meat for consumption on holy days or during Lent. No butcher was to sell any "fleshe . . . being dead, within his said Realm, or Domains." The mayors of cities and towns, also Justices of the Peace and Sheriffs, must comply or risk "his hynesse displeasure, and indignation, & will further answer at their peril." Offenders were to be sentenced to "emprisonment, there safe and surely to be kept, & remain, and & further to be punished."[8]

In 1563 Secretary of State Cecil advocated "the strictest observance of fish days, for policy's sake so the sea-coasts will be strong with men and habitations and the fleet flourish more than ever."[9] Cecil even tried to get Wednesday accepted as a third fish day, a move that would have made half the year meatless. His reasoning was secular, not religious—to save on beef consumption and maintain skilled manpower for a growing navy. The measure failed.

Efforts to enforce fish on Friday continued. On January 24, 1607, King James I issued a proclamation that resulted from disorders in London the previous Lent, during which "much flesh was killed and eaten." Licensed butchers now had to account to mayors and the Privy Council for exactly how much was slaughtered and sold. Offenders were to be imprisoned and the meat they tried to sell given to the poor. All inns and eating places, as well as "Victuallers, Alehouse keepers, and Taverners," were to post bonds of up to £100 and sureties of £30 to ensure they sold no flesh on holy days, except to those allowed it by license or through sickness. All such establishments would be inspected regularly; officials were to be posted at city gates to monitor loads brought from the country into town. "And for that it is to be doubted that the fishmongers, upon the obseruation of the said Orders, will take occasion to inhuate the prices as well of fresh as well as Sea fish, it is thought meete that the Lord Maior shall take order with the sayd fishmongers, that as well the falt as fresh fish shall be uttered at reafonable prices."[10]

In 1621 James I issued another proclamation against meat eating during Lent and on fish days, noting that "the reasons now assigned for this injunction are for the maintenance of our navy and shipping, a principal strength of this island, and for the sparing and increase of fresh victuals."[11] Inevitably the Puritans condemned such proclamations as the "rags of Rome." Lent's forty days were put in abeyance by government decree and remained so until after Oliver Cromwell's death in 1658, when there was another attempt to institute three fish days a week and enforce Lent. The diarist Samuel Pepys, high in the councils of Charles II's government, wrote on February 14, 1661, "The talk of the town . . . is whether Lent shall be kept with the strictnesse of the King's proclamation, which is thought cannot be, because of the poor, who cannot buy fish."[12] Pepys resolved to eat no meat during Lent but wrote some days later, "I did eat fish this Lent, but am resolved to eat as little as I can," this for "a want of other victuals." The king's initiative came to naught.

Generations of monarchs had understood the fisheries as the nursery for the navy. By the seventeenth century, however, the North Atlantic harbored no undiscovered fisheries, and, in any case, agricultural innovations in the Netherlands and England had transformed the food supply situation. Thanks to cold-tolerant crops such as turnips, new cattle and sheep farming practices, and land reclamation, England was self-sufficient in food by the late seventeenth century. The population as a whole turned away from fish toward meat, but this was not enough to kill the cod trade.

French fishers supplied the needs of their markets with wet cod from the Banks, even after the Council of Trent tightened church discipline. Meanwhile, the English now exported nearly all their lightly salted dry cod to the Catholic countries of the south, where Lenten doctrine was still all-important. Cod and herring were also popular in Spain as alternatives to expensive meat. Markets in Seville sold fish at prices that were competitive with those for bread and beans. In Valladolid, over 160 kilometers inland from the Galician coast, fish was cheaper than meat. Dried cod was somewhat more expensive than other fish, but many artisans and shopkeepers ate it regularly. Lightly salted cod was tastier than the saltier "wet" product and kept better in hot environments.[13] By 1620 only 10 percent of the landed cod remained in England. The rest went to Iberia and the Mediterranean, much of it in the holds of sack ships, which collected the processed cod from Newfoundland and sailed direct to the waiting market.

English fishing boats specialized in the sedentary dry cod fishery close inshore, where less salt was required. The economist Lewes Roberts wrote of summer seas that abounded "with Fish in such an abundance that a man may take in an houres space a hundred great Fishes." He described how the fishers would arrive about mid-April, "unrigge their shippes, set up booths and cabanets on the shore in diverse creeks and harbours, and there with fishing provisions and salt, begin their fishing in Shallops and Boats, continue it until September." Once the cold weather came, they would rerig their ships and return home. "They returne contented to their Families; where oftentimes in Winter they merrily spend what in Summer they have painfully fisht for."[14]

Roberts wrote his book over a century after the routine of the dry cod fishery had come into being. It was little changed over the years. Much of this fishery was on the east coast of Newfoundland, Placentia, and the Gaspé Peninsula, where boats assembled every spring when the weather grew mild. The skippers tended to return to the same sheltered bays year after year, where they knew the local waters and the most prolific fishing spots. In time, a custom developed that the first skipper there was the

Processing cod in the inshore fishery. An eighteenth-century drawing that reflects technology and facilities little changed from the early days of the fishery. FROM DUHAMEL DU MONCEAU, *TRAITÉ*, 1769.

"admiral" of the bay for the season, with a choice of the best spots for fishing and for drying racks, known as "flakes." Fierce races across the Atlantic ensued as the westbound ships vied to be the first to anchor. At first the ships were relatively small, with a seventy-ton vessel costing about £200 to build and equip, and carrying a crew of twenty-four, only half of them seamen. But as the fishery became more efficient, the boats grew larger—up to 300 tons with crews of 150, including carpenters, caulkers, and fish processors. A priest and two surgeons shipped out on many larger boats. The mother ship carried longboats, prefabricated at home and then assembled on the beach. In a good season the boat would sell much of its catch to sack ships in Newfoundland, then bring home a full load itself, perhaps as many as 800 quintals being disposed of at the fishery in midseason. The sack ships were purely merchant vessels, so named after the cargoes of wine, or "sack," that they carried back to northern Europe after delivering their fish consignments to Spain, Portugal, or the Mediterranean. Many of them were smaller than the fishing boats they served and thus vulnerable to the pirates of southern Europe, who preyed on them mercilessly for generations.[15]

A shallop—a stout, double-ended rowboat used for fishing and ferrying people to shore—had a crew of five men, two of whom manned the drying stages ashore.* Directly on arrival, the crew would unrig the ships, assemble the prefabricated shallops, then spend two or three weeks building or repairing the cabins, landing stages, and drying flakes that were the shore side infrastructure of the fishery.[16] Sometimes there was little to build on from the previous year. At the end of each season, many crews dismantled the flakes and cabins to use as firewood on the return voyage. Native Americans then moved in and pulled what remained of the iron nails. Still, the fishers generally rebuilt on the same sites, next to gravel or sand beaches or near rock outcrops where they could erect wooden flakes for drying the catch.

The actual fishing lasted six to eight weeks. Every day except Sunday, the boats would leave at dawn. Each carried a crew of three men, a boat master, a midshipman, and a foreshipman, the last usually a fourteen- to sixteen-year-old boy learning the trade. They would row or sometimes sail to spots where cod congregated. Such fishing required an intimate knowledge of the habits of the prey. During the summer cod feed on crustaceans, capelin, and other small fish, plankton feeders. Plankton is most abundant where the south-flowing Labrador Current meets Newfoundland's promontories and islands—exactly where the fishers built their processing stations. Once at a prolific location, the boat either anchored or drifted with the current and wind. The crew would man lines set on each side of the boat, usually baited with mackerel, the paired hooks being set about two meters above the seabed where the cod fed. They would jig the lines, feeling for a bite, then haul the cod in rapidly

---

*Shallops (or *chaloupe,* the French word) varied considerably from one fishery to another. They were up to nine meters long and sometimes shipped across the Atlantic in prefabricated form to assemble at the fishery. Most illustrations show them with high bows and transom sterns, with carvel planking. Five thwarts accommodated rowers, with space between them called "rooms" for fish, especially amidships. A fully laden shallop could hold between 500 and 600 cod. Some were sailed with a sprit rig, the hull treated with a mixture of turpentine and linseed oil. At the end of the season, they were either hidden in the forest or even sunk with boulders for recovery the next year.

and cast it in the bottom boards. Nothing had changed from the Icelandic fishery; the men fished with the same crude iron hooks and lead weights in use for centuries. The fish were so abundant that nothing more elaborate was needed. This medieval fishing technology persisted until the twentieth century.

Fishing continued until late afternoon or until the boat was fully loaded, often with 1,000 fish. Then the crew rowed back to base, a journey that could take an hour or more. At the dock the boat master and midshipman would unload the catch while the foreshipman made the crew's dinner. At this point the catch became the responsibility of the shoremen, who "made" the fish.

As soon as the fish landed on the wharf, boys would lay them on a table, where a shoreman known as the header would gut and decapitate the fish with lightning speed. He threw the livers into a nearby train oil vat, where they fermented into oil in the sun. Another member of the team, the splitter, stood across the table. He split the gutted fish and removed the backbone in a matter of seconds. Some could split as many as "24 score in half an hour," or a fish every four seconds or even faster.[17] Then came the salting, which required expert judgment, since too much salt would burn the fish. The Plymouth ship's surgeon James Yonge, describing the dry fishery in the 1660s, wrote that an excess of salt caused the fish to break, while "wet, too little makes it redshanks, that is look red when dried, and so is not merchantable."[18] This initial salting stabilized the fish, giving time for drying, at the cost of a slight loss of quality.

The cod spent a few days on the salt pile before the shoremen washed them in salt water and then piled them on a platform of stones called a horse. A few days later, they laid out the fish to dry on a pebble beach or on flakes covered with birch bark or fir branches. The gutted fish were heavy, so the flakes were positioned as close to the shore as possible. Every night or in wet weather, the shoremen piled up the fish in covered heaps or turned them skin side up. The cool, windy conditions of the typical Newfoundland summer were ideal for drying lightly salted cod. On hot days extraordinary precautions were taken to guard against burning the fish, and on rainy ones, the fish were hastily covered. After four or five days of good drying, the fish could be stacked in large, layered piles of as many as 1,500 carcasses.

## NEWFOUNDLAND COD CAKES

The Newfoundland cod fishery was established just as demand for fish of all kinds exploded, coming from growing markets in Mediterranean countries where Catholicism was still deeply entrenched, and from the military in an era of endemic warfare. The victualling requirements of naval ships rapidly became standardized, for the authorities knew that fish were not a catch but a commodity of relatively standardized size and weight, even if formal victualling requirements did not come into use until about 1550. In 1565 one naval victualler was contracted to supply 400 grams (¾ lb) stockfish a week. Samuel Pepys of diary fame recorded a victualling contract of 1677 that called for ⅛ of a 60-centimeter (24-inch) North Sea (probably beheaded) cod for each man on Wednesday, Friday, and Saturday, about the same size as the cod eaten on the *Mary Rose* just over a century earlier. Some of the people aboard the doomed warship took hand lines wound around wooden frames with them, to supplement the monotony of fish days with fresh catches.

Fish days would have involved salted fish as well as biscuits, beer, peas, and mustard. Lenten meals, maintained under a Protestant regime probably to encourage the fish industry, were monotonous and often tasteless.

Fish cakes were a convenient way of cooking oddments of fish. They are as old as fisheries. Here's a Newfoundland example.

### ✀ *Newfoundland Cod Cakes*

SERVES 6 TO 8

2¼ lbs/1 kg cod fillets
½ oz/15 ml butter, melted
1 tsp/5 ml salt
Paprika to taste
Generous pinch of garlic powder
1 oz/30 g onion, finely chopped
2 large eggs
4 oz/125 ml potato flakes (or mashed potatoes)
1¾ oz/50 g flour
3 oz/85 ml milk

Poach the cod fillets, then flake and cool. Combine with the other ingredients, form into small patties, and fry about 4 minutes per side. Serve with mustard or applesauce.

Recipe by the Newfoundland Department of Agriculture and Fisheries.

Careful stacking was crucial to the quality of the final product. The work never ended, and everyone had to sleep in small wooden cabins close to the flakes. Apart from actual cod fishing, several boats also had to catch capelin or herring for use as bait, using seine nets set at night.

The fishing stopped in late July or early August; drying continued some weeks longer. This was when the sack ships arrived to collect their cargoes, departing a few days later for ports in Spain and the Mediterranean. Meanwhile the fishers rerigged the ships, loaded them with barrels of train oil, and topped off their holds with wet-cured cod caught too late in the season for drying. Once in England, the fish were recured and sold at a discount. The fishing boats usually sailed direct for home, sometimes with extra migrant fishers as passengers. The average catch per fisher was about forty quintals, about ten tons of fish per person a year.

The English cod fishery enjoyed a sustained boom from the late sixteenth century into the 1720s, with annual catches that may have been around 75,000 tons.[19] This figure was rarely exceeded later in the century. Yet cod stocks were inconsistent. For instance, 1592 was a bad year in both Newfoundland and English Channel waters. The cause was probably not overfishing but climate. The decades of the 1670s to 1690s saw some extremely harsh winters on both sides of the Atlantic. The waters around Iceland, Norway, and the Faeroes became so cold that the cod fisheries failed as the fish moved to warmer water.[20] Newfoundland cod stayed put, for the island and outlying Banks are not at the northern limits of the *Gadus* range, but local temperature changes must have affected their reproduction and their food supply. During the summer that ubiquitous copepod, *Calanus finmarchicus*, grazes near the surface on phytoplankton over the Grand Banks and closer inshore. The minute species attracts millions of cod, but the numbers fluctuate from year to year, falling when the North Atlantic Oscillation is in low mode and the Labrador Current slows, increasing dramatically when the index is high.

Fishers everywhere were accustomed to fluctuations in the catch from year to year, but long-term reductions in fish stocks could have profound economic and social effects. Wars also interrupted the seasonal rhythms of the fishery. As the London merchant John Paige remarked in 1655, "Men being afraid of wars . . . will not adventure upon such a perishing commodity in such uncertain times."[21] The ebb and flow of bad weather years, which affected curing rather than fishing, and the prices of fish relative to other foods were only two of the complex factors that affected the migratory fishery. For all these vicissitudes, the cod fishery was remarkably stable financially. Prices fell in war years but remained level throughout the seventeenth century, when prices of other American goods, like wheat, sugar, and tobacco, fell.

The inshore fishery was by no means confined to the English, who fished the so-called English shore, a stretch of about 230 kilometers from the Bonavista region to Trepassey in the south. Further south lay the French fisheries, from St. Mary's and Placentia Bay into the Gulf of St. Lawrence. The scale of French fishing in Newfoundland was enormous, involving as many as 10,000 men and some 420 vessels averaging ninety tons each.[22]

Many French boats never landed but fished on the banks offshore, exploiting a different cod stock. Their move offshore reduced some of the intense competition in the inshore fishery.

The banks rhythm was even more frenetic, with many boats making two trips a year, sailing in February and then in April. Just crossing to the banks was hazardous because of fog and icebergs. Captains sailed west across the Atlantic at about forty-eight degrees latitude until they reached shallower water in a depth of sixty to 100 meters, found by constant use of the lead and line, a technique that needed fine judgment in the foggy and stormy conditions that so often afflicted the Banks, especially in late winter.

The French used a "green" cure, in which the fish were heavily salted and left wet in the ship's hold. Wet-cured fish were preferred in the French market but unpopular in Spain and the Mediterranean, and consequently three-quarters of the catch went to Paris.

While crossing, the crew would build a special gallery for line fishing along one side of the boat. There they lashed barrels to the deck for the men to stand as they fished, the tops stuffed with straw to protect them from the lethal hooks. Each man wore a leather apron that came up to his

French cod fishers on the Grand Banks in the eighteenth century. (1) The ship, showing the stages, fishing barrels, and holds; (2) gutting the fish; (3) stacking and salting the catch. From Duhamel du Monceau, *Traité*, 1769).

chin and a broad-brimmed hat; he controlled eight to twelve weighted lines about 160 meters long, with different forms of iron hook, one to each line, baited with salted herring or cod guts. The boat drifted with the wind on the starboard (right) side, with just enough sail set to maintain helm control. The fishers jigged the lines at intervals until they got a bite. Then they hauled in the fish, taking hold of the lead first to protect their hands. Behind the fishers, a header and a dresser, also in barrels, seized the fish, lopped off the head, cut out the highly valued tongue, then gutted and cut the body into pieces, throwing it into the hold below. There a salter dressed in canvas laid the fish in thick salt. The cod remained there for twenty-four to forty-eight hours before final stowage, the average catch being about 100–120 cod per man per day.[23]

Banks fishing was brutally hard work with no breaks, even on the roughest days. Regardless of the air temperature, the damp penetrated and chilled every pore. The ship rocked constantly whether anchored or under sail. The crew, usually about fifteen to twenty men and boys, lived in close quarters, where tempers could easily flare, and subsisted on a coarse diet of biscuits, peas, lard, chickens, dried cod, and eggs. Wine and brandy were provided and were undoubtedly necessary. The French novelist Pierre Loti caught the mind-numbing repetitiveness of the fisheries brilliantly in his novel *An Icelandic Fisherman*: "It was not long, for no sooner had they thrown their lines than they lifted them, heavy with shimmering, steel-gray fish. Again and again the live cod were drawn up. Rapid, incessant was this silent fishery." A vast cod shoal passed around and under the boat. "In thirty hours they had caught more than a thousand large cod. At last their strong arms were wearied and they fell asleep. Their bodies alone kept vigil and, of their own volition, carried on the action of fishing, while their minds floated in blissful unconsciousness."[24]

The French were virtually alone in the banks fishery until 1713, when English boats joined them after England and France signed a peace treaty.

For all its abundant marine life, Newfoundland was an unattractive place for permanent settlement. The subarctic winters were far harsher than those in Europe. There were no minerals, nor were the soils exceptionally fertile. The only reason to settle there was the cod. On the face of it, however, that proposition was an attractive one. One could fish year-round, there was a steady market across the Atlantic, and the profits would pay for goods needed to sustain a settlement. Furthermore, the so-called fishing rooms of the migratory fishers could be displaced by establishing permanent settlements with better facilities.

Before 1600 few Europeans overwintered in Newfoundland except involuntarily.[25] The Newfoundland Company, founded by a group of London and Bristol merchants, backed a settlement under merchant John Guy at Cuper's (or Cupid's) Cove in Conception Bay in 1610. The company charter said that the investors wanted to "secure and make safe the trade of fishing." The security the gentlemen dreamed of may have been that of a monopoly. In any event, the tiny colony, harassed by the notorious pirate John Easton, failed to yield the expected profits, partly because many of the settlers were reluctant to fish. Excavations at the site have revealed part of a seventeenth-century wooden house with a massive stone fireplace, also fragments of smoking pipes, glassware, and coarse English earthenware.[26] The principal investors sold their shares to others, who went on to found successor colonies in the 1620s. A few people continued to reside in the cove long after subsidies from England ended. St. John's was probably settled at about this time; there is archaeological evidence of harbor improvements there by 1665.

The best-documented settlement is Ferryland, colonized by Sir George Calvert in 1621 after King James I granted him title to much of the Avalon Peninsula south of St. John's. Calvert was a wealthy man who entrusted his settlement at Ferryland to managers and did not move there until 1627, when he reverted to Catholicism and became Lord Baltimore.[27] After two years he lobbied for a colony in the warmer Chesapeake River area and departed in 1629, leaving behind him some thirty fisherfolk—among the first permanent European settlers of what is now Canada. By 1630 some 200 Europeans lived in Newfoundland during the winter.

Ferryland was intended as a profit-making enterprise, and Calvert's abandonment was probably motivated by the colony's failure to yield adequate returns on investment. In fact, it was hard for a permanent settlement to compete with the seasonal fishing fleet. The overheads were higher because of the costs of overwintering, and it was difficult to market catches from outside the established trading system. Commercial interests in Europe opposed the idea of a permanent fishery, even if their opposition was not as strong as sometimes claimed. Another settlement scheme, Sir David Kirke's Newfoundland Plantation, took over Ferryland in the late 1630s. Kirke set out to fill potentially profitable niches in the migratory fishery such as boatkeeping and other services. The plantation petered out under his arbitrary leadership, which included trying to collect taxes from visiting fishing boats. Those who remained established themselves in sheltered bays where the migrant fishers came, appropriated fishing rooms, and tapped into the transatlantic connections of a resident merchant.[28]

Until now, the destiny of the Newfoundland fishery had lain in the hands of private fishing interests from England's West Country. Bankers and merchants had developed the cod trade as part of the jigsaw of European fisheries stretching from the Baltic to the Levant. The fishing admirals and captains in Newfoundland bays had maintained a rough-and-ready command over the fisheries. For generations, they had handled things in their own way without interference from inquiring officials or royal charters. Having learned their lessons in England, they associated government interest with restriction and regulation. There's an oddly modern ring to this attitude.

But times were changing. During the seventeenth century, dispute after dispute flared between West Country fishing interests and the Crown—over regulation of the trade, over prohibitions on foreign ships carrying English catches, and over the rights of migratory fishers and settlers. In 1634 complaints of disorder and violence in Newfoundland forced King Charles I to confront the issue of whether the island would remain a simple fishing base or become a fortified colony governed by civil authority. In the end, the white flesh of *Gadus morhua* dragged the Crown into Newfoundland. The importance of cod as a strategic commodity and the overwhelming significance of the fishery as a nursery for seamen overrode the demands of religious devotion. Newfoundland's seemingly inexhaustible cod stocks supported the army and navy and had become a priceless strategic commodity. The safety of fishing boats and their crews was thus a national concern. The king issued a Western Charter in 1634, proclaiming that "the Region of the Country called Newfoundland hath been acquired to the Dominion of our Progenitors." The island now came under English law, with a series of regulations that prescribed punishments for murder and other offenses, and also ordered that "devine service . . . bee said by some of the Masters of the Shippes or some others." [29] Newfoundland was now under the protection of British law.

# 16

# "Great Store of Cod-Fish"

Then there were cast out 3 or 4 more [hooks], and the fish was so plentifull and so great, as when our Captaine would haue set saile, we all desired him to suffer them to take fish a while, because we were so delighted to see them catch so great fish, so fast as the hooke came downe . . . one of the Mates with two hookes at a lead at fiue draughts together hauled vp tenne fishes; all were generally very great, some they measured to be fiue foot long, and three foot about.

John Rosier[1]

In 1545 a Frenchman named Pierre Crignon wrote of a "Land of Norumbega" that lay south of the Gulf of St. Lawrence. "Beyond Cape Breton is a land contiguous to that cape, the coast of which travels south-southwest-ward toward the land called Florida, and for a good 500 leagues. . . . The inhabitants of this country are docile people, friendly, peaceful. The land overflows with every kind of fruit; there grow the wholesome orange and the almond, and many sorts of sweet-smelling trees."[2]

We owe Norumbega to the gentleman explorer Giovanni da Verrazzano, who had visited a spot on Maine's Penobscot River in 1524 that he named Oranbega, a corruption of "norumbega," the local word for a quiet place between two rapids. Verrazzano had enthused about the "goodliest people" and fertile soils of Narragansett Bay in New England, but he noted Oranbega merely as a pleasant spot. A picturesque location soon became a golden kingdom situated on a mighty river protected by reefs and islands. Upstream lay a city with "clever inhabitants and a mass of peltries of all kinds of beasts . . . The people use many words that sound like Latin and worship the sun, and they are fair people and tall."[3]

Norumbega was a myth created by the evergreen lure of gold and untold wealth just over the horizon. An English sailor, David Ingram, set ashore with two others on the Gulf Coast of Florida in 1567 and succeeded in walking northward to the Maine coast along Indian trails. It took him two years. Carried back to England by a French ship, he made a living thereafter in taverns telling stories of his journey. He waxed especially lyrical about Norumbega, telling of a "towne halfe a myle longe" with streets broader than those in London, where men wore nothing but skins and hoops of gold and silver on their arms and legs, also pearls, "divers of them as big as one's thumb." Women wore plates of gold like armor and ornaments as elaborate as the men's. Norumbega had a "great abundance of gold, sylver and pearl"; Ingram told of finding nuggets as big as his fist in springs and small water courses.[4]

Through some ten years of lucrative pub crawls, Ingram embroidered his story sufficiently to attract official interest. England laid claim to Norumbega in about 1587 on the basis of Cabot's voyages. By then, English and French fishing boats were catching cod on Maine's banks, with little interest in what lay ashore. The adventurer Sir Humphry Gilbert planned a colony in the heart of Norumbega, sending out two reconnaissance ships in 1579–1580. Though they found no traces of a golden city, one of them returned with reports of a silver mine (actually it was sparkling mica) and a sample of deer and moose hides. In 1604 the French explorer Samuel de Champlain sailed to the limit of navigation on the Penobscot River at the site of present-day Bangor, Maine. He found no traces of a golden city and wrote, "I am convinced that the greater part of those who mention it never saw it, and speak of it only by hearsay. . . . That anyone ever entered the river is unlikely, or they would have described it differently." Champlain also produced the first maps of the New England coast and offlying banks. Norumbega promptly vanished from the stage and now survives, as Samuel Eliot Morison reminds us, only as "a favorite name for hills, yachts, and villas."[5]

But Norumbega—the name was officially changed to Virginia in 1606—had another powerful attraction: the extraordinary bounty of its cod fisheries, which astounded everyone who sailed along the coast. "All the fish of what kinde soever we tooke, were well fed, fat and sweet in taste," wrote English chronicler James Rosier while anchored off Allen Island, Maine, in 1605.[6] Rosier and his fellow crew members had never sailed in such rich waters. Apart from cod, they saw pods of whales, swarms of herring and salmon, tuna, and mackerel. Great mud flats yielded luscious clams as well as extensive shoals rich harvests of mussels and oysters. Huge flocks of seabirds flew overhead, among them puffins and terns. Tastiest of all, flightless great auks crowded rocky headlands and islets.[7]

The Gulf of Maine is a remarkably fertile marine oasis, extending from the banks of Nantucket and Cape Cod in the south to Nova Scotia 725 kilometers to the north. Hundreds of islands lie off the craggy, deeply indented coastline.

This deep bay is bounded to the east by the submerged masses of the Georges and Brown's Banks, which separate the Gulf of Maine from the open Atlantic. Only two channels of any depth connect the Gulf with the ocean. One of them, the Northeast Channel, is only thirty-five kilometers wide. The two great banks deflect tides and currents while providing a vast area of shallow, sunlit seabed for fish and plants. More than sixty rivers fertilize the gulf's waters with billions of liters of nutrient-rich freshwater. Some of the world's most powerful tides sweep through, stirring up and mixing the water, keeping the nutrients suspended in its well-lit surface levels.

The same tides fashioned huge expanses of estuaries, salt marshes, mudflats, and shallows where sea life abounded. Caviar-laden sturgeon swam up the larger rivers, some of them weighing 180 kilograms or more. Alewives, shad, and salmon crowded rivers and streams in spring and fall. But the great attraction lay close inshore and on the banks—incredible quantities of large, well-fed cod, haddock, and halibut. The commercial potential was extraordinary.

You only have to ghost slowly through a Maine summer fog to know what the cod fishers experienced. Sailors have come close enough to the beach to set dogs barking on shore without ever glimpsing land. I've drifted along in these fogs, peering out for shadowy marks, for rocky outcrops that appear momentarily in the pervasive gloom. At least we had a reliable diesel engine under our feet to carry us out of trouble, as well as depth sounders, navigation markers, and a GPS receiver to keep us in safe water. The cod boats had none of these tools, not even charts. They sailed at the mercy of currents and the wind, guided solely by their skippers' experience. But somehow fishing boats from several nations coasted southward from Newfoundland during the sixteenth century.

These pioneers, perhaps ahead of Verrazzano, felt their way slowly through the offshore banks with lead and line, most likely during the summer months when fog is most prevalent. The fog may have prevented serious fishing close inshore, where cod is most abundant. The Maine and New England cod fisheries remained unexploited until the early seventeenth century.

*Gadus* spawned earlier in the south than it did in Newfoundland, so the best time for fishing was between February and May. Waters were slightly warmer and the fish often considerably larger, with forty-five-kilogram adults not uncommon. The best fishing grounds were inshore, close to sheltered bays where flakes could be erected. Both Maine and New England offered better drying conditions, especially the latter, where the summers were warm and sunny. In both places fishers could catch and cure fish almost any time of the year at a considerably lower cost than in Newfoundland. And there was the added attraction of furs, which the local people were already trading north to the St. Lawrence River valley. Even without golden cities, Norumbega offered a good case for permanent settlement, if for nothing else than to fish year-round for the growing Catholic markets of the Iberian Peninsula and Mediterranean.[8]

The first people with ambitions to settle came for the cod and furs. In 1602 an Englishman named Bartholomew Gosnold sailed for New England with two ships, the *Concord* and the *Dartmouth*, and thirty-two people, twenty of whom came as settlers. He made landfall on the Maine coast near Cape Neddick, where he encountered Micmac Indians dressed in European clothes rowing a Basque shallop. The Indians were aware of the Newfoundland fishery and even sketched a map of the coast as far north as Placentia Bay. After this encounter, Gosnold and his party turned south to Cape Cod and Martha's Vineyard, where they found cod in abundance. The Anglican priest John Brereton wrote, "We had pestered our ship so with Cod fish, that we threw numbers of them over-boord againe; and surely I am persuaded that in the months of March, April, and May there is upon this coast, better fishing and is as great plenty, as in Newfound-land." He added that "the places . . . were but in seven faddoms and with less than a league of the shore; where in new-found-land they fish in fortie or fiftie faddome water and farre off." Another member of the group, Gabriel Archer, described how, after rounding a "mighty headland," they anchored in "fifteene fadome, where wee tooke great store of Codfish, for which we altered the name and called it Cape Cod."[9]

Like Gosnold, Archer and Brereton dreamed of a prosperous colony that exported cod and other commodities to Europe. The settlement never materialized, but a year later Martin Pring explored the Maine coast and Massachusetts Bay more thoroughly. In Penobscot Bay he reported "an excellent fishing for Cod . . . better than those of New-found-land . . . Withall we saw good and Rockie ground fit to drie them upon." Pring also reported that salt could probably be manufactured on site. He sent home a cargo of sassafras, which grew wild along the coast.[10]

Cod, furs, sassafras, and a Native American population apparently interested in commerce made for great economic potential.* *Gadus* abounded in intoxicating sizes, to be taken almost any time of the year. Here, unlike

---

*Sassafras *(Sassafras officinale)* is a tree with slender branches and fragrant bark. The roots were said to be a cure for syphilis and rheumatism but were proven ineffective. Sassafras tea, "saloop," made from the leaves, was sold in the early morning on London street corners, mixed with sugar and milk, until the last century.

Newfoundland, it seemed both desirable and possible to establish a permanent English presence before the French expanded from their fur-trading
bases along the St. Lawrence River. In 1605 another English expedition
sailed for New England, this time under the command of George Waymouth. He anchored the *Archangel* in Georges harbor, where "our men
tooke Cod and Hadocke with hooks by our ship side, and Lobsters very
great; which before we had not tried." John Rosier wrote in his account of
the expedition, "It sheweth how great a profit the fishing would be, they
[the fish] being so plentiful, so great and so good, with such convenint drying as can be wished, neere at hand upon the Rocks." Safe anchorages with
good holding ground abounded, an important consideration in an inshore
fishery where ships remained anchored for weeks on end.[11]

Viable settlements required solid financial backing and influence at
court. The critical link between the Crown and the interested merchants
was Sir John Popham, Lord Chief Justice of England, a "huge, heavie,
ugly man," a native of the West Country, and a great believer in the benefits of colonies to his homeland. For more than fifty years, West Country
merchants from Bristol and Devonshire ports had led the way in the
Newfoundland cod trade. Profoundly distrustful of their London counterparts, they had demanded an equal share in the proposed settlement of
"Virginia" in 1606. Popham and others made a strong case for a Virginia
Company that created two separate companies: one located in London
that would establish a colony in the Chesapeake Bay and a second based
in Plymouth that would settle in "Northern Virginia." King James I duly
chartered the Virginia Company on April 10, 1606.*

The first colony was a disaster. Two ships, the *Mary and John* and the
*Gift of God* under Raleigh Gilbert and George Popham, nephew of Sir
John, landed at the mouth of the Sagadohoc River in 1607. They disem-
barked 120 passengers, built a small village of fifty cabins, a chapel, and a

---

*A *royal charter* was a relic of feudalism, a document that granted a specific individual, in medieval parlance a lord, the right to conquer, take possession of, and govern
territories in the Crown's name. Under the terms of such a document, the chartered
individual was a vassal to the Crown. As such he or she ruled not a colony but a private estate.

blockhouse and were quickly overwhelmed by the severity of the Maine winter. Factional quarrels racked the settlement. Many colonists died of scurvy, among them George Popham, forcing the survivors back to England in 1608. According to a French Jesuit, Father Pierre Baird, who visited the ruins of the settlement in 1611, the colonists had been totally unprepared for the savage winter and had refused to trade with the local Indians. He also reported that fishing boats from the Virginia settlements made "a voyage every summer to the fishing grounds of the Peucoit to obtain fish for food during the coming winter."[12] With these annual excursions from the south, the New England cod trade developed an entirely North American dimension.

King James I's Virginia charter also allowed a group of London entrepreneurs to found a settlement in the Chesapeake region of North America; 108 settlers crossed the Atlantic with instructions to find gold and discover an ocean route to Asia. Braving Indian attacks, they established a fort named Jamestown in honor of the king. But the colony was precarious, and when the first supply ship arrived in January 1608 with a hundred new settlers, it found only thirty-eight of the original group still alive. Scurvy haunted the settlement, as did other famine-related diseases. In desperation, the settlers turned to the New England cod fisheries, known by word of mouth from visiting seamen. According to the colonist William Strachey, the fishing there was reported to be better than in Newfoundland.[13] Even before he wrote his report on the colony in 1610, boats from the Chesapeake were sailing to New England waters, not to make money but for simple subsistence.

The Jamestown settlement faltered in part because its backers in London, as well as the settlers themselves, had failed to realize that to be successful the colony had to be self-supporting from the beginning. Although they talked a great deal about bartering with the Indians, no one said anything in the original directions for the settlers about fishing. Jamestown hovered near disaster until the 1620s. It was fortified by a reorganization and an influx of newcomers in 1610, when Captain Samuel Argall was appointed to fish for the new colony. Argall had already pioneered a direct route to Virginia via the Azores and Bermuda that allowed ships to avoid marauding Spaniards. On a voyage to Bermuda for hogs and fish, his pinnaces were blown off course and fished for several days off Cape Cod. They returned to Virginia in August with full holds. From that moment on, the Virginians relied heavily on the New England cod banks. In a reversal of history, what for generations had been a market commodity in Europe once again became an essential subsistence food.[14]

By this time it was common knowledge that the best cod season occurred during the coldest months of the year between December and March, so seasonal camps along the Maine and New England shore made sound commercial sense. Powerful members of the Northern Virginia Company, among them the influential Sir Ferdinando Gorges, petitioned Parliament for a new charter that gave them a fishing monopoly. The result was the Council for New England, established in 1619 and, in the following year, two orders that gave each Virginia colony reciprocal rights to fish at sea within each other's charter areas, with the proviso that the fisheries were used purely for "the sustenation of the people of the Colonies there and for the transportation of people into either Colony." If either party required facilities ashore, these would have to be paid for at "reasonable rates."[15]

The Jamestown colony's fishing boats were active players in the New England cod fishery from as early as 1608 to 1614, but vessels from England's West Country were also sighted in the same waters by Captain John Smith in 1615.

Smith had a colorful past as a mercenary and traveler before sailing to Jamestown in 1606. He had once been enslaved by the Turks but escaped. This decisive, independent man became a member of the Jamestown council, was captured by local Indians, befriended by Chief Powhatan, and released. He proved a firm leader of a settlement plagued by laziness and desertion, asserting that "he who does not work will not eat." He was injured by a gunpowder burn and forced to return to England in 1609. But he lost none of his zeal for further colonization of Virginia. In April 1614 he sailed for the Gulf of Maine with a crew of forty-five to hunt for whales and gold. Landing at Monhegan Island, then the center of fishing activity in the region, he found three English fishing craft and two French boats after cod. He saw no whales and certainly no traces of gold but, ever the opportunist, sent out his men in small boats to catch *Gadus*. His thirty-seven fishers caught and dried nearly 50,000 large fish and made train oil from their livers, a fine cargo that he and his four merchant colleagues sold in England and Spain, clearing £1,500, a staggering profit for a six-month voyage.

Smith named the coast of Maine "New England." He wrote, "Of all the foure parts of the world that I have seene not inhabited, I would rather live here than any where."[16] The captain was a firm advocate for the cod fishery. He wrote a pamphlet urging that a network of fishing and fur-trading stations be established along the New England coast, likening the fishery to a rich mine with an endless lode of "silvered streams" teeming with cod and other fish.

The charismatic explorer made himself unpopular with his company and never returned to Virginia. But he persuaded Ferdinando Gorges to mount a series of expeditions sponsored by the Plymouth Company, which named him admiral of New England. No fewer than three colonization attempts faltered in the face of storms and pirates. He devoted the rest of his life to writing, and his pamphlets and stories spread rapidly through West Country fishing communities.

The number of boats fishing around Monhegan rose from eight or so in 1616 to thirty-seven in 1622. New England's inshore fishery, like Newfoundland's, required extensive facilities ashore. The intense competition for the best beaches and anchorages repeated itself in the Gulf of Maine, so that it was advantageous to leave some men as caretakers over the winter to protect the facilities, repair them if necessary, and prepare for the coming season. Soon, however, the captains discovered that the best fishing was during the cold months. As Christopher Levett, one of Ferdinando Gorges's partners, pointed out, year-round fishing had the potential of doubling profits, since the ships could spend winters as well as summers bringing the catch to market. At the same time, there was more than enough cod to satisfy the subsistence needs of the Virginia colonists, who continued to send ships to Monhegan waters every year.[17]

## PISTOU OF SUMMER VEGETABLES
## WITH POACHED COD

Cod, whether fresh or salted, is something we take for granted on restaurant menus, a king of "must-have," just like Armani suits or Rolex watches. Up to the 1950s, Newfoundland and North American fisheries seemed boundless. But in fact the warning signs of overfishing appeared during the late nineteenth century, when observers complained that the fish were smaller and less plentiful. Today we live with the consequences of centuries of promiscuous fishing. The United Nations Food and Agriculture Organization reports that 47 percent of world fish stocks are fully exploited, 18 percent overexploited, and 10 percent severely depleted. We have fished over 75 percent of the world's marine resources to the limit at a time when fish eating has become fashionable—a lean source of protein. Fattier fish like herring and salmon contain essential fatty acids. We now face the prospect of a lifeless North Sea, with a somewhat better situation in the Bay of Biscay, the English Channel, and the Irish Sea. The cause of this overfishing is not subsistence activity but large-scale industrial harvesting of the ocean using nets that scoop up everything on the sea floor, including critical breeding stocks.

We are caught on the horns of a dilemma. If we ban industrial-scale fishing with its wastage, for the small-scale inshore fisheries that do less damage cannot possibly meet the demand. Part of the future lies in large-scale fish farming of species like salmon, which generates controversy through the large amounts of wild fish meal and oil required to maintain them. Here the solution is organically farmed fish fed on fish meal from fish factory waste and certified sustainable fisheries.

Part of the solution will come from rigorously administered sustainable ocean fisheries, but this is a complex issue that reflects the wide variety of fisheries and fishing conditions around the world. A great deal depends on the educated consumer, who will insist on fish that comes from certified sustainable sources. The long-term future of seafood depends on this. Some restaurants are insisting on sustainable fish, partly because the quality is better, while some big chains in Europe such as Marks and Spencers in England are shifting toward a policy of buying only sustainable catches.

All of us need to play our part to keep seafood on the table. You can identify which fish to eat and which to avoid on the website www.fishonline.org, which is developing a comprehensive database for the informed fish buyer. In the meantime, here's a cod recipe from chef Dan Barber that relies on sustainable cod stocks to encourage you.

New England is rightly famous for its clam chowder, Maine for its lobster. Modern cod recipes seek to enhance the natural freshness of the white meat with innovative sauces, like this contemporary recipe from Blue Hill restaurant at Stone Barns, Pocantico Hills, New York. This stunning recipe combines North American cod with a French-inspired sauce in suitable celebration of the diverse traditions of the Newfoundland and New England fisheries.

*(continues)*

## ⚳ *Pistou of Summer Vegetables with Poached Cod*

A pistou is a traditional French sauce made by pounding or blending vegetables. "Pistou" comes from the Latin *pestare*, to pound. It's often used as a pasta sauce, a *soupe de pistou*, a classic vegetable soup, or, as here, an enhancement for a fish dish.

SERVES 4

### *Pistou*

¼ lb/125 g asparagus, cut into ½ in/1.25 cm pieces and blanched
¼ lb/125 g broccoli, cut into ½ in/1.25 cm pieces and blanched
¼ lb/125 g fava beans, blanched and cleaned
¼ lb/125 g lima beans, blanched and cleaned
¼ lb/125 g peas, blanched
¼ lb/125 g zucchini, seeded and cut into ½ in/1.25 cm pieces
1 bunch basil, cleaned and blanched
8 oz/250 ml olive oil
1 shallot, finely diced
Large handful chopped herbs (parsley, chives)
16 oz/500 ml vegetable stock

Combine blanched vegetables. Place half of them in a blender with the blanched basil. Puree using olive oil.

In a large saucepan, sweat the shallot until translucent. Add the remaining blanched vegetables and the puree. Add vegetable stock until the desired consistency is achieved. Season to taste.

### *Poached Cod*

12 oz/360 g of cod from the center of the fish
68 oz/2 liters olive oil
Salt and pepper to taste
1 sprig thyme
1 clove garlic, peeled
Fleur de sel (natural sea salt from Brittany)
1 cup microgreens

Cut the cod into four 3 oz/scant 100 g portions. Heat the olive oil to 95F/35C. Add thyme and garlic. Season the cod with salt and pepper. Place in olive oil for 8 minutes.

Remove the cooked fish from the oil, season with fleur de sel, and garnish with dressed microgreens.

Recipe from Dan Barber, Blue Hill at Stone Barns, Pocantico Hills, New York.

All this was a logical extension of an inshore fishery that had flourished farther north for more than a century. The sponsors of the ships and crews saw winter settlement as a sensible and profitable move. The men could cultivate crops and tend livestock if the fish were not biting and trade with the local Indians for furs. There was no thought of a permanent colony, merely strategically located fishing stations ashore to serve the international cod trade. They were not intended as self-sustaining communities, although theoretically this was desirable. The inhabitants were there to fish and process the catch on every winter day when fishing was possible.

Thus the first permanent settlement of New England was not the celebrated Plymouth Plantation of the Pilgrim fathers but a series of cod fishing and trading stations along the Maine coast. By 1619 a substantial year-round fishing settlement thrived on Monhegan. Others rose at Pemaquid, on Southport Island, and on Demariscove, a small island 10.5 kilometers west of Monhegan with a snug anchorage and abundant freshwater. A year later there were at least ten temporary fishing stations between Monhegan Island and the mouth of the Charles River.

The men who served at these stations stayed for three years or more, making good money from the ancient share system. In 1620 Smith reported that sailors with a single share "had twenty pounds, and at home again in sevene moneths, which was more than such a one should have got in twenty moneths, had he gone for wages any where."[18] It was also better money than a skilled man would receive in the Newfoundland fishery. Yet far fewer ships sailed for New England than to Newfoundland waters. A customs officer at Plymouth, England, reported in 1621 that 250 boats sailed to the north and only eleven to New England, all of which found "nice fishing places." Two years later, forty-five ships followed in their wake, "all making a better voyage than ever."[19] These vessels, averaging about fifty to 200 tons, sailed for New England waters in January to March, each financed by a consortium of merchants and manned by about fifty men. Outward bound, they carried lumber, salt, and other supplies. Their holds bulged with salted cod on the return voyage. According to Emmanual Altham, who described the cod fishing in 1623, most New England fish were sold immediately in Spain at high prices. When his brother Edward Altham's ship was becalmed in a fog off Patuxet, the crew fished. "In one hour we got 100 great cod." They would have got a full cargo in a week had they not got under way when the fog cleared. "I think we got 1000 in all," Altham reported in a letter to his brother in England. He reported sighting numerous fishing boats. "Every one of them, by their confession, say that they have made good voyages, and now most of them are gone into Spain, to sell their fish where they have ready gold for it."[20]

In a land with no formal government until 1630, occupying a fishing station conferred right of possession during the season. Contemporary observers wrote little about them beyond reporting their presence, so we must turn to archaeology to learn what they were like. The Pemaquid fishing station near Monhegan was a fortified post that began operations as early as 1628 and remained in use until the late seventeenth century, when several farmers and soldiers also lived there. Excavations have revealed the stone-lined cellars of the settlers' homes, as well as some of the artifacts used in the fishery—simple fishhooks like those used to take *Gadus* for centuries, a fish spear, a gaff for handling large cod, and the usual lead sinkers attached to fishing lines.[21]

Damariscove Island, off Pemaquid some five kilometers southeast of Boothbay Harbor, was an ideal location for a fish station—a sheltered anchorage, a freshwater pond, and plenty of space for drying racks ashore. The island had abundant timber for firewood, and it was close to the best fishing grounds. In 1622 John Pory, a Virginia Company official, visited what he called Damerill's Cove, then owned by Ferdinando Gorges. He employed thirteen men who lived there year-round, fishing from two shallops to ensure enough fish to load any visiting ship. They also kept the island "farmed out in Sir Ferdinando's name to such as shall there fish." The fishers lived in fear of attacks by both French rivals and the Indians, so they erected "a strong palisado of spruce trees some ten feet high, having besides their small shot one piece of ordinance and some ten good dogs."[22] Ships from Virginia, Plymouth Plantation, and the West Country also visited the island.

This was a classic sedentary fishery, except that much of the fishing took place in winter. Everything was temporary, for the skippers would assess the potential of local catches each year before deciding whether to stay or move on. In its early days, the Demariscove station was financed by Gorges and other European investors. After 1646 the Gorges monopoly collapsed as groups of independent fishers took over the island, selling their catches to Massachusetts Bay merchants. These villainous middlemen would arrive with "a walking tavern, a bark laden with the Legitimate bloud of the ripe grape," and ply the locals with drink. The fishers would emerge from their carousing with their wages gone, and all too often their fishing operations mortgaged to the merchant.[23] Demariscove flourished until 1676, when it was abandoned during the Indian wars.

An archaeological survey on the island in 1979–1980 uncovered an area of stages and landings by the side of the sheltered harbor, with fish flakes clustered tightly on the gentle slopes nearby.[24] The archaeologists found two triangular fieldstone projections that were once underpinnings for the wooden stages used in the fishery. No signs remained of the palisaded fort, but it most likely stood on the low-lying terrain at the head of the harbor, a restricted area where three or four fishing boats would land their catches.

Studying the archaeology of fishing stations is something like trying to examine medieval fishponds: little survives. Did the Damariscove fishers process the winter fish by allowing them to freeze, then drying them in the summer? Some experts have claimed that winter-cured fish tasted better than those dried and salted in summer. Could the fish have been salted and then stored in some form of cold fish cellar until spring, when they were dried in the sun?

The Trelawney station on Richmond's Island near Casco Bay was originally planned as a trading station but soon became a major fishing center. Between 1633 and 1643, John Walker, Trelawney's agent, employed about forty men there, most of them indentured workers. The majority were engaged in fishing, but a few grew maize, peas, and "English grains," and raised cattle, goats, and pigs in an attempt to make the settlement self-sustaining. Trelawney boasted of substantial housing as protection against the cold months. Walker built himself a house that was "40 foote in length & 18 foot broad within the sides, besides the Chimnay, and the Chimnay is large with an oven in each end of him." Every man had "his close boarded Cabbin [bunk]" and there were substantial storage facilities for ship's sails and dry goods.[25] The station had a pig house, a storage house capable of holding 50,000 dried fish, "4 or 5 akers" of fenced gardens, and apparently some fortifications against the French, but we have no details.

Life at these stations was brutally dangerous and lonely, for the best cod fishing was in winter. The men would head out to sea every day weather permitting except Sundays, fishing from open shallops. They would sail if the wind was favorable or row for kilometers against bitterly cold headwinds. Their thick cotton clothes froze as the boat iced up on subzero days. But the fishing went on, with catches of 350 to 400 fish a day when the cod were biting. *Gadus* does not fight hard, but the sheer labor of hauling in endless fish weighing forty-five kilograms or more must have been exhausting. And when one cod was aboard, the men started the process all over again, the hooks baited anew with fish guts, shellfish, herring, or auk meat. By the time they returned to shore, the fishers would fall asleep over their evening meal or simply collapse into their bunks. Their only relief was Sundays and the many days when the weather was too bad for fishing. Even then, there was work to be done—repairing buildings and stages, assembling barrels, and overhauling fishing gear. Just the labor of collecting firewood required increasing hours of work as the forests retreated ever farther from the station.

The men of the stations cared little for the conventions of society or the faithful worship of God. They were hard-drinking, hard-swearing, self-reliant men who knew no other life, had been in it since they were boys, and had no illusions about its danger. Some of them were family men; others were part-time fishers with work at home in the off-season. But as control of the fishery passed from Europe to shrewd Massachusetts merchants, migrant fishers increasingly began to spend their entire lives on and off the New England coast.

The ever-entrepreneurial Ferdinando Gorges, a passionate royalist, envisaged himself and his friends as feudal lords ruling a royalist America. James I gave them everything they wanted, but the Council for New England was unable to raise the fees and taxes it proposed to levy from fishers and fur trading companies operating in New England waters. With no navy, the council had no operating funds and no way of enforcing its rule. It liquidated its assets by dividing them between the patentees in 1623 and again in 1635 in the face of increasing Puritan colonization.

# 17

# PURITANS AND CAINS

We are all three young men and Can goe when we will and
Com when we will.

Samuel Dutch, 1666[1]

Approve yourselves a religious people, otherwise you will con-
tradict the main end of planting this wilderness!

Sir, you think you are preaching to the people at the Bay;
our *main end* was to catch *fish!*

Exchange, said to be apocryphal, between a
fisherman and Cotton Mather, a minister[2]

The Pilgrim fathers are the very icon of early America, principled settlers
who fled religious persecution to establish a new England based on a social
and political order that hewed to God's will. Like all storied pioneers, they
stand somewhat above the annals of history, remarkable more for their
righteous (and often bigoted) way of life than for their skill at farming or
fishing. The settlers who arrived on the *Mayflower* in 1620 were lamentably
ill-prepared for the realities of life in their new homeland. They were
middle-class folk with no experience of life in the wilderness. Unlike Sir
Ferdinando Gorges in Maine, who dreamed of a feudal New England ruled
by noble gentry, the Pilgrims were austere commoners who believed that
their labor would glorify God. Coming to America "to serve God and to
fish," they knew nothing of the latter. Captain John Smith, one of the
greatest advocates for the New England fisheries, remarked of the Pilgrims

that "it is a wonder [how the colonists] could subsist, fortifie themselves, re-sist their enemies, and plant their plants." They were "wanting most neces-sities for fishing and fowling." Yet at their doorstep were some of the richest fisheries in the world.[3]

The Pilgrims settled at Plymouth on the Massachusetts south shore in late December 1620 after rejecting Cape Cod as a settlement site and stealing some corn from the local people.* They set out immediately to build a village, using the *Mayflower* as a base. As the weather deteriorated, so did their health. By spring 1621, the great sickness—a combination of various diseases including scurvy—had taken over half the community. The forty who survived subsisted off ship's stores, plundered grain, and shellfish. Yet a short distance away in the Gulf of Maine, winter fishing stations abounded in salted cod. The Pilgrims learned the hard way that a new colony, however well financed, could not survive without trade and regular communication with home.

Come spring, the survivors planted cereal crops, including corn, but only with the help of local Indians did they get through the first year. Their indigenous neighbors showed them where to collect clams and har-vest eels, how to distinguish between edible and poisonous plants, and how to hunt deer. Still, the 1621 harvest fell lamentably short, and Ply-mouth endured its second winter on reduced rations. The situation be-came desperate in May 1622 with the arrival of thirty-five new settlers on the *Fortune*. The newcomers brought no supplies or tools with them, and food quickly ran out. In desperation, Edward Winslow and some of the other men took Plymouth's one shallop on a 240-kilometer trip to beg for food from the fishing stations.[4] The fishers filled their boat with dried cod and refused to accept payment. Conditions improved with the arrival of new settlers in 1623. By 1630 some 300 Pilgrims lived at Plymouth, en-joying a degree of comfort and maintaining a rigidly disapproving attitude toward their dissolute and morally flawed neighbors in Maine.

The Pilgrims could be devout to the point of eccentricity. Members of a minority Puritan sect known as Separatists, they believed that membership

---

*I have chosen to use the spelling Plymouth rather than Plimoth.

Drying cod. FROM DUHAMEL DU MONCEAU, *TRAITÉ*, 1769.

in the Church of England violated biblical expectations for true Christians. In England, where church and state were one, such beliefs were treasonous. To avoid persecution, the Pilgrims fled to Amsterdam and Leyden, where they lived for eleven years. But they were uncomfortable in Holland and decided to settle in North America. They obtained a grant to settle in the Hudson Valley from the Virginia Company, negotiated a safe conduct from the English Crown, and mortgaged themselves heavily to London merchants for the expenses of setting up a colony. While the Londoners were hard-nosed businessmen expecting a rapid profit, the Pilgrims were neither fishermen nor expert farmers, but upright middle-class people with deep religious convictions and a profound belief in godly discipline, orderly family life, and churchgoing. They expected discomfort and suffering but were unprepared for the New England winters they encountered. Still, the Plymouth community survived crop failures, dishonest backers in England, and the loss of its first export cargo to a "Turks man of warr" in 1625.[5]

There were other organized settlements too, all of them, like Plymouth, indebted to English merchants trying to cash in on the vast natural resources of North America. The settlers' backers labored under unrealistic expectations of immediate profits like those of the Newfoundland fisheries. But bad harvests in England produced rumblings of civil strife between the king and Parliament, and money for speculative ventures was in short supply. The merchants behind the new plantations soon backed away from the mounting cost of keeping them afloat. As their financial backing dissolved, the settlers were forced to sell fish and furs at low prices and pay premium prices for the equipment and essential supplies they needed.[6]

As the organized companies fell apart, New England trade fell into the hands of a few leading colonists and adventurers from England. The latter would form partnerships, outfit a few ships, and sail to North America on their own initiative. Once there, they either sailed home with a quick profit from fish or furs or settled down to acquire wealth as expeditiously as possible, with little reference to the austerely respectable Pilgrims. Many of these adventurers were violent men with few scruples about selling arms and liquor to the Indians. The Puritan settlers heartily disapproved of such people.

Until 1630 these rowdy folk and the Maine fishers effectively controlled the commerce in New England. As a visitor to one of the fishing stations remarked, "If a man of quality chance to come where they are roistering and gulling in *Wine* with a dear felicity, he must be sociable and *Roly-poly* with them, taking off their liberal cups as freely, or be gone."[7] New England was slowly becoming an adjunct to the Newfoundland fisheries, its trade in the hands of West Country merchants.

Profound change began in the 1630s, when diminishing chances of reform at home turned the thoughts of thousands of Puritans to America. There, free from interference, they could create a righteous England and order their lives according to God's word.

The great Puritan migration transformed the colonies. Some 65,000 English settlers emigrated to North America and the West Indies between 1630 and 1640; 20,000 of them came to New England. They arrived in well-organized fleets, fishing vessels, and individual trading ships, as families and individuals. Most of them were poor and many were escaping religious persecution, recruited by commercial companies needing settlers for their concessions on the far side of the Atlantic. These enterprises proliferated in the 1620s, many of them imploding rapidly or merging with others, like the Dorchester Company, a pious fishing community on Cape Ann founded in 1624 and folded into the New England Company in 1628. Of the failure of this enterprise, John White remarked that "no sure fishing place in the Land is fit for planting, nor any good place for planting found fit for fishing, at least neere the Shoare."[8] Almost invariably, the backers of such projects were prominent merchants of Puritan inclination interested in fostering the true religion while making a profit. Some of these businessmen, having obtained a patent from the Council for New England for land between the Charles and Merrimac Rivers, incorporated themselves as the Massachusetts Bay Company.

When King Charles I dissolved Parliament in 1629 and effectively took power into his own hands, a group of devout Puritans saw an opportunity. In a brilliant political move, they turned the Massachusetts Bay Company into a self-governing colony, where authority lay not with the company back in England but with a group of leaders who emigrated to govern it. These leaders included men like John Winthrop and Thomas Dudley, intensely religious people whose lives were devoted to a quest for righteousness.[9] Life was a moral experience in which people worked both for themselves and for the common good, as sinners seeking salvation. From the commercial point of view, this meant charging fair prices and honoring debts, while paying scrupulous attention to the realities of supply and demand. Higher prices for scarce commodities were the workings of God's hand in the community. In other words, the Puritans insisted that business be conducted within the structure of a society created by God. In contrast, the North Atlantic fishery was a purely commercial enterprise, governed by cutthroat competition and few moral boundaries.

By the time the Massachusetts Bay Company became self-governing, hunting grounds lay far inland, the trade subject to intense competition from the St. Lawrence region. The company moved rapidly to assume a commanding position in the fur business and planned on doing the same with the fishery. A vision of lucrative fisheries had attracted English investors since John Smith's day. In theory, conditions were ideal. The New England fishing grounds could be worked winter and summer; the catch was much closer inshore, and the climate was ideal for the kinds of lightly salted and dried cod that appealed to the lucrative Spanish and Mediterranean markets. Although the Dorchester and New England Companies had failed to make a profit, the dream persisted.

During the first decade of Puritan government, the leaders had much on their minds besides fisheries. Matthew Cradock, the Bay Company governor, remarked in 1640 that some form of cooperative venture involving the fishery was the only way the colony would be able to pay its debts in England.[10] Nothing came of his proposal, but individual fishers helped feed the settlers in the early, hungry years.

At first, most of the fish consumed in the colony came from English and European fishing boats that sailed each year to New England waters. Trelawney's fishing station on Richmond Island flourished off the cod trade; numerous fishers settled in isolated bays and inlets along the Gulf of Maine. After a lull in the 1630s, Bristol merchants took a renewed interest in the New England fisheries, but as a sideshow to the Newfoundland enterprise. As always, their profits came from Catholic Europe's dinner tables, by now mostly in southern Europe. They made little from the Puritans, who obtained fish from independent, often migrant fishers along the New England coast.

Then came the Civil War in 1642, which pitted Charles I against Parliament. The war spread to the sea as both sides commandeered fishing boats and crews for naval service. Although the royalists held much of Devon and Cornwall, most of the coastal towns stood for Parliament. Fighting erupted; ports were besieged. Bristol changed hands twice between 1642 and 1644. Ships from both sides pursued one another far from England's shores. With fewer boats crossing the Atlantic for cod, the Newfoundland fisheries declined and the West Country's long ties to the New England fishery finally withered away.

ᕙᕃ

The ripples of civil war soon washed ashore in New England. Settlers needed food, and merchants were eager for exchange commodities. Fishers and farmers seeking winter employment began exploiting local waters, often with primitive equipment. New Englanders settled on Monhegan, on the Isle of Shoals, at Marblehead and Hog Island. Most of them were young men who preferred a life of casual labor to indentured service in a Puritan household. The Puritans considered them beyond the social pale: outsiders, little more than "wild creatures, ruffians, Cains and the like."[11] The fishers lacked godly discipline, which could only be imposed under the supervision of upright communities, where churchgoing, orderly behavior, and regular hard work contributed to the common good. John Winthrop went so far as to proclaim that earlier colonies in Newfoundland and Virginia had failed because they "used unfit instruments . . . a multitude of rude and misgoverned persons, the very scumme of the land."[12] But the fisheries were profitable. In 1641, 300,000 cod came to land. Six years later £4,000 worth of fish sold at Marblehead.

The founders of the Massachusetts colony would have liked to isolate themselves and their people from the evils of the outside world, but their communities were heavily indebted to merchants at home. They were used to expensive goods that could only come from England, including good ironwork and gunpowder. Consequently, they had to organize an export trade to satisfy their debts and buy these items, which meant relying on workers with little interest in the Puritan life or its narrow, often bigoted values. John Winthrop's papers tell us the Pilgrims were well aware that New England cod was a "knowen and staple Commodotie." But the Pilgrims were not fishers.

At first they turned to migrant fishermen, the same people recruited in West Country ports for the Newfoundland fishery. The Massachusetts Bay Company, as well as the occasional individual merchant, recruited and equipped the fishers on yearly contracts that mirrored the practices of English traders. The migrants operated out of fishing bases on the north shore of Massachusetts, sailing for England with the catch in the fall. Even as late as 1636, hardly any settlers were proficient fishers, and the few who were demanded high wages. Migrant fishers from Europe, whose contracts were agreed before they left home, worked for considerably less. Many of them, when their term of employment ended, promptly demanded pay to match the "great wages" paid to the settlers.

The Puritans created what historian Daniel Vickers calls a "servant fishery," controlled by agents and merchants who did not adhere to the high standards of loyalty, obedience, and personal honesty expected in colonial society. Many fishermen were drunken roisterers who spent their leisure hours in dissipation. Even worse, many of them adhered to the doctrines of the Church of England propagated by a handful of eloquent preachers who cared nothing for the austerity of Puritan doctrine. Finally, almost all the profits left New England and ended up in the hands of distant merchants.

In the mid-1630s the Puritans took the first steps toward a resident fishery. They made colonial vessels taking and transporting fish exempt from taxation. In 1635 the Puritans' General Court permitted fishers who would settle in Marblehead to "plant and improve such grounde as they stand in neede of."[13] Dozens of fishermen promptly enclosed as much land as they could and settled down to become farmers, glad to be quit of the cold, hazardous ocean. Later attempts to limit holdings to 0.8 hectares a family and recruit only married men failed to have the desired result, since land was too easy to acquire and life was safer ashore. The few migrant fishers who took up the Puritans' offer and continued to fish remained as dissolute and profane as ever.

At first the Puritans were unfamiliar with the intricacies of the international cod trade. Bringing *Gadus* to market depended on a vast network of personal contacts, between merchant and merchant, merchant and skipper, as well as ample supplies of capital to pay the fishers and equip their boats. It was an industry built on seasonal rhythms that ran off lines of credit and close personal relationships that extended over thousands of kilometers of Atlantic sailing routes. The trade depended on profound trust between people living long distances away from one another. The only way the New Englanders could plug into the cod trade was as purveyors of catches, which they organized, processed, and delivered to English ships when they arrived on the coast. This required an intricate choreography between fisher and merchant, and the production of enough quintals of processed fish to fill the holds of arriving ships promptly and efficiently.

A New England merchant working the fish trade normally employed fishers as independent contractors, advancing provisions and equipment against an undertaking to purchase the catch at the going rate. The fishers had little freedom, whereas the merchant had a sure way of transforming his credit into a profitable commodity at the end of the season at the lowest possible cost. Invariably the traders had the upper hand, since their prices were dictated by changing demand in the international market. Since the cost of outfitting a four-man company consisting of three fishers and a shoreman ran between £100 and £150 a year in the mid-seventeenth century, there was no way most fishers could ever break free of this exploitative relationship.[14]

The life of a cod fisher who belonged to one of these companies was driven by the prices of landed fish. They were highest at the end of spring and in late autumn, just before the major fleets sailed for Europe, and prices fell sharply thereafter, with no demand for what was often a glut of deteriorating catches. There was enormous pressure to be the first at the fishing grounds and the first to return to port. Very early in the year, the companies readied their shallops and outfitted them with salt and empty barrels, hooks, lines, and bait, bread and salted meat, peas and flour, and hogsheads of brandy, beer, and rum. Many of the crews departed for the Gulf of Maine in the depths of winter, often encountering savage weather and freezing winds that sheathed their boats in ice. The crews accepted the risks and the high casualty rates just as their ancestors had done on the Grand Banks, in Icelandic waters, and in the North Sea. The voyage to Monhegan and other stations took a few days in fine weather, weeks in foul. Once there, the men built sleeping cabins and prepared stages and flakes in the familiar routine.[15]

As soon as the cod came in, the crews fished virtually without stopping, eighteen to twenty hours a day, in an endless round of hauling heavy lines from depths of fifty meters or more. In good weather the work was exhausting; in midwinter it could be life threatening. Hypothermia was a constant threat: a dunking was fatal within minutes. Life in the fishing camp was one of extremes—days of idleness waiting for fish and then frenetic weeks seemingly overwhelmed with fish.

The entire business was personal and transitory. Daniel Vickers describes how two fishers, John Roads and Peter Greenfield, purchased an open shallop for £100 in 1659.[16] George Corwin of Salem outfitted them in 1661. After hiring William Ford as the third man, they sailed for Monhegan after Christmas. They set up camp and hired a shoreman to dry the fish. In April they returned to Salem, delivered their catch, and bought more provisions. Then they hurried back to Maine to fish the remainder of the spring season, returning in June for good, settled up with Corwin, and dissolved their partnership. Their experience was typical—months of brutally hard labor along an isolated coastline often in savage weather conditions, and usually without female company. One can hardly blame the fishers for taking to drink and carousing, or for the violence that broke out in disputes over stages and prime drying spots.

Most New England fishermen came from the huge pool of migrant workers who made a living from the cod fisheries and arrived merely to fish. Word of the high wages and easy credit from Pilgrim interests soon reached Newfoundland, where employers began sending their men south at the end of the season to save the expense of shipping them home. There was intense competition for good fishers, recruited by liberal credit, sometimes interest-free if the man would agree to work exclusively for one agent or merchant. Sometimes the merchants advanced the equivalent of several years' earnings, establishing a firm claim over the income of their clients in an environment where labor was in chronically short supply.

Unlike many English fishers who farmed at home and often owned hectarage and animals, few New England fishermen ever acquired land. A prejudiced society did not allow them to move inland from the coastal ports where they worked. Even if they aspired to the security of landowning, they could not get it in Puritan territory, where they were always on the periphery. New England fishing communities were governed by convenience, friendship, respect for talent, and the need for flexibility in a business driven by two outside forces—the seasons of cod and the demands of a marketplace thousands of kilometers distant. The fishers, who lived in constant fear of sudden, random death, were often religious in a thoroughly traditional way that had them invoking patron saints and the

Lord's benevolence. But they had no respect for the Puritans' belief that good fortune was God's reward for virtue.

In time, Puritan influence weakened, and the periphery became part of the core as more and more fishers settled permanently in the colony. Fishing settlements grew and cod created great wealth. Artisans and tradesmen served the needs of a growing indigenous fishing industry. *Gadus* became a main prop of the colonial economy.

For over a century, the Newfoundland fisheries were in the hands of West Country ports having the experience, capital, ships, people, and equipment to outdistance the competition. The New England fishery was another matter; by the mid-1640s, settlers were heavily engaged in both fishing and processing the catch. A number of London merchants, anxious to expand into the North American fishery, saw an opportunity in New England.

In 1646 Robert Houghton, a brewer, pledged to two other London merchants, George Gifford and Benjamin Whetcomb, that Charles Sedgwick of Charlestown, Massachusetts, would load 1,500 quintals of fish on their ship within twenty days of its arrival.[17] New Englanders would provide the fish, but Londoners would own the consignment while in transit. The entire transaction called for the merchants to export manufactures to New England and then carry the fish to Spain or the Wine Islands (the Azores, Madeira, and Canary Islands), returning to England with either bills of exchange or subtropical products. In other words, the Londoners financed a sack ship, an arrangement similar to what Dutch and French merchants were doing in the Newfoundland trade. The voyage was a success thanks to Houghton's Puritan contacts—Charles Sedgwick was his brother-in-law. Houghton soon became one of New England's leading fish merchants.

London merchants played another critical role in the development of the New England fishery by introducing their North American counterparts to the southern markets that were now the staple of the cod trade.

New Englanders became part of the triangular trade across the Atlantic—
from Europe to North America with goods and luxuries, then eastward
with fish (and other commodities like furs), before the ships brought
wine and other southern products like fruit back to England. At first the
settlers had only a small part of the trade. They were middle parties, with
a limited share in the profits. But they soon expanded their operations by
financing joint ventures with one another to carry fish to southern European ports and return with wine and other subtropical commodities.
They never achieved total control, since the English merchants always
retained ownership of their exported goods until they were sold upon arrival. But New Englanders' efforts paid off. By the time King Charles II
was returned to the throne in 1660, the settlers controlled their own fishery and also a growing fleet of ships that exported the catch to Spanish
and Mediterranean markets.[18]

A generation after the landing at Plymouth Rock, New England's fishing trade was a cornerstone of the colonial economy. Profits from cod and
the contacts obtained from shipping it brought demands for other commodities—timber for barrels and other by-products of the wine trade,
agricultural produce, even wooden house clapboards, a cargo of which was
sent to Malaga in Spain by Samuel Maverick of Noddles Island in Massachusetts Bay in 1641. He received cash and oranges in return, while paying for English manufactures from Bristol with whale oil.

By 1643 New England was rapidly becoming an independent trading
force, with voyages as far as Spain and the Canary Islands, thanks in part
to cheap salt prices. The Crown made an important concession to normal
practice, which forced the colonists to import everything through England, and permitted ships carrying salt to sail directly from Europe to
New England. A quintal of fish in Boston purchased more than five times
its weight in salt but was far more expensive in Europe, which made for a
most attractive trade. This was the year when a New England ship made
the first triangular voyage, with fish and other goods to the Canary Islands, then to Barbados where the skipper purchased tobacco "in exchange
for Africoes, which she carried from the island of Maio." This enterprise,
as well as gossip from visiting Dutch ships, opened the eyes of New Eng-

landers to the potential of the West Indies trade, where European colonies had mushroomed after 1625. In 1645 George Downing spent five months in the Caribbean and reported to his cousin John Winthrop Jr. on the potential of the Barbados slave trade, where "the more they buie, the better able they are to buye, for in a yeare and halfe they will earn . . . as much as they cost."[19] The West Indies colonies lacked the commodities that New England ships were carrying to the Wine Islands and Spain. For their dried and salted fish, timber, and other products, New Englanders could obtain cotton and tobacco. After 1644 New England became increasingly immersed in the West Indies trade. Poor-quality salt cod, which sold at half the price of "merchantable" fish, turned out to be highly marketable in the Caribbean. This refuse catch—salt burned, spotted, "carelessly ordered," and often rotten—was considered the ideal food for the slaves who cultivated the islands' growing sugar plantations.

Between 1620 and 1650, the mercantile nations of Europe turned the Atlantic basin into a single huge trading area, where salted fish, slaves, and sugar flowed along distant shipping routes with increasing predictability. England played a leading role in this commerce, part of a polygon of trade connections that linked Newfoundland, New England and other American ports, the West Indies, the Wine Islands, and Europe in an intricate lattice. The seed of this crystalline structure was the most ancient trade of all, in the fish required by devout Catholics to fulfill their religious obligations.

Nourished by the fish trade and the business that went with it, New England's commercial centers thrived. By the 1650s, Boston, founded by the Massachusetts Bay Company in 1630, was a prosperous mercantile community with over 3,000 inhabitants, "four full companys of Foote and Troope of horse."[20] Boston merchants acquired a reputation for greed and injustice, for imposing their terms on farmer and fisher alike. Observer after observer complained about high prices charged by the "damnable rich" Massachusetts merchants, about how they cheated Maine fishers by getting them drunk. There were so many charges of poor-quality cures, of quintals brought to market too quickly, that Newfoundland fish acquired a reputation for better quality—most of the time. Curing practices were sometimes irregular there too, more often in the hands of the British than the French.

## ACKEE AND SALTFISH

New England is the land of clam chowder and scrod, of clam bakes, lobsters, and other delicacies. There seems little point in traveling this familiar culinary path, so we journey instead to the Caribbean, where black slaves developed a distinctive cookery that survives to this day in both simple and elaborate forms. Traditional island cuisine comes from a melding of cultural influences. Native Americans like the Arawaks and Caribs fabricated grills with green sticks called *barbacoa* and used chilis to flavor their food. They cultivated corn and other tropical crops, such as taro from South America. Columbus and the conquistadors introduced sugar cane, onions, garlic, and other European crops. West African foods came to the islands from the African slave trade, among them okra, pigeon peas, plantains, and ackee. Mexico brought avocados, chayote, cocoa, and papaya.

The New Englanders traded salt cod of inferior quality—often moldy or rotten—to the islands. The slaves served it with ackee, the national fruit of Jamaica, whose name comes from the West African *Akye fufo,* the evergreen tree introduced to the Caribbean in the eighteenth century. Only the fleshy arils around the seeds are edible. When boiled, drained, and simmered in oil with salted dried cod, vegetables, and peppers, it has the consistency of scrambled eggs. Many people eat it at breakfast or as an entrée.

Like many cod dishes, ackee began as a basic subsistence staple. Today it has an important place in Caribbean cuisine, one of the many consequences of an industry that supplied salted fish to people far from Newfoundland and New England.

Here's a classic Jamaican dish that's served for breakfast throughout the island and wherever there are Jamaicans. Canned ackee is hard to find outside Jamaican neighborhoods, and fresh is unobtainable outside Jamaica.

### ✂ *Ackee and Saltfish*

SERVES 4

2 oz/60 g boneless salted codfish
3 strips bacon, cut into 1-in/2.5-cm pieces
1 oz/28 g butter
1 medium onion, chopped
6 cloves garlic, minced
2 medium tomatoes, chopped
1 16 oz/500 g can Jamaican ackee*
$\frac{1}{16}$ oz/5 g Jamaican pepper sauce, or to taste

---

*Canned ackee is very fragile and should be gently stirred with a fork.

*(continues)*

*Ackee and Saltfish (continued)*

Desalt the codfish by placing it in boiling water to cover and cook for 5 minutes. Drain and cool under running water. Flake the fish with your fingers and set it aside.

In a large skillet, fry the bacon until crisp. Add the butter and heat until it foams slightly. Add the onion and garlic and sauté until the onion is transparent. Add the tomatoes and pepper sauce and continue to cook for five minutes. Stir in the salt fish, cover, lower the heat, and cook for three minutes. Check flavor. Gently stir in the ackee, cover, and cook until the ackee is cooked through and has absorbed the flavor. You may need to add a bit of water to keep it from sticking. Serve hot.

Recipe from Jessica B. Harris, professor at Queens College, New York, and author of many books on the foods of the African diaspora.

Bostonians also acquired a reputation for rapacious dealings in the West Indies, where sugar proved highly profitable for New England's growing rum distilleries. At the same time, with the local fishery well under their thumb, Boston's merchants expanded into Newfoundland waters. At first interested in cargoes of fish that they could ship out to their usual markets, they found a growing market in Newfoundland itself for provisions of all kinds, including timber, tobacco, and tropical products. They also supplied the migratory fishers with food and cheap rum, to the point that English authorities became concerned about the effects of New England liquor on the "debauchery" of the fishers. The newcomers also impinged on a cod trade that was now an arena of competition between London merchants who supplied settlers ashore and West Country interests that controlled the migratory fishery. The West Country merchants in particular complained that New Englanders were corrupting the fishers with drink, entangling them in debt, and encouraging them to desert for an easier life in New England.

The Canso Islands at the northeastern tip of Nova Scotia have rocky beaches and lie close to cod-rich offshore banks. Basque and French ships visited there year after year during the seventeenth century. One Basque fisher is said to have sailed to the area forty-three times. New England ships went there in small numbers in the 1690s, but the islands came into their own after the Treaty of Utrecht (1713) between Britain and France transferred the islands to British sovereignty.[21] Some twenty or thirty New Englanders lived on the Cansos during the winter, protected by a small military garrison. But hundreds of fishers, almost all from New England, descended on the islands during the summer cod season.

After 1713 the Canso fishery was entirely in New England hands. Each winter, large sack ships, almost all owned by New England merchants like Peter Faneuil, sailed for English and Mediterranean ports in late winter laden with American and Caribbean goods.[22] They loaded salt, provisions, and other supplies in Europe, then sailed direct to the Cansos. Some merchants supplied Canso from Boston, selling cargoes of livestock, rum, sugar, and New England salt. In late summer, the same ships carried the processed merchantable fish from Canso to Spanish and Mediterranean ports, and "refuse fish" damaged during processing to the West Indies.

The Canso fishery produced as many as 50,000 quintals of fish a year during the 1720s and 1730s, requiring as many as 5,000 hogsheads of salt to process the cod. By this time, the Iberian marketplace alone was consuming 300,000 quintals of merchantable cod a year, and the Italian peninsula an equal amount. Canso reached its peak in the 1720s and then declined owing to unsettled political conditions, gluts of cod in Europe and the West Indies in the 1730s, and frequent complaints about the quality of the fish, which was subjected to hasty curing by merchants after a quick profit.

For all their problems with quality, fluctuating prices, and occasional gluts, New Englanders were now major players in the international fish trade, which flourished through the eighteenth and nineteenth centuries into the modern era, using technology little changed from medieval times.

The craft of fishing unfolds far from the magnifying glass of history. A traveler to Egypt once remarked that pharaohs, caliphs, pashas, and prime ministers came and went over the millennia, but the farmers by the banks of the Nile remained unaffected.[23] The world of the fisher was also timeless, an unceasing confrontation with the harsh realities of the brutal ocean. The fisherfolk persevered through the slow generational shift of religious doctrine and the faster ebb and flow of supply and demand. History accelerated and slowed, changed course, and brought prosperity or suffering, but people still had to eat and conform to religious teachings. So the fishing boats left port in fair weather or foul, summer and winter, sometimes in the face of gale-force winds. Each night the herring fishers hauled in their nets, fingers numb with cold, backs breaking from the weight, feet awash in a cascade of silvery fish. Spray broke over the bow, the boat surged in the waves, and everyone was wet through, snatching brief naps when the nets were set. Far offshore, cod fishers lined the sides of a deep sea boat, hooking their prey and hauling the heavy fish aboard, fish after fish, for ten, twelve, fifteen hours a day. The routine never changed, the rhythm of the fisheries never altered from one papal reign to the next. Like Egyptian farmers, the fishers who supplied the fish consumed by the devout were part of the anonymous backdrop of history. But their nameless, unending labors were the advance guard of European expansion. It was not the sudden inspiration of famous names that brought Europeans to North America—not Columbus or Cabot or the settlers at Plymouth Rock—but the thousand-year journey in pursuit of fish.

# Acknowledgments

In writing a book of this nature, I've drawn on the work of dozens of researchers to produce a synthesis that is, in the final analysis, my own take on a complex subject. I am, of course, entirely responsible for the conclusions and the accuracy of this book. I've done everything I can to document my narrative on the grounds that some readers may want to follow up on what is often a magnificent specialized literature, as well as avoid the wilder claims about Atlantic exploration that pervade the popular literature on the Age of Discovery. As part of the process of synthesis, many scholars have helped me navigate through an enormous, complex multidisciplinary literature, answering seemingly endless questions patiently, and, above all, encouraging me along the way. It's impossible to name everyone, but a long list includes Alison Locker, Michael Barkham, James Barrett, Michael Hoffmann, Evan Jones, Laurence Kant, Maryanne Kowaleski, John Leather, Tom McGovern, George Michaels, Sophia Perdikaris, Peter Pope, Andrew Selkirk, Chris Scarre, Vicki Szabo, David Starkey, Andrew Wolstenholme, and Arlen Zoharis.

John Moyes took me on a memorable tour of St. Johns and was a mine of information on local conditions. Some years ago, I had the privilege of touring the Red Bay Basque whaling sites in Labrador and the Ferryland settlement in Newfoundland with James Tuck—a unique and fascinating experience. Thanks also to the many friends who have sailed with me over the years in boats of all sizes through many of the waters described in these pages.

I owe a great debt to my old friend and passionate food expert Daphne Derven for assembling the chefs and food authorities who have contributed recipes to the book and for testing the historic dishes that adorn these pages. She has enriched my life and served me some mouthwatering repasts over the years. My thanks as well to the distinguished food authorities and chefs who contributed their innovative recipes to this book.

Dan Starer of Research for Writers helped me immensely with the basic research for the book, especially on the symbolism of fish in early Christianity. As always, Shelly Lowenkopf was a tower of strength during the writing process. He helped me avoid many potential minefields. Mystery writers Aaron and Charlotte Elkins were prized colleagues on a trip across the North Atlantic, providing me with literary inspiration at a critical moment in a way that only writers understand. I'm grateful to Crystal Cruise Lines for an invitation to lecture aboard *Crystal Symphony* on a memorable voyage through the North Atlantic, when we followed in the wake of the Norse voyagers and John Cabot, among others. The crew was kindness itself.

My profound thanks go to Bill Frucht, my editor at Basic Books, without whom this book would never have reached fruition. Our friendship now extends over four books and countless fascinating discussions that always reveal something new. During the writing of this book I discovered, to my delight, that he is not only the "man with the black pen," as he is known in my household, but also an expert small boat sailor. I value his critical sense and friendship more than I can say.

*Fish on Friday* owes its birth to my agent, Susan Rabiner, who persuaded me to undertake what turned out to be an engrossing journey. I am deeply grateful for her creativity and encouragement. The least I can do is dedicate the book to her.

Last, deep homage to Lesley and Ana, who suffered through this project, as they have earlier ones. I appreciate their tolerance and occasional teasing, to say nothing of their esoteric tastes in cats and rabbits.

# Notes

1. Leo Walmsley, *Three Fevers* (London: Collins, 1932), p. 2.
2. Samuel Eliot Morison, *Admiral of the Ocean Sea* (Boston: Little, Brown, 1942), p. 226.
3. James A. Williamson, *The Cabot Voyages and Bristol Discovery Under Henry VII* (Cambridge: Hakluyt Society, 1962), p. 64.

## Part One

1. The Blickling Homiliary is a late tenth- or eleventh-century collection of eighteen sermons for Sundays and saints' days, perhaps written for a monastic house near Lincoln, England. It came into the possession of the Marquis of Lothian of Blickling Hall, Norfolk (whence its name), but was sold to Princeton University in 1932. Quote from Michael Swanton, ed., *Anglo-Saxon Prose* (Totowa, N.J.: Rowman & Littlefield, 2002), pp. 67–69.

## Chapter 1

1. Quintus Septimus Florens Tertullian was born in about A.D. 160 to a centurion in Carthage and became an attorney. He was a pleasure-loving pagan until middle age. In 197 he became an ardent Christian, was appointed a priest, then quarreled with the Church and eventually founded a sect of his own, living to a ripe, and unknown, old age. His written works are of great importance to the students of early Christian doctrine. *De Baptismo*, date uncertain, defends Christianity against a female gnostic preacher of the Cainite cult, whom he calls a "poisonous viper." Translated by Ernest Evans (London: SPCK, 1962), p. 1. Tertullian's other major work, the *Apologeticum*, is a defense of Christianity against pagan criticism composed in A.D. 197, addressed to the provincial governors of the Roman Empire.
2. Matthew 13:47–50.
3. Oppian, *Halieutica* 1:702–733. Oppian wrote his *Halieutica* in about A.D. 176.

4. A complex academic literature surrounds the garum industry. For a comprehensive survey, see Robert I. Curtis, *Garum and Salsimenta* (Leiden: Brill, 1991).

5. In writing Chapters 1–2, I drew on Andrew McGowan, *Ascetic Eucharists: Food and Drink in Early Christian Ritual Meals* (Oxford: Clarendon, 1999); and Laurence Harold Kant, "The Interpretation of Religious Symbols in the Graeco-Roman World: A Case Study of Early Christian Symbolism" (Ph.D. diss., Yale University, 1993). I'm grateful to Professor Kant for kindly permitting me to make use of, and to quote from, his important study. Quote from p. 158.

6. Polycrates was tyrant of Samos, c. 535–522 B.C. He turned the island into a formidable naval power in the Aegean Sea. The story of the fish is in Herodotus, *Histories* 3.42, trans. Robin Waterfield (Oxford: Oxford University Press, 1998), p. 187.

7. Kant, "Interpretation," p. 127.

8. The annalist and antiquarian Fenestella (52 B.C.–A.D. 19) wrote a Roman history in at least twenty-two books, which is now lost except for fragments. He had wide antiquarian interests and excellent critical abilities. Many authors, among them Pliny the Elder, used his works.

9. Spanish-born Marcus Valerius Martialis (Martial) (c. A.D. 38–c. 101) was an epigrammist, intellectual, and poet. His *Epigrammaton liber* appeared in A.D. 80. Quote from 13.81.

10. Claudius Aelianus (Aelian) (A.D. 165/70–230/5) was a writer admired for the purity of his Attic diction. His *Varia historia* in fourteen books comprises anecdotes of human life and history. Quote from 1.28.

11. Avercius was a priest of Cybele, perhaps a member of a part-gnostic, part-heathen sect. He commissioned his inscription in about A.D. 200. Archaeologist W. M. Ramsey found a fragment of the stone at the ancient mineral baths near Hieropolis, Turkey, in 1883. The wording of the inscription is cryptic, for professing Christianity was dangerous at the time. G. Ficker translation at www.ccel.org/s/schaff/encyc/encyc01/contrib.386.htm.

12. "Pectorius of Autun," in *Catholic Encyclopedia*.

13. Kant, "Interpretation," p. 163.

14. This is a complex issue, and I have followed Kant, "Interpretation," pp. 526ff. here. The biblical quotation in this paragraph is from John 13:15.

CHAPTER 2

1. Tertullian *Apologeticum* 11.2.
2. Genesis 12:19.
3. Leviticus 16:34.
4. Genesis 9:3–4.
5. Leviticus 11:9.

6. 1 Corinthians 9:25.

7. Acts of the Apostles 15:29.

8. Matthew 26:26.

9. The Didache (Teachings of the Twelve Apostles) is a short treatise of un-known date, perhaps written as early as A.D. 50. The text instructs a Christian community how to treat itinerant prophets and gives guidance on appropriate behavior for the faithful. Quote from chap. 8.

10. St. Irenaeus (A.D. 177–202) was a priest of the Church of Lyons in what is now France and later became bishop. He was a missionary and pastor who campaigned against what he considered the heresy of gnosticism, the doctrine of salvation by knowledge. Gnostics believed they "knew" the mysteries of the universe, making them superior beings. Gnosticism originated somewhere in southwestern Asia before Christianity and went into rapid decline after A.D. 250.

11. See www.ewtn.com/library/PAPALDOC/P6PAEN.htm.

12. St. Augustine of Hippo in Roman North Africa (354–430) became a Christian in 384 after grappling with basic philosophical questions for many years. He became bishop of Hippo in 396, residing in a monastery where he lived a communal life with monks bound to poverty. His doctrinal writings were very influential, preaching austerity, charity, and the belief that every work of God is good. Quote is from St. Augustine, *De Oratione et Jejunio, Sermo* 220.20.

13. Basil, bishop of Caesarea, was a distinguished teacher and theologian celebrated for his ascetic lifestyle and piety. His surviving writings include sermons on morals. Quotes from *De Jejunio Homiliae* 1.3–4; *De Renuncio* 7. For discussion, see Philip Rousseau, *Basil of Caesarea* (Berkeley: University of California Press, 1994), pp. 360–363. Also Teresa M. Shaw, *The Burden of the Flesh: Fasting and Sexuality in Early Christianity* (Minneapolis: Fortress, 1998), pp. 196–198.

14. Galatians 5:26.

15. Galen of Pergamum was the son of a wealthy architect who became a physician in the imperial Roman service and served five emperors. He made ambitious efforts to encompass the entirety of medicine in his prolific writings, which covered anatomy, physiology, and philosophy. See Shaw, *Burden of the Flesh*, pp. 58–59.

16. St. Jerome devoted much of his life to writing, living an austere existence in a monastery, where he spent much time translating and annotating the Scriptures. Quotes from *Adversus Jovinianum* 2.7; *Epistles* 79.7. See www.newadvent.org/fathers/3009.htm.

17. See www.newadvent.org/fathers/3009.htm. For modern dietary research, see summary in Shaw, *Burden of the Flesh*, pp. 126–127.

18. Antioch-born John Chrysostom became a controversial bishop of Constantinople, famous for his eloquence and austerity. See Shaw, *Burden of the Flesh*, pp. 132–135; John Chrysostom, *Discourses Against Judaizing Christians*, trans. Paul W. Hawkins (Washington, D.C.: Catholic University of America Press, 1979), p. 111.

19. Revelation 1:8; 22:13.

20. Salminius Hermias Sozomen, a fifth-century advocate in Constantinople, wrote a continuation of Eusebius Scholasticus's *Historia Ecclesiastica* covering the history of the church to 439. His work comprises nine books and is especially rich on the early history of monasticism. See Joseph Bidez and Léon Parmentier, eds., *The Ecclesiastical History of Evagrius* (London: Methuen, 1898), p. 30. Eusebius (260–339) is a major source on the reign of the Emperor Constantine and wrote a notable history of the early church.

21. Bidez and Parmentier, *Ecclesiastical History*, p. 30.

22. Shaw, Burden of the Flesh, pp. 126–127.

23. *Regula Magistri*, the Rule of the Master, is much longer than the subsequent Rule of St. Benedict, which draws extensively on the earlier document. Its authorship is the subject of much discussion. Quote from Luke Eberle, trans., *The Rule of the Master = Regula Magistri* (Kalamazoo, Mich.: Cistercian, 1977), 53:213.

24. The quotes from *The Rule of St. Benedict* in these pages come from an English translation by Boniface Verheyen (1949), www.osb.org/rb. For a discussion, see St. Benedict, *Households of God: The Rule of St. Benedict with Explanations for Monks and Lay-People* (Kalamazoo, Mich.: Cistercian, 1980).

25. The anonymous author of the *Regula Magistri* stressed the value of the communal monastic life. Quote from Maria Dembinska, "Fasting and Working Monks: Regulations of the Fifth to Eleventh Centuries," in Alexander Fenton and Eszter Kisbán, eds., *Food in Change* (Edinburgh: John Donald, 1986), p. 155.


PART TWO

1. "The Nun's Priest's Tale," from Geoffrey Chaucer, *The Canterbury Tales*, trans. David Wright (Oxford: Oxford University Press, 1985), p. 203.


CHAPTER 3

1. Lady (or Dame) Juliana Berners was one of the earliest women writers in English. Tradition states that she was the prioress of a nunnery at Sopwell near St. Albans, Hertfordshire. According to the eighteenth-century author John Hawkins, she was a "lady of noble family and celebrated for her learning and accomplishments." Her treatise on fishing appeared in *The Boke of St Albans*, published in 1496. The *Treatyse of Fysshynge wyth an Angle* has been oft reprinted. Quote from John McDonald, *The Origins of Angling* (New York: Lyons, 1997), pp. 30–31. The same volume includes a thought-provoking essay on the genre of sporting books and early sport fish literature.

2. *Rule of St. Benedict.* Quotes in these paragraphs are from an English translation by Boniface Verheyen (1949). Available at www.osb.org/rb. See also Dembinska, "Fasting and Working Monks."

3. A brief discussion is found in C. Anne Wilson, *Food and Drink in Britain* (Chicago: Academy Chicago Publishers, 1991), pp. 25ff.

4. *Anguilla anguilla* has a fascinating life cycle, so unlikely that it seems almost like space fiction. Quite where eels came from remained a mystery until 1924, when the great Danish biologist Johannes Schmidt traced their tiny larvae back to their spawning grounds in the seaweed-infested Sargasso Sea in the eastern Atlantic. Millions of these larvae spread out in all directions, many reaching North America, others riding the Gulf Stream to Europe and the Mediterranean. At this point they look like curled-up leaves, known to biologists as *leptocephali*. When they reach European waters, the larvae metamorphose into wormlike objects—glass eels or elvers. The almost transparent elvers now come together in broods, straggling along for kilometers in cordons known as *eel-fares*, pushing up rivers and streams at night by the million. Nothing stands in their way—vertical walls, lock gates, the living climbing on the backs of the dead. They populate even the smallest bodies of water, can penetrate the narrowest cracks in sluice walls.

For the next six to twenty years, sometimes much longer, the eels feed and grow to maturity in freshwater. They consume small fish and invertebrates, their growth determined by water temperature, available food, and the density of the eel population itself. In many rivers, the densest stock is downstream, which is where male eels tend to congregate, while the larger females flourish upstream where there is less crowding.

As the eels reach maturity, they grow fatter and their heads broader; their underskin turns silver, a change that adapts them for the long sea journey ahead. When conditions are right, the fat, silver eels swim downstream with the current in their thousands and begin their long swim back to the Sargasso Sea, where they breed and die as the entire cycle begins all over again.

For eels, see F.-W. Tresch, *The Eel: Biology and Management of Anguillid Eels*, trans. Jennifer Greenwood (London: Chapman & Hall, 1977); also Richard Schweid's charming *Consider the Eel* (Chapel Hill: University of North Carolina Press, 2002).

5. C. C. Dyer, "The Consumption of Fresh-water Fish in Medieval England," in Michael Aston, ed., *Medieval Fish, Fisheries, and Fishponds in England*, British Archaeological Reports 182(i) (Oxford: British Archaeological Reports, 1988), pp. 27–38.

6. The Venerable Bede's *Historia Ecclesiastica Gentis Anglorum* is one of the seminal works of early Christianity in Britain. See Bede, *A History of the English Church and People*, trans. Leo Sherley-Price (Baltimore: Pelican, 1955), 4.134.223.

7. "Piscatores," quoted by Charles L. Cutting, *Fish Saving: A History of Fish Processing from Ancient to Modern Times* (New York: Philosophical Library, 1955), p. 54. "Godly men": see Mike Smylie, *Herring: A History of the Silver Darlings* (Stroud, U.K.: Tempus, 2004), p. 24.

8. A lively trade in salted whale meat flourished in Paris in the form of *craspois*, strips of salt-cured meat from the fattier parts of the whale—somewhat like inferior

bacon. Not that it was a desirable food by today's standards. *Craspois* required at least a day's boiling to soften it before it was eaten with peas. Rouen merchants sold *craspois* as an expensive luxury in England. They brought in so much that King Athelred II taxed both whale meat and French wine at London Bridge in 982. For *craspois*, see Mark Kurlansky, *Salt: A World History* (New York: Penguin, 2003), pp. 111–112.

9. Medieval fishing methods are briefly summarized at www.regia.org/fishing.htm. See also J. M. Steane and M. Foreman, "Medieval Fishing Tackle," in Aston, *Medieval Fish,* pp. 137–186.

10. Steane and Foreman, "Medieval Fishing Tackle," p. 140.

11. Tresch, *Eel,* chap. 5.

12. Willy Louis Braekman, *The Treatise on Angling in The Boke of St. Albans* (Brussels: Scripta, 1980), p. 27.

13. Richard Hoffmann, "Medieval Fishing," in Paolo Squariti, ed., *Working with Water in Medieval Europe: Technology and Resource Use* (Leiden: Brill, 2000), pp. 331–393, discusses eel traps and other fishing methods. The Otto case is mentioned on p. 369.

14. King Charlemagne of France (742–814) is a classic larger-than-life historical figure, surrounded as much by mythology as historical truth. Apocryphal stories of his conquests, his devotion to the Church, his reforms, and his promiscuity abound. But there can be no question that he exercised a profound influence on the future course of Christianity in Europe, so much so that Pope Leo III crowned him Emperor of the Holy Roman Empire in St. Peter's, Rome, on Christmas Day 800. Charlemagne used his administrative and military authority, also the power of his own example, to enforce Christian discipline. In this, he followed the counsel of his close adviser, the Anglo-Saxon monk Alcuin, who reminded him constantly that the king's most important task was to lead his subjects and combat abuse with justice. It's questionable just how much influence Charlemagne had on the enforcement of Church doctrine of the day. Certainly, like Pope Nicholas I a half century later, he was adamant about meat-free Lents and was careful to maintain good fish stocks on his estates.

A useful biography is Matthias Becher, *Charlemagne,* trans. David S. Bachrach (New Haven: Yale University Press, 2003).

15. Ernest Perels, *MGH Epistolae,* vol. 6, trans. W. L. North (Berlin: Springer, 1925), pp. 568–600.

16. Hoffmann, "Medieval Fishing," p. 365.

17. Quoted, with sources, by Hoffmann, "Medieval Fishing," p. 337.

18. Hugh Magennis, *Anglo-Saxon Appetites: Food and Drink and Their Consumption in Old English and Related Literature* (Dublin: Four Courts, 1999), p. 88.

19. The paragraphs that follow are based on Richard Hoffmann, "Cod, Carp, Connections," in Mary J. Henninger-Voss, ed., *Animals in Human Histories* (Rochester, N.Y.: Rochester University Press, 2002), pp. 3–55.

20. Dyer, "The Consumption of Fresh-water Fish," pp. 27–38. See also Aston, *Medieval Fish*, pp. 137–186.

21. J. M. Steane, "The Royal Fishponds of Medieval England," in Aston, *Medieval Fish*, pp. 39–68.

22. C. J. Bond, "Monastic Fisheries," in Aston, *Medieval Fish*, pp. 92–93. See also Bond, "Production and Consumption of Food in the Medieval Monastery," in Graham Keevill, Mick Aston, and Teresa Hall, eds., *Monastic Archaeology: Papers on the Study of Medieval Monasteries* (Oxford: Oxbow, 2001), pp. 54–87.

23. Hoffmann, "Carp, Cod," describes the beginnings of fish farming.

24. Both quotes come from Bond, "Monastic Fisheries," p. 94 n. 17.

25. C. K. Currie, "Medieval Fishponds in Hampshire," in Aston, *Medieval Fish*, pp. 267–290.

## CHAPTER 4

1. Quoted from Maguelonne Toussaint-Samat, *History of Food* (Oxford: Blackwell, 1992), p. 466.

2. Few authors have tackled herrings for a popular audience, but see Smylie, *Herring*. Classic accounts are A. Samuel, *The Herring: Its Effect on the History of Britain* (London: John Murray, 1918); and W. C. Hodgeson, *The Herring and Its Fishery* (London: Routledge & Kegan Paul, 1957).

Herring rarely appears on American menus, but if you are near Jamesville, North Carolina, between January and April, head for the Cypress Grill, where river herring is served during the spawning season. I have never eaten there, but acquaintances of mine rave about the fish. The Cypress Grill is the last survivor of numerous riverside places where you could eat fresh herring. Fifty years ago, local fishers would catch as many as 500,000 herring in a single day, using nets more than a kilometer long. Now a drift net may catch no more than twenty.

3. Jane Grigson, *Jane Grigson's Fish Book*, 2nd ed. (London: Michael Joseph, 1993), is the bible of fish cookery, larded with sound advice and historical background on every fish imaginable. Quote from p. 85.

4. Isabella Beeton, *Mrs Beeton's Book of Household Management* (London: Chancellor, 1982). This is a reprint of the original 1861 edition and a mine of information on Victorian cuisine and, for that matter, household management.

5. Cutting, *Fish Saving*, is still the best source on the history of fish preservation. Quote from p. 72.

6. These paragraphs are based on Cutting, *Fish Saving*, pp. 57ff. Lobster is even harder to preserve and defeated the best efforts of New England fishers centuries later.

7. Matthew 5:13.

8. 2 Kings 2:20–21.

9. Mark Kurlansky, *Salt,* offers a wide-ranging, thinly researched history, on which I drew for these paragraphs.

10. Cutting, *Fish Saving,* describes herring curing in detail. See also Wendy R. Childs, "Fishing and Fisheries in the Middle Ages: The Eastern Fisheries," in David J. Starkey, Chris Reid, and Neil Ashcroft, eds., *England's Sea Fisheries: The Commercial Sea Fisheries of England and Wales Since 1300* (London: Chatham, 2000), pp. 19–23.

11. D. H. Cushing, *The Provident Sea* (Cambridge: Cambridge University Press, 1988), chap. 9.

CHAPTER 5

1. Petter Dass (1647–1707) was vicar of Alstadhaug in Northland and Norway's greatest seventeenth-century writer. He composed hymns and poetry. His most renowned work was a small book, *The Trumpet of Northland,* printed in 1739, long after his death. He looked on everything in Northland as God's creation. See Theodore Jorgenson, *The Trumpet of Nordland, by Peter Dass, and Other Masterpieces of Norwegian Poetry from the Period 1250–1700,* trans. Theodore Jorgenson (Northland, Minn.: St. Olaf College Press, 1954). The quote comes from the introduction to the poem, p. 10.

2. A huge literature surrounds faerings. Two good articles by Jean-Pierre Guillou, "The Faerings of Norway," appear in *Maritime Life and Traditions* 19 (2002); 21 (2003), covering both handling and construction, with excellent pictures. B. Faeroyvik and O. Faeroyvik, *Inshore Craft of Norway* (London: Conway Maritime, 1979), is a collection of nineteenth-century illustrations of traditional craft and well worth studying in this connection.

3. Cod have generated much more prose than *Clupea,* probably because of the seeming romance of the Grand Banks fisheries. Mark Kurlansky's *Cod* is a widely read, if superficially researched starting point for the general reader. See also Albert C. Jensen, *The Cod* (New York: Crowell, 1972).

4. The description of *Gadus* in Bruce B. Collette and Grace Klein-MacPhee, *The Fishes of Maine,* 3rd ed. (Washington, D.C.: Smithsonian Institution Press, 2002), pp. 223–260, is exemplary and applies to most Atlantic Gadidae.

5. The most accessible general sources on the Lofoten Islands are on the Web. The Norwegian Fishing Village Museum website provides an admirable introduction: www.lofoten-info.no/fiskmus.htm.

6. Ian A. Simpson et al., "Cultural Sediment Analyses and Transitions in Early Fishing Activity at Langenesvaeret, Vesterålen, Northern Norway," *Geoarchaeology: An International Journal* 15, no. 8 (2000): 743–763, which supplies other references.

7. These paragraphs are based on Sophia Perdikaris, "From Chiefly Provisioning to Commercial Fishery: Long-Term Economic Change in Arctic Norway," *World Archaeology* 30, no. 3 (1999): 388–402. For Vågan, R. Bertelsen and P. Urbanczyk,

"Two Perspectives on Vagan in Lofoten," *Acta Borealia* 5 (1988): 98–110; Perdikaris, "Scaly Heads and Tales: Detecting Commercialization in Early Fisheries," *Archaeofauna* 5 (1996): 21–33, describes the methodology behind analyzing stockfish bones.

8. Quote from Lofoten Fisheries Museum, *Brief History of the Lofoten Fishery.* See www.lofoten-info.no/fiskmus.htm. Also P. Urbanczyk, *Medieval Arctic Norway* (Warsaw: Institute of the History of Material Culture/Polish Academy of Sciences, 1992).

9. Sophia Perdikaris, *The Transition to a Commercial Economy: Lofoten Fishing in the Middle Ages: A Preliminary Report,* Seventh ICAZ Conference Proceedings, *Anthropozoologica,* September 1994, pp. 505–510.

10. Ottar (Ohthere), and his fellow seaman, Wulfstan, are heavily chronicled. I drew on Niels Lund, *Two Voyagers at the Court of King Alfred: The Ventures of Ohthere and Wulfstan,* trans. Ole Crumlin-Petersen (York, U.K.: Sessions, 1984).

## CHAPTER 6

1. Ermentarius (or Armentarius) was born in England and served as a monk at Noirmoutier in France, coveted by the Norse because of its salt. He subsequently became a hermit on Mount Scobrit near the Loire River. Neil S. Price, "Laid Waste, Plundered, and Burned: Vikings in Frankia," in William W. Fitzhugh and Elisabeth I. Ward, eds., *Vikings: The North Atlantic Saga* (Washington, D.C.: Smithsonian Institution Press, 2000), p. 119.

2. Colleen E. Batey and John Sheehan, "Viking Expansion and Cultural Blending in Britain and Ireland," in Fitzhugh and Ward, *Vikings,* p. 127. Diedre O'Sullivan and Robert Young, *The English Heritage Book of Lindisfarne* (London: Batsford, 1995), is an excellent introduction for the general reader.

3. The scholar and theologian Alcuin (c. 735–804) was of Northumbrian birth and served as a teacher. In 781 he became Charlemagne's "Master of the Palace School," educated the monarch's sons, and served as one of the king's most influential advisers. In 796 he retired to become abbot of St. Martin's at Tours, where he set up a model monastic school. Alcuin exercised a profound influence on the religious and secular affairs of his day and even prompted a poem by Sigfried Sassoon (1886–1967), "Awareness of Alcuin":

> *At peace in my tall-windowed Wiltshire room,*
> *(Birds heard overhears from March twilight's close)*
> I read, translated, Alcuin's verse, in whom
> *A springtide of resurgent learning rose.*

Alcuin also proclaimed that *Vox populi, vox Dei,* "the voice of the people is the voice of God."

4. This paragraph is based on Sophia Perdikaris and Thomas H. McGovern, "Cod Fish, Walrus, and Chieftains: Economic Intensification in the Norse N. Atlantic," in T. Thurstan et al., eds., *New Perspectives on Intensification* (New York: Kluwer Academic/Plenum, in press). I am grateful to the authors for permitting me to see this paper in advance of publication.

A huge and ever-growing literature surrounds the Norse, endowed as they are with a romantic aura, some of it generated from such Hollywood extravaganzas as *The Vikings*, with, inevitably, Kirk Douglas in the starring role. An excellent overview for the general reader is Fitzhugh and Ward, *Vikings*, which features authoritative essays on all aspects of Norse society. The references in this volume give an excellent guide to more specialized literature. Another sound account is contained in Eric Christiansen, *The Norsemen in the Viking Age* (Oxford: Blackwell, 2002).

5. *The Anglo Saxon Chronicles*, part 2, A.D. 750–919. See http://sunsite.berkeley.edu/OMACL/Anglo/part2.html.

6. On the Norse expansion through western Europe, see part 2 of Fitzhugh and Ward, *Vikings*.

7. Sean McGrail, *Ancient Boats in Northwest Europe* (London: Longman, 1987), is a definitive account of early ships in the North Sea and Baltic based on archaeological and historical sources. The Nydam ships are well described in John Haywood, *Dark Age Naval Power: A Reassessment of Frankish and Anglo-Saxon Seafaring Activity* (Hockwold-cum-Wilton, U.K.: Anglo-Saxon Books, 1999), pp. 94ff.

8. Sutton Hoo is a spectacular site, with a magnificent visitor center and museum that is worth going a long way to enjoy. The royal burial itself is well published. For a technical monograph, see R. L. S. Bruce-Mitford, *The Sutton Hoo Ship Burial*, vol. 1, *Excavation, Background, the Ship, Dating, and Inventory* (London: British Museum Publications, 1975). Martin Carver, *Sutton Hoo: Burial Ground of Kings?* (Philadelphia: University of Pennsylvania Press, 1998) is a more popular, up-to-date account.

9. E. Gifford and J. Gifford, "The Sailing Characteristics of Saxon Ships as Derived from Half-Scale Working Models with Special Reference to the Sutton Hoo Ship," *International Journal of Nautical Archaeology* 12 (1995): 121–131.

10. A. W. Brøgger and H. Shetelig, *The Viking Ships*, 2nd ed., trans. Katherine John (Oslo: Dreyer, 1953). These two researchers connected the T-shaped Norse keel with the use of sailing boats in northern waters.

11. The Roskilde Museum with its vibrant traditional boatbuilding programs should be on everyone's visiting list. Ole Crumlin-Pedersen, "The Skuldelev Ships," *Acta Archaeologica* 38 (1967): 73–174, is a definitive source on the Roskilde vessels. For a brief summary, the museum booklet *The Viking Ship Museum in Roskilde* is an admirable starting point.

12. For instance, see Thomas Gillmer, "The Capability of the Single Square Sail Rig: A Technical Assessment," in Sean McGrail, ed., *The Archaeology of Medieval*

*Ships and Harbors in Northern Europe,* British Archaeological Reports International Series, no. 66 (Oxford: British Archaeological Reports, 1979), pp. 167–182.

13. A discussion of knarrs appears in Owain T. P. Roberts, "Descendants of Viking Boats," in Robert Gardiner, ed., *Cogs, Caravels, and Galleons* (London: Conway Maritime Press, 1994), pp. 11–28.

14. On the Gokstad voyage, see A. E. Christiansen, "Viking: A Gokstad Ship replica from 1893," in Ole Crumlin Pedersen and M. Vinner, eds., *Sailing into the Past* (Roskilde: Viking Ship Museum, 1986), pp. 68–77.

15. The quotes in this paragraph are from G. J. Marcus, *The Conquest of the North Atlantic* (Woodbridge: Boydell, 1980), pp. 47, 49. See also Gwyn Jones, *The Norse Atlantic Saga,* 2nd ed. (Oxford: Oxford University Press, 1987).

16. Climatic information summarized in Brian Fagan, *Little Ice Age,* chap. 3. See also Astrid Oglivie et al., "North Atlantic Climate ca. AD 1000," *Weather* 55 (2000): 34–45.

Ice conditions around Iceland were often hazardous during the Little Ice Age. In 1654 the twenty-two-gun escort ship *Marigold* from Bristol was unable to sail along the stormy north coast of Iceland because of pack ice in mid-June. The local people told the captain that there was "noe passage for ship nor boote" to the west. I'm grateful to Dr. Evan Jones for drawing my attention to his transcript of the ship's journal: www.bris.ac.uk/Depts/History/Maritime/marigold.pdf.

17. Brian Fagan, *Ancient North America: The Archaeology of a Continent,* 4th ed. (New York: Thames & Hudson, 2005), chap. 1, offers a broader summary of Norse exploration and contact with North America, and of the L'Anse aux Meadows site.

18. Markland is almost certainly southern Labrador. The identity of Vinland remains a mystery, which will probably never be satisfactorily answered. The controversy is irrelevant to this story.

CHAPTER 7

1. Olaus Magnus, *A Description of the Northern Peoples (Historia de gentibus septenrionalibus),* was published in Rome in 1555. Magnus (1490–1557) was the last Catholic archbishop of Uppsala, Sweden. Despite spending the second half of his life in exile, he was completely devoted to his cultural heritage. The twenty-two books with their 778 chapters illustrated with 480 woodcuts cover a vast range of topics, everything from snowflakes to werewolves. The *Historia* remains a major source for modern scholarship about conditions in Scandinavia before the Reformation. Quote from P. G. Foote, ed., *Olaus Magna: A Description of the Northern Peoples* (London: Hakluyt Society, 1998), 2:36.

2. The latest archaeological evidence is admirably summarized by James H. Barrett, Alison M. Locker, and Callum M. Roberts, "Dark Age Economics Revisited: The English Fish Bone Evidence AD 600 to 1600," *Antiquity* 78 (2004): 616–638.

3. A popular account is Smylie, *Herring;* also, at a more technical level, Cutting, *Fish Saving,* chaps. 3–4.

4. Cutting, *Fish Saving,* chaps. 3–4, offers a useful account of fish preservation. See also Kurlansky, *Salt.*

5. David Kirby and Merja-Liisa Hinkkanen, *The Baltic and the North Seas* (London: Routledge, 2000), p. 165.

6. On the Skänia herring fishery, see Poul Holm and Maibritt Bager, "The Danish Fisheries, c. 1450–1800: Medieval and Early Modern Sources and Their Potential for Marine Environmental History," in Poul Holm, Tim D. Smith, and David J. Starkey, eds., *The Exploited Seas: New Directions for Marine Environmental History* (St. Johns, Newfoundland: International Maritime Economic History Association, 2001), pp. 97–122.

7. The Burgundian councilor Philippe de Mézières (c. 1327–1405) was a well-known crusader and diplomat. See Philippe de Mézières, *Le Songe d'un vieil pèlerin,* 2 vols., ed. and trans. G. W. Coopland (Cambridge: Cambridge University Press, 1969), 1:249–250.

8. Cutting, *Fish Saving,* pp. 54ff.

9. Historian James Campbell has calculated that if the herring inventories in the Domesday Book represented about a twentieth of the annual catch, then the total English catch may have been as high as 3,298,000 fish in the late eleventh century. See Maryanne Kowaleski, "The Commercialization of the Sea Fisheries in Medieval England and Wales," *International Journal of Maritime History* 15 (2003): 177–231, which lists primary sources.

10. Kowaleski, "Commercialization," p. 179, where primary sources are found.

11. Barrett et al., "Dark Age Economics," summarizes the evidence.

12. Hoffmann, "Medieval Fishing," p. 338, is the source for these two paragraphs.

13. Childs, "Fishing," p. 19.

14. Cutting, *Fish Saving,* p. 35.

15. Cutting, *Fish Saving,* p. 72. The quote is from Thomas Nash, *Lenten Stuffe* (Cambridge: Chadwyck-Healey, 1997).

CHAPTER 8

1. Comte de Lacépède (1756–1825) was a French naturalist, a disciple of Buffon, who later became a politician. The quote comes from *Natural History,* 1817–1818, p. 100.

2. John Milverston, interview by the author, September 15, 2004.

3. Kirby and Hinkkanen, *Baltic and North Seas,* chap. 8.

4. Childs, "Fishing," pp. 18–23. Quote from p. 19. The paragraphs that follow are based on this article. See also A. Saul, "The Herring Industry at Great Yarmouth c. 1280–c. 1400," *Norfolk Archaeology* 38 (1981–1983): 33–43.

5. Childs, "Fishing," pp. 20–21.

6. Childs, "Fishing," p. 20.

7. A history of Great Yarmouth is found at www.ukonline.co.uk/members/gwoodcock/gyarm/history/history.htm.

8. Childs, "Fishing," p. 21.

9. The Bremen cog has generated a huge literature. This account is based on Detlev Ellmers, "The Cog as Cargo Carrier," in Gardiner, *Cogs, Caravels, and Galleons*, pp. 29–46. Also Siegfried Fliedner, *The Cog of Bremen* (Bremen: Landesmuseum Bremen, 1971). A popular account is Gabriele Hofman and Uwe Schnall, "The Bremen Cog: A Portrait of a Ship's Type," *Maritime Life and Traditions* 27 (2005): 12–25.

10. Richard Unger has analyzed the van Beukels invention in a closely argued paper: "The Netherlands Herring Fishery in the Late Middle Ages: The False Legend of Willem Beukels of Biervleit," *Viator* 9 (1978): 335–356. This must be regarded as the definitive word on the subject.

Emperor Charles V (1500–1558) ruled so many European lands from the Low Countries to Germany and Spain that it was said that the sun never set on his domains. He founded Spain's influential Council of the Indies and introduced important financial reforms in the Netherlands that benefited the cloth industry.

11. Childs, "Fishing," p. 22.

12. Childs, "Fishing," p. 22.

13. This discussion is based on Hoffmann, "Carp, Cods," and "Medieval Fishing."

14. Hoffmann, "Carp, Cods," p. 3.

15. Hoffmann, "Medieval Fishing," pp. 339–340.

16. Based on Barbara Harvey, *Living and Dying in England, 1100–1540* (Oxford: Clarendon, 1993), pp. 38ff.

17. Roy Strong, *Feast: A History of Grand Eating* (New York: Harcourt, 2002), pp. 52ff.

18. This paragraph is based on Alison Locker, *The Role of Stored Fish in England, 900–1750 A.D.: The Evidence from Historical and Archaeological Data* (Sofia, Bulgaria: Publishing Group, 2001), pp. 95ff.

19. Strong, *Feast,* p. 67.

20. Hoffmann, "Medieval Fishing," pp. 28–29, was the basis for this paragraph and the quote.

21. For a summary of the North Atlantic Oscillation, see Fagan, *Little Ice Age*, chap. 3.

CHAPTER 9

1. From a fifteenth-century treatise. C. Anne Wilson, *Food and Drink in Britain: From the Stone Age to the 19th Century* (Chicago: Academy Chicago Publishers, 1991), p. 36.

2. Natalis de Wailly, ed., *The Life of St. Louis by John of Joinville,* trans. René Hague (London: Sheed & Ward, 1955), pp. 47–48. For a discussion, see Strong, *Feast,* pp. 69–71.

3. Strong, *Feast,* p. 71.

4. Strong, *Feast,* p. 88.

5. Terry S. Reynolds, *Stronger Than a Hundred Men: A History of the Vertical Water Pump* (Baltimore: Johns Hopkins University Press, 1983), was the source for this discussion of water mills. His book is the definitive study of the technology. For general economic aspects, see Lynn White Jr., *Medieval Technology and Social Change* (Oxford: Oxford University Press, 1962).

6. J. McDonnell, "Inland Fisheries in Medieval Yorkshire 1066–1300," *Borthwick Papers* 60 (1981): 23.

7. Hoffmann, "Medieval Fishing," p. 365.

8. Hoffmann, "Medieval Fishing," is the best source for medieval fish farming. I drew on it heavily here. For monastic landscapes, see James Bond, *Monastic Landscapes* (Stroud, U.K.: Tempus, 2004).

9. For the introduction of carp into central and western Europe, see Hoffmann, "Carp, Cods," where primary sources are found.

10. Hoffmann, "Medieval Fishing," pp. 381ff. The carp information came from London's Royal Botanical Gardens website: www.rbg.ca/pages_sci_conserv/sci_conserv_carp.html.

11. Jan Dubravius (c. 1486–1533) was the author of *A Nevv Booke of good Husbandry, very pleasaunt, and of very great profite both for Gentlemen and Yomen: Conteining, the Order and maner of making of Fish-pondes,* originally written in Latin in Zurich in 1559 and translated into English "by the special request of George Churchey, fellow of Lions Inne" (London: W. White, 1599).

12. Once again, information from Hoffmann, "Medieval Fishing," pp. 388ff.

13. For Trebon carp farming, see Hoffmann, "Medieval Fishing," pp. 390ff, and also http://otter.trebone.cz/carpfishing.htm.

14. Discussion in Hoffmann, "Carps, Cods," pp. 12ff.

CHAPTER 10

1. Ivan Turgenev (1818–1883), novelist, *Little Poems in Prose,* 23.

2. Gordon Jackson, "State Concern for the Fisheries, 1485–1815," in Starkey et al., *England's Sea Fisheries,* pp. 46–53.

3. Maryanne Kowaleski, "Fishing and Fisheries in the Middle Ages: the Western Fisheries," in Starkey et al., *England's Sea Fisheries,* pp. 23–28. See also Kowaleski, *The Havener's Accounts of the Earldom and Duchy of Cornwall, 1301–1356* (Exeter, U.K.: Devon and Cornwall Record Society, 2001).

4. Maryanne Kowaleski, "The Internal and International Fish Trades of Medieval England and Wales: The Internal Fish Trade," in Starkey et al., *England's Sea Fisheries,* pp. 29–33.

5. Kowaleski, "Internal and International," pp. 30–31.

6. Wendy R. Childs, "The Internal and International Fish Trades of Medieval England and Wales: The International Trade," in Starkey et al., *England's Sea Fisheries*, pp. 33–35.

7. E. H. Weatherly, ed., *Speculum Sacerdotale* (Oxford: Old English Text Society, 1935), old series 200, 4.

8. Bridget Ann Henisch, *Fast and Feast* (University Park: Pennsylvania State University Press, 1976), p. 33.

9. E. L. Guilford, *Select Extracts Illustrating Sports and Pastimes in the Middle Ages* (New York: Macmillan, 1920), p. 52.

10. W. Nelson, ed., *A Fifteenth Century Schoolbook* (Oxford: Clarendon, 1956), p. 8.

11. 1 Timothy 5:23.

12. The sermon was preached by Robert Rypon, an eminent cleric of his day and a contemporary of the poet Geoffrey Chaucer. Discussed in G. R. Owst, *Literature and Pulpit in Medieval England* (Oxford: Basil Blackwell, 1961), p. 435.

13. Pieter Breughel, *Fight Between Carnival and Lent,* was painted in 1559 and can be seen at the Kunsthistorisches Museum, Vienna.

14. B. White, ed., *Alexander Barclay: Eclogues* (Oxford: Early English Text Society, 1928), old series, 9.1 (From the First Eclogue.)

15. Henisch, *Fast and Feast,* pp. 46ff.

16. C. M. Woolgar, "'Take This Penance Now, and Afterwards the Fare Will Improve': Seafood and Late Medieval Diet," in Starkey et al., *England's Sea Fisheries,* pp. 36–44.

17. Pope Benedict XII (1334–1342) was the third of the Avignon pontiffs. He was a Cistercian and devoted much attention to monastic reform. On dietary boundaries, see Barbara Harvey, *Living and Dying*, pp. 40–41.

18. Woolgar, "Take This Penance," p. 38. See also Bond, "Production and Consumption," p. 73.

19. Barbara Harvey, *Living and Dying*, part 2, was the major source for this section and its dietary analyses.

20. Woolgar, "Take this Penance," p. 37.

CHAPTER 11

1. William Shakespeare, *Henry IV* 1.2.4.222–223.

2. See Chapter 5 for herring curing methods. For an excellent history of Dutch fisheries, see A. Beaujohn, *The History of the Dutch Sea Fisheries* (London: Williams, 1883).

3. Richard W. Unger, *Ships and Shipping in the North Sea and Atlantic, 1400–1800* (Brookfield, Vt.: Ashgate Variorum, 1997); and Unger, "Northern Ships and the Late Medieval Economy: Columbus and the Medieval Maritime Tradition," *American Neptune* 53, no. 4 (1993): 247–253.

4. The buss is summarized in Richard W. Unger's two works cited above; and Unger, "The Fluit: Specialist Cargo Vessels 1500 to 1650," in Gardiner, *Cogs, Caravels, and Galleons*, pp. 120–121. During and after the seventeenth century, smaller boats often carried the processed herring barrels to shore. For a brilliant analysis of the wider implications of the buss, see Jan de Vries and Ad van der Woude, *The First Modern Economy: Success, Failure, and Perseverance of the Dutch Economy, 1500 to 1815* (Cambridge: Cambridge University Press, 1997).

5. The painting is in the Royal Cabinet of Paintings, Mauritshuis, The Hague, Netherlands.

6. Cutting, *Fish Saving*, p. 91. For the wider economic implications of the Dutch herring trade, see de Vries and van der Woude, *First Modern Economy*, chap. 7.

7. 2 Thessalonians 3:10.

8. A *smack* is a fishing boat that operates close to shore, often with a hold to carry live fish.

9. I'm greatly indebted to John Leather for his unpublished notes on doggers. My reconstruction is based on his thoughtful analysis. Thanks also to yacht designer Andrew Wolstenholme for helpful discussion.

10. The author of *The Seafarer* is unknown, but the manuscript was inscribed in about 975, surviving in *The Exeter Book*, a codex bequeathed to Exeter Cathedral by Archbishop Leofric in 1072:

> The dark night deepens, northern snow
> hardens the soil and hail hits earth
> like cold corn
> Yet my heart hammers now, yearning anew
> wanting the steep salt-water road
> longing with lust to roam rough seas alone
> to seek out some far foreign shore
> The mood to wander mills within my mind
> But none on earth may be so proud
> so prodigal or yare in youth
> nor so express in action
> nor smiled on by so mild a master
> that he embark with unconcern
> what end for him the Master may intend.

Translation by Charles Harrison Wallace, *Artes International*, Stockholm, 1999.

Ezra Pound wrote a poem of the same title in 1912 based loosely on the Anglo-Saxon original.

11. Eric McKee, *Working Boats of Britain: Their Shape and Purpose* (London: Conway Maritime Press, 1983), chap. 2.

12. John Collins, *Salt and Fishery* (London: Godbid & Playford, 1682), esp. p. 87. Summary in Evan Jones, "England's Icelandic Fishery in the Early Modern Period," in Starkey et al., *England's Sea Fisheries*, pp. 105–110.

13. This passage is based on John Leather's unpublished notes.

CHAPTER 12

1. George Townsend Warner, ed., *The Libelle of Englysche Polycye* (Oxford: Clarendon, 1926), p. 41.

2. Discussion in Marcus, *Conquest*, a major source for this chapter. See also J. A. Gade, *The Hanseatic Control of Norwegian Commerce in the Late Middle Ages* (Leiden: Brill, 1951). Another useful work is Bruce E. Gelsinger, *Icelandic Enterprise: Commerce and Economy in the Middle Ages* (Columbia: University of South Carolina Press, 1983).

3. On Little Ice Age conditions in the north, see Fagan, *Little Ice Age,* chaps. 3–4.

4. See Marcus, *Conquest*, p. 126.

5. Some Faeroese still do. For early Faeroes history, see G. V. C. Young, *From the Vikings to the Reformation: A Chronicle of the Faroe Islands up to 1538* (London: Shearwater, 1979).

6. Maryanne Kowaleski, "The Commercialization of the Sea Fisheries in Medieval England and Wales," *International Journal of Maritime History* 15, no. 2: 177–232.

7. Childs, " Internal and International Trade," p. 22.

8. Warner, *Libelle*, p. 41.

9. First quote, Jones, "England's Icelandic Fishery," p. 108. Remaining quotes: *The North Sea Pilot* (London: Admiralty Hydrographic Office, 1875), p. 121.

10. Jones, "Icelandic Fishery," p. 108.

11. Cutting, *Fishing Saving*, p. 124. For Iceland and England, see Kirsten Seaver, *The Frozen Echo: Greenland and the Exploration of North America, ca. A.D. 1000–1500* (Stanford, Calif.: Stanford University Press, 1996), chap. 7.

12. Marcus, *Conquest*, p. 126.

13. Jones, "Icelandic Fishery," p. 108.

14. Marcus, *Conquest,* p. 130, has primary references.

15. Marcus, *Conquest*, p. 130.

16. Marcus, *Conquest*, p. 131.

17. Childs, "Eastern Fisheries," p. 22.

18. Marcus, *Conquest*, p. 145.

19. Both quotes in this paragraph are from Marcus, *Conquest*, p. 147.

20. Collins, *Salt and Fishery*, pp. 87ff.

21. This account is drawn from Jones, "Icelandic Fishery," pp. 109–110.

22. Based on Marcus, *Conquest*, chap. 20.

23. Jones, "Icelandic Fishery," p. 106.

24. Jones, "Icelandic Fishery," p. 106.

25. A composite quote from Marcus, *Conquest*, p. 149.

26. Discussed by Jones, "Icelandic Fishery," p. 107, where the quote is found.

27. Jones, "Icelandic Fishery," p. 107.

28. Quotes in this paragraph from Jones, "Icelandic Fishery," p. 107.

PART THREE

1. James A. Williamson, *The Cabot Voyages and Bristol Discovery Under Henry VII* (Cambridge: Hakluyt Society, 1962), pp. 17–18.

CHAPTER 13

1. Letter from John Day to the Grand Admiral (Christopher Columbus), December-January 1497–1498. David B. Quinn, ed., *New American World: A Documentary History of North America to 1612*, vol. 1, *America from Concept to Discovery: Early Exploration of North America* (New York: Arno/Hector Bye, 1979), p. 98.

2. This section is based on J. H. Bettey, "Late-Medieval Bristol: From Town to City," *Local Historian*, February 1998, pp. 3–15. See also Patrick McGrath, *Bristol and America, 1480–1631* (Bristol: Historical Association, 1997); and David Harris Sacks, *The Widening Gate: Bristol and the Atlantic Economy, 1450–1700* (Berkeley: University of California Press, 1991).

3. I urge those imbibing readers who have not tried it to sample Bristol milk sherry. The wine is exquisitely smooth and an ideal preprandial aperatif. You're following in the footsteps of diarist Samuel Pepys. He wrote in his diary for Saturday, June 13, 1668: "Then walked with him [Butts] and my wife and company round the quay, and to the ship; and he shewed me the Custom-house, and made me understand many things of the place, and led us through Marsh Street, where our girl was born. But, Lord! The joy that was among the old poor people of the place, to see Mrs. Willet's daughter, it seems her mother being a brave woman and mightily beloved! And so brought us a back way by suprize to his house, where a substantial good house, and well furnished; and did give us good entertainment of strawberries, a whole venison-pasty, cold, and plenty of brave wine, and above all Bristoll milk." Project Gutenberg: www.gutenberg.org/dirs/4/1/9/4190.txt.

The end of the Hundred Years War between England and France (1337–1453) brought major changes to the wine trade, as Bordeaux came under French rule. It was an episodic struggle with long periods of peace interspersed with violent battles, including a naval battle at Sluys (1340), Crecy (1346), Poitiers (1356), and Agincourt (1415) (immortalized by Shakespeare in *Henry V*). The war ended with England losing its final toehold on the Continent.

4. Kowaleski, "Western Fisheries," pp. 27–28.

5. Kowaleski, "Western Fisheries," pp. 27–28. I'm grateful to Dr. Evan Jones for discussion (by e-mail) on Bristol's involvement with the Icelandic stockfish trade.

6. These pages on western fisheries are based on Kowaleski, "Western Fisheries," pp. 27ff.

7. For pilchards, see Michael Culley, *The Pilchard: Biology and Exploitation* (New York: Pergamon, 1971).

8. Kowaleski, "Western Fisheries," pp. 27–28.

9. On Hy-Brasil, see Morison, *European Exploration*, pp. 102–105.

10. Mark Kurlansky, *The Basque History of the World* (New York: Walker, 1999), offers a summary account of Basque history for a general audience. Roger Collins, *The Basques*, 2nd ed. (Oxford: Basil Blackwell, 1990), pp. 131–132. For an authoritative account of offshore fishing at a specialist level, see Michael Barkham, "The Spanish Basque Offshore Fisheries during the Early Modern Period," in Jon Th. Thor et al., *A History of the Traditional Histories of the North Atlantic Ocean* (Bremerhaven: German Maritime Museum, in press). I'm grateful to Dr. Barkham for allowing me to consult this paper in advance of publication.

11. Kurlansky, *Basques*, p. 53.

12. Trausti Einarsson, "Sobre los primeros balleneros vascos en Islandia" [About the First Basque Whalers in Iceland], in Selma Huxley, ed., *Los vascos en el marco Atlántico Norte: Siglos XVI y XVII* [*The Basques in the North Atlantic in the 16th and 17th Centuries*] (San Sebastián: Editorial Etor, 1987), pp. 287–288. Einarsson tracked down the reference to Basque fishing vessels in publications of the later 1800s and 1900s and concluded that the reference was a corruption of an earlier published reference to about thirty *foreign* ships fishing off Iceland.

13. Selma Huxley, "Los vascos y las pesquerías transatlánticas, 1517–1713" [The Basques and the Transatlantic Fisheries, 1517–1713] in Huxley, *Los vascos en el marco Atlántico Norte*, pp. 26–210.

14. Gerrit de Veer, *Three Voyages of William Barents to the Arctic Regions (1594, 1595, and 1596)* (London: B. Franklin/Hakluyt Society, 1964), 1st series, no. 54.

15. Selma Barkham, "The Documentary Evidence for Basque Whaling Ships in the Strait of Belle Isle," in G. M. Story, ed., *Early European Exploration and Settlement and Exploitation in Atlantic Canada* (St. Johns: Memorial University of Newfoundland, 1982), p. 53. The same author's article on early Basque merchants and their attitudes to native Americans and the trade is well worth reading: Selma Huxley Barkham, "The Mentality of the Men Behind Sixteenth-Century Spanish Voyages to Terranova," in Germaine Warkentin and Carolyn Podruchev, eds., *Decentering the Renaissance: Canada and Europe in Multidisciplinary Perspective 1500–1700* (Toronto: University of Toronto Press, 2001), pp. 110–124.

16. Controversies over possible Bristol predecessors to Cabot have raged for centuries. The debate is unresolved and will remain so until definitive historical records come to light, which may never happen. Some eminent scholars, like Samuel Eliot Morison in his magisterial *European Discovery*, dismiss pre-Cabot voyages out of hand. Many modern authorities are similarly dubious. On the other side of the debate, James A. Williamson, *Cabot Voyages*, argues for earlier voyages, as does David Beers Quinn in *England and the Discovery of America, 1481–1620* (New York: Knopf, 1974), probably the most thorough analysis ever undertaken. The reader is referred to these for a thorough briefing; also to Peter E. Pope, *The Many Landfalls of John Cabot* (Toronto: University of Toronto Press, 1997). My speculative venture into these intellectually shark-infested waters is mostly based on these sources and involves triangulating off many indirect clues.

17. For the customs records, see E. M. Carus-Wilson, *The Overseas Trade of Bristol in the later Middle Ages* (New York: Barnes & Noble, 1967), pp. 71–73. Also recorded in William of Worcester's *Itineraria Symonis Simeonis et Wilhelmi de Worcestre*, which appears in James A. Dallaway, ed., *Antiquities of Bristow in the middle centuries; including the topography by William Wyrcestre, and the life of William Canynges* (Bristol: Mirror Office, 1834). Only the Bristol portions of the *Itineraria* appear in this volume.

18. Marcus, *Conquest*, p. 164, gives the primary source. See also Carus-Wilson, "Overseas Trade," pp. 157–158.

19. Marcus, *Conquest*, p. 165. The Island of the Seven Cities was a popular legend of the time. The fabled isle had allegedly been found by a Portuguese ship that was blown by a gale far out into the Atlantic from the Strait of Gibraltar in 1447. There were said to be seven cities there, inhabited by people who spoke Portuguese, refugees from the Islamic invasions. And (of course) a sand sample yielded gold. Columbus, among others, collected tales of islands to the west as part of the research for his voyage, as perhaps, did John Cabot before his northern venture.

20. The name John Day was an alias for Hugh Say, a member of a London merchant family who dealt in textiles in Bristol and Spain. See Alwyn A. Ruddock, "John Day of Bristol and the English Voyages Across the Atlantic Before 1497," *Geographical Journal* 132 (1966): 225–233. For the letter, see L. A. Vigneres, "The Cape Breton Landfall: 1494 or 1497? Note on a letter by John Day," *Canadian Historical Review* 33 (1957): 226–228. A more accessible translation is found in David B. Quinn, *New American World*, pp. 98–99. This remarkable volume is a mine of information on original sources relating to early European exploration.

21. On caravels, a summary appears in Carla Rahn Phillips, "The Caravel and the Galleon," in Gardiner, *Cogs, Caravels, and Galleons*, pp. 91–114.

22. McGrail, *Boats of the World*, pp. 245–247.

23. A total of twelve vessels, among them the *San Juan* and two other large ships, are known in the waters of Red Bay. Parks Canada and the Red Bay community have taken steps to ensure their permanent conservation. For instance, the *San Juan's* timbers have been returned to the seabed after recording. See Robert Grenier,

B. Loewen, and J.-P. Proulx, "Basque Shipbuilding Technology, c. 1560–1580," in C. Westerdahl, ed., *Crossroads in Ancient Shipbuilding: Proceedings of the Sixth International Symposium on Boat and Ship Archaeology, Roskilde, 1991* (Oxford: Oxbow, 1993), pp. 137–141. A popular account can be found in Robert Grenier and James Tuck, "A Sixteenth-Century Basque Whaling Station in Labrador," *Scientific American* 245 (1981): 180–188.

24. Thomas Oertling, "The Concept of the Atlantic Vessel," *Proceedings of the International Symposium on the Archaeology of Medieval and Modern Ships of Iberian-Atlantic Tradition*, 1998, pp. 233–240.

25. Figures quoted by José Luis Casado Soto, "The Spanish Ships of the Ocean Expansion: Documentation, Archaeology and Iconography," *Proceedings of the International Symposium*, p. 142.

26. This argument is based on Oertling, "Atlantic Vessel." See also John Steffy, "The Development of Ancient and Medieval Building Techniques," *Proceedings of the International Symposium on the Archaeology of Medieval and Modern Ships of Iberian-Atlantic Tradition*, 1998, pp. 49–61.

27. T. F. Reddaway and A. A. Ruddock, eds., "The Accounts of John Balsall, Purser of the *Trinity* of Bristol, 1480–81," *Camden Miscellany* 23 (1969): 1–27.

28. Seaver, *Frozen Echo*, chapters 7–9, offers an extended analysis. See also Fin Gad, *History of Greenland*, vol. 1 (London: David Hurst, 1970), for a balanced discussion.

29. Perdikaris and McGovern, "Cod Fish, Walrus, and Chieftains," discuss the contrasts between Icelandic and Greenland Norse economies.

30. Morison, *Admiral*, pp. 24–26. For a fictional look at the unlikely notion of Columbus crossing the Atlantic with Norwegians, see Roland Huntford, *Sea of Darkness* (New York: Scribners, 1975).

CHAPTER 14

1. David B. Quinn, "Newfoundland in the Consciousness of Europe in the Sixteenth and Early Seventeenth Centuries," in Story, *Early European Settlement*, p. 9. As he points out, the same sentiment was expressed by Thomas Morton in *New England Canaan*, published in Amsterdam in 1637.

2. William Canynges (c. 1399–1474) was born into a wealthy family of cloth manufacturers. He expanded the business and became one of the richest Englishmen of his day, owning ten ships and employing some 800 people. For a while, by special license from the king of Denmark, he enjoyed a complete monopoly on the fish trade between Iceland, Finland, and England. Canynges was five times mayor of Bristol and a member of Parliament on two occasions. He and his wife financed the reconstruction of the famous church of St. Mary Redcliffe, employing up to a hundred workers on the task for many years. After the death of his spouse, he took holy orders and became dean of Westbury in 1469.

3. Morison, *Admiral*, pp. 91–92.

4. Morison, *European Discovery*, chapter 6, is a good summary of Cabot's career and adventures. See also James A. Williamson, *The Cabot Voyages;* and Pope, *Many Landfalls*. The latter is a superb introduction for the informed general reader.

5. Letters-patent granted to John Cabot and his sons, March 5, 1496. Quinn, *New American World*, pp. 93–94.

6. How John Cabot would have craved the twentieth-century replica, which is equipped with a 200 horsepower Caterpillar diesel engine with two propellers, GPS and full navigational electronics, two enclosed toilets, a cold-water shower, and a fully equipped galley with propane stove, oven, and refrigerator. The modern-day *Matthew* is an active seagoing vessel, with a schedule of voyages each summer that offers participation on a fee-paying basis. See www.matthew.co.uk.

7. This account based in part on Morison, *European Discovery*, chap. 6. The old Norse route eventually gave way to others. By the seventeenth century, most ships sailed west southwest from western England until west of the Azores at about forty-six degrees north. They then sailed westward until soundings brought them to the 100-fathom (183-meter) line on the Grand Banks. The crossing distance was much shorter for English and Breton boats and typically lasted about five weeks, although thirty-day crossings were not uncommon. Ian K. Steele, *The English Atlantic, 1675–1740* (New York: Oxford University Press, 1986), pp. 79ff., has an informed discussion of sailing routes.

8. This is perhaps a controversial interpretation of Cabot's landfall, which has engaged the close attention of historians for a long time. Many authorities favor Cape Breton as the point of first contact. Here I follow Samuel Eliot Morison's carefully reasoned interpretation, which to me as a sailor seems straightforward and logical, but I'm quite prepared to admit that I'm wrong. For the purposes of this book, the important point is that Cabot sighted Newfoundland and found an abundance of *Gadus morhua*. Two good starting points for the general reader are Morison, *European Discovery*, chap. 6; and Pope, *Many Landfalls*. The latter examines not only the historical evidence but also the complex motives behind different interpretations of Cabot's voyage.

9. Letter from Raimondo de Soncino to the Duke of Milan dated December 18, 1497. Included in English translation in Quinn, *New American World*, the quotes in this paragraph and the next being from pp. 97–98.

10. The pope sent the Italian administrator and historian Polydore Vergil (c. 1470–1555) to England in 1501. He became close to King Henry VII, was appointed archdeacon of Wells, and commissioned to write his *Anglia Historia* (1512–1513), which is especially valuable on Henry VII's reign. The book became a classic, for Vergil was one of the first writers to compile a detailed, carefully weighed historical narrative. Quoted from Quinn, *New American World*, p. 102.

11. Morison, *European Discovery*, chap. 7, quotes from p. 215.

12. Robert Fabyan (?1450–1513) was a London clothier and alderman as well as chronicler. Fabyan's *The Concordaunce of Hystoryes* appeared posthumously as *The New Chronicles of England and of France* (London: Pynson, 1516).

13. History has not been kind to Sebastian Cabot (c. 1474–1557). He has acquired a reputation as an expert self-promoter, a talker rather than a doer, who had the gift of charming the right people. He may have led an expedition to Labrador in 1508. In later life, he became a gifted pilot and cartographic adviser to several European governments. Whether one believes in his earlier exploits is a matter of considerable and unresolved debate, admirably summarized by Peter Pope, *Many Landfalls*, chap. 4, where he distinguishes nicely between "Sebastiolators" and "Sebastiophobes."

14. See Peter E. Pope, *Fish into Wine: The Newfoundland Plantation in the Seventeenth Century* (Chapel Hill: Omohundro Foundation/University of North Carolina Press, 2004), p. 15. Chapter 1 of this book has an excellent, analytical account of the early Newfoundland fishery. Chapters on various nations' Newfoundland cod fisheries are found in James E. Candow and Carol Corbin, eds., *How Deep Is the Ocean? Historical Essays on Canada's Atlantic Fishery* (Sydney, N.S.: University of Cape Breton Press/Louisbourg Institute, 1997).

15. An excellent account of *Gadus morhua* can be found in Collette and Klein-MacPhee, *Fishes of the Gulf of Maine*. Harold A. Innis, *The Cod Fisheries* (Toronto: University of Toronto Press, 1955), is the bible for all students of cod and its fisheries. Although now somewhat outdated, its research is authoritative, comprehensive, and outstanding. For a popular account, see Kurlansky, *Cod.*

16. L. Sabine, *Report on the Principal Fisheries of the American Seas* (Washington, D.C.: U.S. Treasury, 1853), p. 183.

17. Adolphe Bellet, *La Grande pêche de la morue à Terre-Neuve* (Paris: Challamel, 1902), pp. 5ff.

18. D. E. Ruzzante, C. T. Taggert, and D. Cook, "A Nuclear DNA Basis for Shelf- and Bank-Scale Population Structure in Northwest Atlantic Cod *(Gadus morhua)*: Labrador to Georges Bank," *Molecular Ecology* 7 (1998): 1663–1680.

19. Morison, *European Discovery*, chaps. 7–8, has a useful summary on which this passage is based. The *La Pensée* belonged to Jean Ange, a veritable merchant prince in Dieppe, who handled wool, cloth, and merchandise of every kind, including fish. He owned merchant ships, small vessels, and fishing boats. His ship captains often served as privateers and captured over a million ducats worth of prizes in a mere twenty years between 1520 and 1540.

Ange was to finance important expeditions to North American waters, among them those of Giovanni Verrazzano and Jacques Cartier. Giovanni Verrazzano (1485–1528) sailed from Dieppe and traversed the east coast of North America from about Cape Fear to Newfoundland in 1524. He perished on a later expedition, murdered by Carib Indians in the Lesser Antilles in 1528. Jacques Cartier (1491–1557) was a Saint-Malo mariner who explored the Gulf of St. Lawrence in 1534 and penetrated the great river as far upstream as Hochelaga, the site of modern-day Montreal, where he encountered the Huron Indians in 1535–1536. A third expedition in 1541–1542 was an abortive attempt to establish a trading station. Cartier is regarded as the founder of Canada.

20. Guienne, its capital Bordeaux, was retaken by the French in 1453. Brouage in Charente-Maritime was the hometown of the explorer Samuel de Champlain, a town with its own salt pans.

21. Basque boats are said to have been cod fishing in Newfoundland waters as early as 1511 and certainly by 1517. Quinn, "Newfoundland," p. 17.

22. Michel Mollat du Jourdain, *Europe and the Sea*, trans. Teresa Lavender Fagan (Oxford: Blackwell, 1993), pp. 54ff., has a discussion.

23. Quoted by Innis, *Cod Fisheries*, p. 14. Anthony Parkhurst (dates unknown, active 1561–1583) was a Bristol merchant who became an entrepreneur in the Newfoundland fishery. He accompanied his own ship on three good and one unsuccessful seasons between 1575 and 1578, spending a great deal of time exploring the "harbors, creekes and havens and also the land." He advocated colonization of Newfoundland in a famous letter to Richard Hakluyt in 1578 but did not take part in any efforts himself.

24. Morison, *European Discovery*, p. 268.

25. Pope, *Fish into Wine*, p. 20. For Bordeaux, see Laurier Turgeon, "Bordeaux and the Newfoundland Trade During the Sixteenth Century," *International Journal of Maritime History* 9 (1997): 1–28.

26. The Council of Trent, convened from 1545 to 1563, was an attempt to define the doctrines of the Catholic Church in the face of Protestantism and reform abuses in the inner life of its operations.

## Part Four

1. Thomas Henry Huxley, "Inaugural address of the Fishery Conferences," *Fisheries Exhibition Literature* 4 (1884): 18.

## Chapter 15

1. Robert Perret, *La géographie de Terre-Neuve* (Paris: E. Guilmoto, 1913), p. 183.

2. Marc Lescarbot (1570–c. 1629) was a French lawyer turned explorer who visited New France (Canada) in 1606. He spent over a year there and on his return resumed the practice of law. He also wrote his lively and well-informed *Histoire de la Nouvelle France*, which appeared in 1609. This is an important source of information about conditions on the Canadian frontier at the time. For a translation, see H. P. Biggar and W. L. Grant, eds., *History of New France by Marc Lescarbot* (Toronto: Champlain Society, 1907–14); quotes from pp. 304–307.

3. Lewes Roberts, *The Marchants Map of Commerce* (London: R. Mabb, 1638), pt. 1, p. 57.

4. Pope, *Fish into Wine*, pp. 17ff., is an excellent beginning point for this complex literature.

5. David J. Starkey and Michael Haines, "The Newfoundland Fisheries, c. 1500–1900: A British Perspective," in Holm et al., *Exploited Seas*, pp. 4–5. Statistics on catches from the seventeenth to nineteenth centuries appear on pp. 10–11. See also the essays in Candow and Corbin, *How Deep Is the Ocean?*

6. Morison, *European Discovery*, pp. 646ff.

7. Both quotes from Cutting, *Fish Saving*, p. 33. Diarmaid MacCulloch, *The Reformation: A History* (New York: Viking, 2004) offers an excellent analysis.

8. Proclamation of King Edward VI, February 13, 1552.

9. Cutting, *Fish Saving*, p. 33.

10. Proclamation of King James I, March 24, 1607.

11. Cutting, *Fish Saving*, p. 33. See also David J. Starkey, "The West Country-Newfoundland Fishery and the Manning of the Royal Navy," in Robert Higham, ed., *Security and Defense in South-West England Before 1800* (Exeter: Center for South-Western Historical Studies, University of Exeter, 1987), pp. 93–101.

12. Pepys quotes are from Cutting, *Fish Saving*, p. 34.

13. A proliferating literature discusses Spanish diets. See A. R. Mitchell, "The European Fisheries in Early Modern History," in E. E. Rich and C. H. Wilson, eds., *The Cambridge Economic History of Early Modern Europe*, vol. 5, *The Economic Organization of Early Modern Europe* (Cambridge: Cambridge University Press, 1977), pp. 172–178. For specialized references, see Daniel Vickers, *Farmers and Fishermen: Two Centuries of Work in Essex County, Massachusetts 1630–1850* (Cambridge: Harvard University Press, 1994), pp. 86–87.

14. Quotes from Roberts, *Marchants Map*, pp. 57ff.

15. Discussion of ships in Gillian T. Cell, *English Enterprise in Newfoundland, 1577–1660* (Toronto: University of Toronto Press, 1969), pp. 3–4. For sacks, see Pope, *Fish into Wine*, chap. 3, "Adventures in the Sack Trade," a definitive summary.

16. An excellent account of the dry fishery can be found in Pope, *Fish into Wine*, pp. 22ff., which I drew on here. He gives an admirable summary of such topics as equipment, provisions, and so on. Our knowledge of the inshore fishery comes from a composite of accounts, all of them from the seventeenth century or later, but little appears to have changed over the years. The fishery was highly effective as long as cod were abundant. I also consulted the seventeenth-century writer Nicholas Deny's (1598–1688) account, by far the best contemporary description of the fishery, written in 1671, which appears in W. F. Ganong, ed., *The Description and Natural History of the Coasts of North America (Acadia) by Nicholas Denys* (New York: Greenwood, 1968). (This is a facsimile of 1908 edition by the Champlain Society.)

17. Pope, *Fish into Wine*, p. 26.

18. James Yonge's journal is an important source of information on both the sedentary fishery and the Ferryland settlement described below. Yonge (1641–1721) had a long career as a talented surgeon (by the standards of the day). See F. N. L. Poynter, ed., *The Journal of James Yonge (1647–1721), Plymouth Surgeon* (London: Longman,

1965), p. 57. See also Pope, *Fish into Wine*, pp. 24ff. Pope comments, "*Merchantable fish* was a premium grade; *not merchantable*, or *refuse, fish* was in fact salable, but of a cheaper grade" (p. 27).

19. Pope, *Fish into Wine*, pp. 33–39.

20. Fagan, *Little Ice Age,* chap. 8.

21. John Paige quote from Pope, *Fish into Wine*, p. 39, where a discussion is found.

22. Pope, *Fish into Wine*, p. 209.

23. Summarized by Cushing, *Provident Sea*, pp. 56ff.

24. Pierre Loti was the nom de plume of French naval officer Julian Viaud (1850–1923), who spent forty years in naval service, two of them along the Brittany coast, where he gathered the background for this novel about Breton fishers and their wives or girlfriends back home. The novel is actually about cod fishing off Iceland, but I have no compunction about transferring this quote to the banks, where conditions were virtually identical. Pierre Loti, *An Icelandic Fisherman*, trans. Guy Endore (Alhambra, Calif.: Braun, 1957), p. 8.

25. The discussion of early Newfoundland settlement that follows is based on two admirable sources that are fully referenced. Cell, *English Enterprise*; and Pope, *Fish into Wine*, which concentrates on the archaeology and history of Ferryland, provide an excellent overview.

26. John Easton was just one of many pirates who preyed on fishing boats. Pirates and privateers were a constant scourge of the seventeenth-century Newfoundland fisheries. Barbary pirates lay in wait for Newfoundland boats in spring and fall, even short distances off English Channel harbors. They attacked ships in the Severn Estuary and preyed on vessels taking cod to Spain, Portugal, and the Mediterranean. The presence of warships and convoying offered some security, but the Royal Navy was stretched thinly over huge distances and could be little more than a vague deterrent. Discussion in Pope, *Fish into Wine*, p. 209.

27. On Ferryland, see Pope, *Fish into Wine*, which is a study of the colony.

28. Sir David Kirke (1597–1654) was a colorful, controversial figure. He and his brothers captured both Nova Scotia and Quebec in 1628, receiving the island of Newfoundland as compensation when peace was signed. Kirke died a pauper after a tangle of lawsuits over his grabbing of Ferryland engulfed him. Discussion in Cell, *English Enterprise*, pp. 114–117.

29. Keith Matthews, *Collection and Commentary on the Constitutional Laws of the Seventeenth Century Newfoundland.* (St. John's: Memorial University of Newfoundland: Maritime History Group, 1975), pp. 71–75.

CHAPTER 16

1. David B. Quinn and Alison M. Quinn, *The English New England Voyages, 1602–1608* (London: Hakluyt Society, 1993), pp. 300–301. Rosier's account is *A True*

*Relation of the most prosperous voyage made this present yeere 1605 by Captaine George Waymouth in the Discouery of the land of Virginia* (London: George Bishop, 1605).

2. Morison, *European Discovery*, p. 465.

3. Norumbega is discussed by Richard D'Abate, "On the Meaning of a Name: Norumbega and the Representation of North America," in Emerson W. Baker et al., eds., *American Beginnings: Exploration, Culture, and Cartography in the Land of Norumbega* (Lincoln: University of Nebraska Press, 1994), p. 75.

4. Morison, *European Discovery*, pp. 467–468.

5. Marc Lescarbot, *Nova Francia: A Description of Acadia, 1606*, trans. P. Erondelle (New York: Harper, 1928), describes Champlain's visit, with quotes, pp. 48–54. (His book was written in 1609.) Also Morison, *European Discovery*, p. 469.

6. Quinn and Quinn, *English New England Voyages*, p. 300. My account of the Gulf of Maine also draws on Colin Woodard, *The Lobster Coast* (New York: Viking, 2004), pp. 55ff. Woodard's book is an admirable popular account of Maine's beginnings. I also consulted Lincoln P. Paine, *Down East: A Maritime History of Maine* (Gardiner, Me.: OpSail Maine, 2000).

7. The great auk, *Pinguinus impennis*, was a flightless, penguinlike seabird that once gathered in enormous numbers on the rocky islands and coasts of Greenland and northeastern America, also Iceland, Britain, and Scandinavia. The birds wintered as far south as Florida and southern Spain. Great auks became extinct as a result of promiscuous hunting for their food, fat, and feathers by cod fishers and whalers, then became a favored prey for collectors in search of skins and eggs. The last living pair and one egg were taken in Iceland in 1844. See Jeremy Gaskell, *Who Killed the Great Auk?* (New York: Oxford University Press, 2001).

8. An authoritative essay on early New England cod fisheries is Faith Harrington, "Wee Tooke Great Store of Cod-fish": Fishing Ships and First Settlements on the Coast of New England," in Baker et al., *American Beginnings*, pp. 191–216. I drew on this important summary for this section of the chapter. See also Harrington, "Sea Tenure in Seventeenth-Century New Hampshire: Native Americans and Englishmen in the Sphere of Coastal Resources," *Historical New Hampshire* 40, no. 1–2 (1985): 18–33.

9. Quoted from Harrington, "Wee Tooke," p. 194. See also Henry S. Burrage, ed., *Early English and French Voyages* (New York: Scribners, 1932), p. 331.

10. Charles E. Levermore, *Forerunners and Competitors of the Pilgrims and Puritans* (Brooklyn, N.Y.: New England Society, 1912), p. 61.

11. Harrington, "Wee Tooke," p. 195. In the early days, lobsters were so plentiful that they could be taken by hand in shallow water. The flesh could not be cured, so they were eaten locally.

12. According to Harrington, "Wee Tooke," p. 198, Peucoit was the nearby Matinicus Islands. Baird's account (also quoted by Harrington) appears in Richard E. Thwaites, ed., *The Jesuit Relations and Allied Documents* (1897; New York: Pageant, 1959), 2:253.

13. William Strachey (1572–1621) was educated at Cambridge and sailed to Virginia in 1609, being shipwrecked during a hurricane in Bermuda en route. He stayed in Virginia for nearly a year and then became secretary of the Jamestown colony. He wrote his *Historie of Travaile into Virginia Britannia* (London: Hakluyt Society, 1951) for the Virginia Society, a primary source for early Virginian history. His vivid account of the Bermuda shipwreck is said to have been the source for Shakespeare's play *The Tempest.*

14. Sir Samuel Argall (1580–1626) was an expert sailor who knew his fisheries. He later became admiral of Virginia and drove the French from nascent settlements in Maine. He was appointed deputy governor of Jamestown in 1619, but there were many complaints about his severity. Argall subsequently became admiral for New England and a member of the king's war council.

15. Discussion in Harrington, "We Tooke," p. 200, where quotes appear. Sir Ferdinando Gorges (c. 1566–1647) was a seaman and soldier who became keeper of the castle and fort at Plymouth. He developed an interest in North America, sponsored several expeditions and attempts at settlement, and received the royal charter for Maine in 1639. See J. P. Baxter, ed., *Sir Ferdinando Gorges and His Province of Maine,* 3 vols. (Boston: Prince Society, 1890).

16. This passage is based on Harrington, "Wee Tooke," pp. 203ff.; also Innis, *Cod Fisheries,* p. 72. Captain John Smith (1580–1631) was a proud and boastful man given to exaggeration and as such was vilified by his many foes. But there is no question that he was an energetic leader of great ability. Quote from Innis, *Cod Fisheries,* p. 72. See also John Smith, *Description of New England* (Boston: Massachusetts Historical Society Collections, 1837), 3rd series, 6.

17. Woodard, *Lobster Coast,* p. 84.

18. Innis, *Cod Fisheries,* p. 72.

19. Harrington, "Wee Tooke," pp. 204–205.

20. Emmanuel Altham was an early visitor to Plymouth Plantation during the first few years of the Pilgrim settlement. His letters to his brother Sir Edward Altham in England of September 1623 can be found at www.mayflowerhistory.com. The quotes here come from that source.

21. Harrington, "Wee Tooke," p. 209.

22. Sydney V. James, ed., *Three Visitors to Early Plymouth* (Plymouth, Mass.: Plimoth Plantation, 1963), p. 25.

23. John Josselyn, *An Account of Two Voyages to New-England, Made During the Years 1638, 1663* (Boston: William Veazie, 1865), p. 161.

24. Alaric Faulkner, "Archaeology of the Cod Fishery: Damariscove Island," *Historical Archaeology* 19 (1985): 57–86, is a preliminary account of the archaeological research.

25. James P. Baxter, ed., "The Trelawney Papers," in *Documentary History of the State of Maine,* vol. 3 (Portland: Maine Historical Society, 1884).

CHAPTER 17

1. Quoted from Daniel Vickers, "Work and Daily Life on the Fishing Periphery of Essex County, Massachusetts, 1630–1675," in David D. Hall and David Grayson Allen, eds., *Seventeenth-Century New England* (Boston: Colonial Society of Massachusetts, 1984), p. 83.

2. Cotton Mather, *Magnalia Christi Americana; or The Ecclesiastical History of New England* (New York: Russell & Russell, 1967), 1:65–66. Originally published in 1702; reprint of 1853 edition published by S. Andrus, Hartford, Conn.

3. H. Roger King, *Cape Cod and Plymouth Colony in the Seventeenth Century* (Lanham, Md.: University Press of America, 1994), offers a summary of the founding of the colony and its predecessor voyages. Quote from Harrington, "We Tooke," p. 205.

4. Edward Winslow (1595–1655) became governor of Plymouth in 1633. He was widely admired for his diplomatic skills when dealing with local Indian communities and acted as the colony's frontman in dealings with England. He subsequently returned there, worked for Oliver Cromwell's government, and died on an expedition to the West Indies.

5. John White, *The Planters Plea* (Boston: Massachusetts Historical Society, 1930), p. 73. Reprint of 1630 edition published by William Jones, London. John White (1575–1648) was an Anglican priest with moderate Puritan beliefs who helped found the Massachusetts Bay Company; he never visited America.

6. A discussion of these developments is found in Bernard Bailyn, *The New England Merchants in the Seventeenth Century* (Cambridge: Harvard University Press, 1955), pp. 2ff.

7. Bailyn, *New England Merchants*, p. 14.

8. White, *Planters Plea*, p. 74.

9. John Winthrop (1587–1649) was an intensely religious Puritan attorney, one of the powers behind the Cambridge Agreement of 1629, which authorized the establishment of the Massachusetts Bay Company as an autonomous entity. Winthrop sailed to the new colony in 1630 with a fleet of eleven ships. Elected governor many times, he was a moderate voice in a colony filled with fanatics, who would execute people for heresy without hesitation and propose other excesses, such as the veiling of women.

Thomas Dudley (1576–1653) was fifty-four years old when he landed in New England. He was a touchy personality but became an influential figure in colonial society and was elected governor or deputy governor for seventeen years. He signed the original charter of Harvard College in 1650.

10. Bailyn, *New England Merchants*, p. 77.

11. This section draws on Vickers, "Work and Life," pp. 83ff. Quote from p. 86. Vickers, *Farmers and Fishermen,* offers a more complete study of early settlement in Essex County.

12. Vickers, "Work and Life," p. 87.

13. Quoted from Vickers, "Work and Life," p. 90. This discussion is based on his analysis.

14. Vickers, "Work and Life," p. 95.

15. Vickers, "Work and Life," p. 96, gives sources and describes the fishery cycle.

16. Vickers, "Work and Life," p. 98. George Corwin of Salem (1610–1685) was born in England but emigrated in 1638, becoming a wealthy merchant and land speculator. At his death, he was one of the richest, most aristocratic men in New England.

17. Bailyn, *New England Merchants*, pp. 79–80, on which this paragraph is based.

18. King Charles II (1630–1685) ascended the throne after the Declaration of Breda declared an amnesty for supporters of Oliver Cromwell's Commonwealth, which was in danger of dissolving into chaos after the Protector's death. The king landed in England and assumed the throne amid general rejoicing on May 25, 1660. Known popularly as the "Merry Monarch," Charles was a controversial ruler, an impulsive, pleasure-loving king who fostered science and navigation, and enhanced Britain's navy. His forces captured New York from the Dutch in 1664.

19. The quotes in this paragraph are from Bailyn, *New England Merchants*, pp. 83–84. New England trade with the Caribbean is the subject of an extended literature, including Richard Pares, *Yankees and Creoles: The Trade Between North America and the West Indies Before the American Revolution* (Cambridge: Harvard University Press, 1956). Also useful is James G. Lydon, "Fish and Flour for Gold: Southern Europe and the Colonial American Balance of Payments," *Business History Review* 39 (1965): 171–183; and Larry D. Gregg, "The Early New England–Barbados Trade," *Historical Journal of Massachusetts* 17 (1989): 177–200.

20. Bailyn, *New England Merchants*, p. 97.

21. The Canso fishery is described by Judith Tullock, "The New England Fishery and Trade at Canso, 1720–1744," in Candow and Corbin, *How Deep Is the Ocean?* pp. 65–73.

The Treaty of Utrecht between England and France concluded the War of Spanish Succession (1701–1714) and ceded Newfoundland, Acadia, and Hudson Bay to England.

22. Boston merchant Peter Faneuil (1700–1743) gave his home city the public market and hall named after him in 1742. It burned down in 1761 and was rebuilt, becoming the scene of many revolutionary meetings, a "cradle of liberty." Faneuil Hall is still now a beautifully restored market, meeting place, and museum.

Many of Canso's provisions came from Ireland: John Mannion, "Victualling a Fishery: Newfoundland Diet and the Origins of the Irish Provision Trade, 1675–1700," *International Journal of Maritime History* 12 (2000): 1–60.

23. Robin Fedden, *Egypt: Land of the Valley* (London: John Murray, 1977), p. 13.

# RECIPE REFERENCES

Daphne Dervan used the following sources when researching and testing the recipes in this book.

Ballerini, Luigi, ed. *The Art of Cooking: The First Modern Cookery Book, Maestro Martino of Como.* Berkeley: University of California Press, 2005.

Banham, Debby. *Food and Drink in Anglo-Saxon England.* Stroud, U.K.: Tempus, 2004.

Bottero, Jean. *The Oldest Cuisine in the World: Cooking in Mesopotamia.* Chicago: University of Chicago Press, 2004.

Crewe, Rudolf, and Constance Hieatt, eds. and trans. *Libellas de Arte Coquinaria: An Early Northern Cookery Book.* Temple: Arizona Center for Medieval and Renaissance Studies, 2001.

Davidson, Alan. *North Atlantic Seafood: A Comprehensive Guide with Recipes.* 3rd ed. Berkeley: Ten Speed, 2003.

Fleming, Stuart J. *Vinum: The Story of Roman Wine.* Glen Mills, Pa.: Art Flair, 2001.

Frere, Frances, ed. *A Proper Newe Booke of Cookery.* 1575. Reprint, Cambridge: W. Heffer and Sons, 1913.

Giacosa, Ilaria Gozzini. *A Taste of Ancient Rome.* Chicago: University of Chicago Press, 1992.

Hagen, Ann. *A Handbook of Anglo-Saxon Food: Processing and Consumption.* Hockwold-cum-Wilton, U.K.: Anglo-Saxon, 1995.

_____. *A Second Handbook of Anglo-Saxon Food and Drink: Production and Distribution.* Hockwold-cum-Wilton, U.K.: Anglo-Saxon, 2002.

Henisch, Bridget Ann. *Fast and Feast: Food in Medieval Society.* University Park: Pennsylvania State University Press, 1976.

Hieatt, Constance, Brenda Hosington, and Sharon Butler. *Pleyn Delit: Medieval Cookery for Modern Cooks.* 2nd ed. Toronto: University of Toronto Press, 1996.

McGovern, Patrick. *Ancient Wine: The Search for the Origins of Viniculture.* Princeton: Princeton University Press, 2003.

Olson, S. Douglas, and Alexandra Sens. *Archestratos of Gela: Greek Culture and Cuisine in the Fourth Century BCE.* Oxford: Oxford University Press, 2000.

Powell, Owen. *Galen on the Properties of Food Stuffs.* Cambridge: Cambridge University Press, 2003.

Redon, Odile, Françoise Sabban, and Silvano Serventi. *The Medieval Kitchen: Recipes from France and Italy.* Chicago: University of Chicago Press, 1998.

Schweid, Richard. *Consider the Eel: A Natural and Gastronomic History.* Chapel Hill: University of North Carolina Press, 2002.

Scully, D. Eleanor, and Terrance Scully. *Early French Cookery: Sources, History, Original Recipes, and Modern Adaptations.* Ann Arbor: University of Michigan Press, 2002.

Vehling, Joseph, ed. and trans. *Apicius Cookery and Dining in Imperial Rome.* New York: Dover, 1977. Facsimile of the 1936 edition.

Warner, Richard. *Antiquitates Culinariae or Curious Tracts Relating to the Culinary Affairs of the Old English.* 1791. Reprint, Oxford: Prospect, 1983.

Wheaton, Barbara Ketchum. *Savoring the Past: The French Kitchen and Table from 1300–1789.* Philadelphia: University of Pennsylvania Press, 1983.

Wood, Jacqui. *Prehistoric Cooking.* Stroud, U.K.: Tempus, 2001.

# INDEX